150 Palestinian Tales

Tom S. van Bemmelen

150
Palestinian Tales

Facts to better understand
the Arab-Israeli Conflict

Aspekt Publishers

150 Palestinian Tales
© 2016 Tom S. van Bemmelen
© 2016 Aspekt Publishers
Aspekt Publishers | Amersfoortsestraat 27
3769 AD Soesterberg | The Netherlands
info@uitgeverijaspekt.nl | www.uitgeverijaspekt.nl

ISBN: 978-9463-38-100-0
NUR: 680

Coverdesign: Maarten Bakker
Lay-out: Paul Timmerman

All rights reserved. No part of this book may be reproduced or translated in any form, by print, photoprint, microfilm, microfiche or any other means without written permission from the publisher.

Introduction

You've heard the many slogans of Palestinian propaganda. They sound something like this:
"Palestinian terror is a logical result of the occupation."
"Israel was established because of the Western guilt over the Holocaust."
"The settlements make peace impossible."

However, just because these mantras are repeated often does not mean that they are true.

This book covers the 150 most commonly repeated accusations against Israel. We investigate the extent to which each of these allegations is true, based on fact. This examination found that each allegation proved to be factually incorrect or much distorted. Often the accusations are not only false, but projections: it turns out that Israel is not guilty as charged, but the Palestinian side is.

The list of false accusations – or Tales – is almost endless, so we have picked the 150 most frequently encountered in the press. We made sure that every section is self-contained, and that each section gives a complete picture of the subject. As a result, the book can be read in any order. The Tales are furthermore sorted alphabetically by keyword. Thus, the book can also be used as a reference guide.

In writing this book I have been helped by the experienced editorial team of Likud Netherlands. The other authors would rather not be listed by name, given the current uncertain security situation in Europe. This team in recent years produced more than five hundred articles in many Dutch media outlets, including the major Dutch newspapers.

Footnotes have been omitted to keep the book as readable as possible, because everybody can easily check the facts on the Internet. For example, all cited television broadcasts can be found on YouTube as well as on the website of Likud Netherlands. In addition, for the sake of readability, we use the most commonly accepted terms, even when these have an anti-Israel slant (such as "West Bank" instead of the historically correct geographical name "Judea and Samaria").

Does this mean that we claim that Israel never does anything wrong? Of course not. Israeli leaders are not exempt from making mistakes. Governing in the middle of a hostile region, these leaders often have to decide matters of life and death. They sometimes face existential dangers related to the survival of the country and the half of the global Jewish population that lives there. In your own life, how often do you think – with perfect vision in hindsight – that you could have made a better decision or found a more perfect solution?

One hundred and fifty nonsensical and yet ever-recurring accusations against Israel. It shows how deep the hatred against her is – against Israel, and therefore often also against the Jewish people.

This book attempts to make clear that there can only be real peace – genuine coexistence between Arabs and Jews – when this hatred and demonization is stopped. Because until now, while there have been several peace treaties signed, the hatred toward Israel appears hardly to have diminished. Not in Egypt, not in Jordan and not among Palestinians.

To stop this hatred, to combat propaganda, a better knowledge of the facts is needed:
> *"As a teenager I learned to hate Jews without ever having seen one. I felt a deep hatred. The Israeli flag I used as a doormat at home for my room…*
> *[Later] I read a lot and wanted to know everything about the history of the Palestinian people, Israel, Islam, the Western policy in the region. By gaining knowledge, I was able to free myself from all my hate."*
> – Montasser Al-De'emeh, a Muslim living in Belgium who had undergone Jihad training and had planned to go to Syria

What this peace will look like, the authors of this book do not know. But we *do* know that peace requires a stop to the hatred. By debunking tales with facts, we hope this book will make a contribution to the solution, however modest.

Contents

Introduction 5

1	Apartheid	13
2	Arab anti-Semitism	16
3	Arab treatment of Palestinians	19
4	Arabs in Israel	22
5	Arafat	24
6	Archaeology	27
7	Atomic bomb	29
8	Beasts (wild)	32
9	Blood libel	33
10	Borders	35
11	Boycott	37
12	Caliphate	39
13	Chosen people	41
14	Christians	42
15	Civilian casualties	44
16	Collaborators	47
17	Colonialism	49
18	Conflict	52
19	Conspiracy theories	55
20	Criticism of Israel	58
21	Death cult	60
22	Democracy, Israel	63
23	Democracy, Palestinians	65
24	Destruction of Israel	67
25	Development aid	70
26	Economy, Israeli	73
27	Economy, Palestinian	75
28	Emigration	78
29	European Union	79
30	Expulsion now	83
31	Expulsion of 1948	84
32	Fatah	89
33	Gaza blockade	91

34	Gaza densely populated	93
35	Gaza hunger	95
36	Gaza open-air prison	97
37	Genocide	99
38	Greater Israel	101
39	Hamas	103
40	Hamas founding	107
41	Hebron	108
42	Herzl	110
43	Holocaust	113
44	Holocaust denial	115
45	Holy places, access	118
46	Holy places, respect	121
47	Human rights organizations	124
48	Islam	128
49	Islamic State (IS)	131
50	Jerusalem capital	133
51	Jerusalem East	134
52	Jerusalem history	137
53	Jerusalem Judaization	140
54	Jesus	143
55	Jewish lobby	145
56	Jewish refugees	147
57	Jewish state	150
58	Jewish state creation	152
59	Jewish terror	155
60	Jews in Arab countries	157
61	Khazars	160
62	Land development	162
63	Land for peace	166
64	Land, population	169
65	Land promise	171
66	Land theft	173
67	Likud	175
68	Media	176
69	Motherly love	179
70	Muslim fundamentalism	181
71	Natural resources	185
72	Nazis	186
73	Nazism	188

74	Normalization	193
75	Occupation Gaza Strip	195
76	Occupation Golan	197
77	Occupation Lebanon	199
78	Occupation West Bank	201
79	Olive trees	203
80	Organ theft	205
81	Origin	207
82	Orthodox Jewish power	208
83	Orthodox Jews	210
84	Oslo Accords	212
85	Palestinian leaders	214
86	Palestinian people	216
87	Palestinian state is missing	220
88	Palestinian state, future	222
89	Palestinian state, history	224
90	Palestinian state, viability	228
91	Palestinian state, wish	230
92	Partition Plan	233
93	Peace	235
94	Peace education	239
95	Peace from the right	243
96	Peace negotiations	245
97	Philistines	247
98	Pigs	249
99	Poisoning Arafat	250
100	Poisoning wells	252
101	Population growth	254
102	Prisoners	256
103	Rabin murder	258
104	Racism	260
105	Refugee problem	263
106	Refugees, numbers	266
107	Resistance	269
108	Right of return	272
109	Right to exist	274
110	Roadblocks	276
111	Sabra and Shatila	277
112	Safety fence, construction	279
113	Safety fence, necessity	280

114	Saudi peace initiative	282
115	Second Intifada	284
116	Settlement construction	286
117	Settlements	289
118	Sexual harassment	291
119	Six Day War	266
120	Suffering of the Palestinians	297
121	Suicide bombers	301
122	Talmud	304
123	Temple Mount	306
124	Terror, cause	309
125	Terror, right to	311
126	Terrorists	313
127	Torah	316
128	Tourism	318
129	Two-state solution	320
130	United Nations	324
131	UN Human Rights Council	327
132	UN peacekeepers	330
133	UN UNRWA	331
134	United States	333
135	Victim culture	335
136	Violence	338
137	War crimes	340
138	War crimes, Hamas	344
139	War of Independence in 1948	346
140	Water shortage	349
141	Water theft	351
142	West Bank claims	355
143	West Bank services	358
144	West Bank withdrawal	360
145	White phosphorus	362
146	World domination	363
147	Yom Kippur war	366
148	Zionism and anti-Semitism	368
149	Zionism history	370
150	Zionism self-determination	373

Bibliography	375
Illustration Credits	377
About the Editor	379

1. Apartheid

The Palestinian Tale: Israel is an apartheid state.

In Israel, Jews, Christians, Muslims, Druze, and others live together. They all have the same rights; they all occupy the highest positions in Israeli society. Not a Jew but an Arab Druze, Raslan Alian, is currently the highest commander of the elite Golani unit of the Israeli army. The Catholic Arab Salim Joubran is a Supreme Court justice. Arabs occupy more than 10 percent of the seats in the Knesset, the Israeli parliament. The current majority Likud party has had several Arab MPs, including Ayoub Kara. Israel's ambassador to Norway, Naim Araidi, is an Arab. In 2013, Miss Israel was a very beautiful black Ethiopian woman, Yityish Aynaw; in 1999, the winner was the Muslim Rana Raslan. The highest commander in the Israeli Navy until 2011 was Eli Marom, a Chinese Jew. Not race nor creed, but hard work determines where you end up in Israel.

Israel is in actuality one of the most multicultural countries in the world! There is almost no country with such a mixed population: Arabs, Russians, Europeans and Ethiopians all live amongst each other. They lie next to each other in hospitals, picnic with each other in parks and study in the same universities. Over 400 Arab-Israeli soldiers have died in the defense of the State of Israel since 1948. Nowhere is access prohibited for certain groups of the population, as was the case under the apartheid regime in South Africa.

Ismail Khaldi, the first Muslim Bedouin to serve as a diplomat at Israel's Ministry of Foreign Affairs, said:

"The Bedouin in Israel are an example of the contribution that one can give to this democratic and free state; that is why we are proud to be part of it. I am a proud Israeli – along with many other non-Jewish Israelis such as Druze, Bahai, Bedouin, Christians and Muslims, who live in one of the most culturally diversified societies and the only true democracy in the Middle East. Like America, Israeli society is far from perfect, but let us deal honestly. By any yardstick you choose – educational opportunity, economic development, women and gay rights, freedom of speech and assembly, legislative representation – Israel's minorities fare far better than in any other country in the Middle East."

The term apartheid is often referred to specifically in conjunction with the security fence, the "wall" west of the West Bank. But before it was built, Palestinians could travel freely to Israel and many Palestinians worked in Israel. The wave of suicide attacks in the 1990s made a stricter admission policy unfortunately unavoidable. That has nothing to do with apartheid; it is one of many examples of how Arabs, by using violence, become victims of their own actions.

The accusation of apartheid is a case of projection, where Israel is blamed for a phenomenon that is widespread in the area where the Palestinians have self-government (in the West Bank and Gaza). In autonomous Palestinian territory there is indeed discrimination: no Jews are allowed to live there, and in some places – for example in the Palestinian Bir Zeit University – no Jews are even allowed to visit. For Palestinians under these authorities, selling a house to a Jew is punishable by death. Another example of discrimination: Arab-Jewish soccer games were called *"a crime against humanity"* by the president of the Palestinian Soccer Association.

Apartheid is very common in the Arab countries. Distinctions are made between the various sectors of society, and in many areas the male heterosexual Sunni minority rules violently over the rest of the population. Slavery is still very common, especially in the African Muslim countries, such as Sudan, Chad, Niger, Mali and Mauritania. In the latter country, at the moment, as much as 20 percent of the population is living under traditional slavery. Women from Cameroon are being "exported" as slaves to Kuwait and Saudi Arabia. Slavery involves an estimated 750,000 people in the Middle East and North Africa. This is in line with Islamic *Sharia* law, which states that slavery is permissible and apartheid should be applied to women and "infidels."

Discrimination and abuse of women in Arab countries are well documented. "Honor" killings of wayward relatives are commonplace. Female circumcision is very common. According to a UNICEF report from 2013, virtually all women in Somalia, Egypt, Chad, Mali, Sudan and Yemen are circumcised – or, more accurately, mutilated.

Under *Sharia* law women have few legal rights. The Norwegian Marte Dalelv very painfully discovered this in 2013. She reported her being raped in Dubai, but over the course of the lawsuit she herself was convicted to sixteen months in prison for *"extramarital sex."* This is a consequence of the fact that the testimony of a woman, according to *Sharia* law, has much less value than that of a man.

Compare that with Israel. In 2011 Israel's Jewish president, Moshe Katsav, was convicted of rape and sentenced to seven years in jail based on women's testimony. Moreover, that verdict was pronounced by the above-mentioned Arab judge Salim Joubran.

> *The World has no right to assume that Jewish statesmanship is unable to create as decent a regime as created by English, Canadian or Swiss statesmanship. After all, it is from the Jewish sources that the World has learned how the 'stranger within the gates' should be treated.*
> – Ze'ev Jabotinsky, ideological father of the Likud, 1940

Tale: Israel is an apartheid state.
Fact: In Israel, Muslims and Jews live together.
Photo: Jerusalem train to Tel Aviv.

2. Arab anti-Semitism

The Palestinian Tale: Arabs cannot be anti-Semites because they themselves are Semites.

The word anti-Semite was conceived at the end of the nineteenth century because the word Jew-hater sounds nasty. It has nothing to do with the word Semite, which indicates a people that lived thousands of years ago, and from which, according to the Bible, both Jews and Arabs are descended.

That no Arab anti-Semitism exists is utter nonsense. Anti-Semitism in almost all Arab countries is government policy. In a worldwide study on anti-Semitism in 2014, it was found that 75 percent of the population of the Middle East and North Africa has strong anti-Semitic views. In the Palestinian territories the study revealed an alarming 93 percent (for comparison, in the United States it was 10 percent). Anti-Semitism is found among the whole of Arab society, from high to low. Thus the Egyptian state television showed how even Egyptian President Morsi in a mosque prayed for the destruction of the Jews.

Islam is used as the foundation of this hatred. The head of the Fatwa department of the Al-Azhar University in Cairo – the most authoritative Islamic institution – published a list of twenty bad characteristics of Jews *"based on the Koran."* Jews, according to his list, are among other things, *"deceitful, wicked, vulgar, murderous and cursed by Allah."*

> *"Throughout history, Allah has imposed upon the Jews people who would punish them for their corruption. The last punishment was carried out by Hitler. By means of all the things he did to them – even though they exaggerated this issue – he managed to put them in their place. This was divine punishment for them. Allah willing, the next time will be at the hand of the believers.*
> *We wait for the revenge of Allah to descend upon them, and Allah willing, it will be by our own hands.*
> *Allah, do not spare a single one of them. Oh Allah, count their numbers, and kill them, down to the very last one."*
> – Statements on Al-Jazeera TV on January 30, 2009, by Yousouf Al-Qaradawi, dean of the Faculty of Sharia and Islamic Studies at the University of Qatar, also the president of the International Union of Muslim Scholars

and the European Council for Fatwa and Research. His television program on Al-Jazeera attracts 60 million viewers worldwide

Former Dutch MP Ayaan Hirsi Ali, currently a fellow of the Kennedy School of Government at Harvard University, writes in her autobiography *My Freedom* about her early childhood in Saudi Arabia – a country on whose ground Jews may not set foot:

"In Saudi Arabia, all that was bad was caused by Jews. If the air conditioning was broken or no more water came from the tap, the Saudi neighbors blamed the Jews. Their children had to pray for the health of their parents and the destruction of the Jews.
When we went to school, our teachers complained endlessly about all the devilish things the Jews had done against Muslims and all they were planning to do."

And on her teenage years in Kenya:

"As a teenager I was still a devout Muslim, I regularly made my ritual ablutions. And with each splash of water I cursed the Jews. I covered my body, spread a prayer rug facing Mecca and asked Allah to protect me from the evil that Jews spread...
With every petition that formed the imam to Allah, we shouted in unison, "Amen," and every time he called Allah destroy the Jews, I said with as much enthusiasm: "Amen."
I heard one teacher after another explain that the Jews had declared war on Islam. I learned that the Prophet Muhammad – the holiest of holy men, whose footsteps all Muslims are expected to follow – had warned of the insidious and despicable behavior of the Jews. They had betrayed him and tried to murder him. Every Jew, wherever he is, forges nefarious plans to overthrow Islam.
The Jews were the masters of the world and we had to be pure to resist their evil influence. Islam was attacked and we had to take action.
Only when all Jews would be destroyed could Muslims live in peace."

Tale: Arabs cannot be anti-Semites.
Fact: Arab anti-Semitism is widespread.
Photo: Egyptian cartoon, shortly before the Six-Day War.

3. Arab treatment of Palestinians

The Palestinian Tale: The Israelis are to blame for all Palestinian ills.

Discrimination against the Palestinians by other Arabs is widespread. Other Arabs blame the Palestinians for not fighting hard enough against the Jews in 1948, but rather fleeing. In addition, the Arab countries want to use the continuing refugee status of the Palestinian people as a means of pressure on Israel (by demanding their "right of return"). In 1959, therefore, the Arab League passed Resolution 1457:

"The Arab countries will not grant citizenship to applicants of Palestinian origin in order to prevent their assimilation into the host countries."

The Arab countries did not integrate the Palestinian refugees, despite the fact that they are co-religionists and, until 1917, were co-inhabitants of the Turkish Ottoman Empire. On the contrary, Arabs have systematically discriminated against Palestinian Arabs for generations.

Some examples:

The Gaza Strip was occupied by Egypt between 1948 and 1967. The Egyptians made Gaza a closed camp. It was almost impossible for Palestinians to leave Gaza. Severe restrictions in the areas of employment and education, for example, were imposed on the people of Gaza, both its original residents and the refugees. Every evening there was a curfew. Egypt also opposed a UN proposal to resettle 150,000 refugees in Libya, as all proposals for resettlement of refugees were blocked by the Arab countries.

In a radio broadcast in Saudi Arabia:

"Imagine, Arabs, how Nasser, who claims to be the pioneer of Arab nationalism, is behaving towards the miserable Arabs of Gaza, who are starving whilst the military governor and his officers enjoy the riches of the Strip."

The same situation, more or less, developed in the West Bank under Jordanian rule. A resident of the West Bank said in an interview with the Lebanese daily *Al Hawadith* on April 23, 1971:

> *"We lived for a long time under the humiliation of the Arab nationalism and it hurts to say that we had to wait for the Israeli conquest in order to become aware of human relations with civilians."*

In Syria, Palestinians could not own property until 1968. Under Syrian law, all Arabs can receive Syrian citizenship, except Palestinians – even if they were born in the country and the family has been living there for generations.

In Lebanon, two-thirds of Palestinians still live in camps. Lebanese hospitals refuse to treat Palestinian patients. Of the refugees in Lebanon, 56 percent are unemployed. That is the highest rate not only among Palestinians but of the entire Arab world. Those who do work, have low-paying jobs. This is the result of legally established discrimination. A series of Lebanese laws limits the Palestinians' right to citizenship, to own property and to practice certain professions, such as legal, medical and journalistic professions.

In 1970-1971 the Jordanian king Hussein set out to violently break the power of the Palestinians and of their armed militias. Estimates of the number of Palestinian deaths vary widely. According to Yasser Arafat more than 20,000 Palestinians were killed (which are more Palestinian deaths than have been caused in the conflict with Israel).
In 1988, Jordan withdrew Jordanian nationality from millions of Palestinians.

In Kuwait in 1991, 30 percent of the population was Palestinian. However, Palestinian leader Yasser Arafat chose the side of Iraqi leader Saddam Hussein when the latter invaded Kuwait. After Kuwait was liberated from Iraqi occupation, an anti-Palestinian campaign began, including persecutions, arrests and show trials. Eventually, 450,000 Palestinians were expelled from Kuwait, almost as many as had fled Israel in 1948. But in contrast, the expulsion of Palestinians from Kuwait is a forgotten chapter in history.

The Libyan Muammar Gaddafi also expelled 30,000 Palestinians because he was angry that the Palestinians had concluded peace treaties with Israel during the 1990s.

In other Arab countries, similar discriminatory measures apply. While discrimination against minorities in the Arab world is not unheard of, it is notable in the case of the Palestinians; they are considered as belonging to the Arab nation, brothers of sorts, whereas the Copts in Egypt or the Kurds in Syria are indeed minorities.

Tale: Arabs treat Palestinians in their countries well.
Fact: Palestinians are treated harshly in Arab countries.
Photo: Destruction by the Lebanese army of the Palestinian camp Nahr al-Bared in 2007, where more than 200 Palestinians were slain.

4. Arabs in Israel

The Palestinian Tale: The Arabs in Israel have a tough life.

Arabs constitute about 20 percent of the population in Israel. Approximately 90 percent of Arabs are Muslim and 10 percent are Christian.

Life expectancy is considered to be the best indicator of the health of a population, because it indicates whether people are socio-economically well off and have clean water and access to proper medical facilities. The life expectancy of Arab citizens in Israel originally lagged behind that of Jews due to socio-economic causes. In 1980, Arab-Israeli life expectancy was 72 years, two years less than that of Americans, which was then 74 years. The life expectancy of Americans increased by four years to 78 years of age in the thirty-year period since. That of Arabs in Israel, however, rose during the same period by no less than seven years and is now 79 years. So, on average, Israeli Arabs live longer than Americans. The life expectancy of Arabs in Israel is indeed higher than that of Arabs in Europe.

Opinion research confirms that many Arab Israelis are happy that they live in Israel. A survey conducted in 2012 showed that a clear majority (68 percent) of Arabs would rather live in Israel than in any other country in the world. Seventy-one percent of Arab respondents said Israel is a good place to live, while 60 percent described Israel as a "homeland." That is a lot better than, for instance, the Moroccans in the Netherlands. Of these, only 48 percent consider themselves Dutch!

In an opinion poll conducted in 2014 by Israeli television station Channel 10, Israeli Arabs were asked under which government they would prefer to live, the Israeli or the Palestinian Authority. A whopping 77 percent chose Israel! More than three quarters of the Arab citizens in Israel would rather live under Israeli rule than under Arab rule. Another study in 2015 found that 68 percent of the Arabs in Israel are proud to be Israeli citizens.

Consider the arbitrariness, corruption and terror regimes under which Arabs in countries such as Syria and Saudi Arabia live, and you will understand the preference of the Israeli Arabs. This applies equally to the Palestinians under the regimes of Hamas, the rulers of Gaza, and Fatah, which controls the West Bank.

So this is a case of projection, whereby Israel is accused of something of which Arab countries themselves are guilty.

Tale: The Arabs in Israel have a tough life.
Fact: Arabs in Israel can reach any position, including the Arab Salim Joubran (photo), a judge in the Israeli Supreme Court.

5. Arafat

The Palestinian Tale: Arafat was a peacemaker.

Yasser Arafat was born in Cairo on August 24, 1929. In his youth he traveled extensively with Haj Amin al-Husseini, a big supporter of Adolf Hitler. Al Husseini lived in Berlin during World War II and admiringly described the gas chambers of Auschwitz (see Tale: Nazism). Arafat affectionately called Al Husseini his "uncle."

Yasser Arafat's biography mainly consists of a very long list of terrorist attacks. He started his career in 1965 with terror attacks on Israel even before Israel took hold of the West Bank and the Gaza Strip (in 1967), before even one "settlement" existed. In the early 1970s the Fatah party Arafat led changed its terror tactics and focused on a series of hijackings to receive more global attention.

Some of the most notorious terror attacks have been perpetrated by Fatah (the largest organization within the PLO): a bomb aboard a Swissair plane to Tel Aviv killed 47 (1970), three teachers and nine students were murdered by a missile aimed at an Israeli school bus (1970), 27 people were slain in a shooting at an Israeli airport (1972), eleven Israeli athletes were murdered at the Olympic Games in Munich (1972), 26 people were murdered in an attack on a school in northern Israel, including 21 children (1974), and 37 Israeli civilians were killed in the hijacking of a bus, including 12 children (1978).

In 1993, Yasser Arafat signed the Oslo Accords, in which he renounced terror and violence. But he never adhered to the agreement.

Evidence which Israel has intercepted shows that Arafat continued to support and finance terrorist attacks. It also appears that since 1997 – and possibly earlier – he agreed with other terrorist organizations like Hamas and Islamic Jihad to continue to carry out attacks despite the peace accords. His own terror groups continued to conduct terrorist attacks, such as the notorious Al-Aqsa Martyrs' Brigades of his Fatah movement. From the start of the second intifada, which Arafat planned and organized (see Tale: Second Intifada) in 2000, Fatah terror was openly visible.

In 2002, Israel intercepted the ship Karine-A, loaded with 50 tons of mortars, rocket launchers, anti-tank mines and many more weapons. The captain explained that he was acting on orders from Arafat.

To Arab audiences Arafat continuously insisted that he did not take seriously the peace treaties he had signed. He declared not long after the signing, in a private speech at a mosque in Johannesburg, South Africa (which leaked an audio recording):
"The Jihad will continue.
I can't do it alone.
No! You have to come, and to fight and to start the Jihad to liberate Jerusalem, your first shrine.
This agreement, I am not considering it more than the agreement which had been signed between our prophet Mohammed and Koraish, and you remember the Caliph Omar had refused this agreement and [considered] it a despicable truce. But Muhammad had accepted it and we are accepting now this peace accord."

Arafat was comparing the Oslo accords with a ten-year truce signed by Mohammed with the tribe that originally controlled Mecca. However, two years later, when Muhammad's army had become stronger, he went ahead and attacked and captured Mecca.

In 1996, Arafat said in a speech in the Swedish capital Stockholm (also leaked):
"We Palestinians will take over everything, including all of Jerusalem.
You understand that we plan to eliminate the State of Israel and establish a purely Palestinian State. We will make life unbearable for Jews by psychological warfare and a population explosion; Jews will not want to live among us Arabs! I have no use for Jews, they are and remain Jews!"

In the same year, Arafat spoke publicly in Bethlehem:
"We know only one word, jihad, jihad, jihad. Whoever does not like it can drink from the Dead Sea or from the Sea of Gaza."

To Abd Al-Bari Atwan, editor of the Arab newspaper *Al-Quds* Al-Arabi, Arafat said:
"By Allah, I will drive them crazy. I will make these [Oslo] Accords a disaster for them [Israel]. It won't be in my lifetime, but you will see the Israelis run away from Palestine. Have a little patience."

To the Western world, Arafat continued to claim he was pursuing peace. For the Americans that tale was finally finished in 2002, when Arafat denied that he was involved with the ship that smuggled 50 tons of weapons, despite abundant evidence to the contrary. (About the violence organized by Arafat see Tale: Second Intifada.)

It is obvious that Arafat signed the peace agreements to get land transferred from Israel, but never wanted to give back real peace. He was not a second Nelson Mandela. Instead, Arafat acted fully in accordance with the *Plan for the phased destruction of Israel* that the PLO, under his leadership, adopted in 1974:

"The Palestine Liberation Organization will employ all means, and first and foremost armed struggle, to liberate Palestinian territory and to establish the independent combatant national authority for the people over every part of Palestinian territory that is liberated.

Once it is established, the Palestinian national authority will strive to achieve a union of the confrontation countries, with the aim of completing the liberation of all Palestinian territory, and as a step along the road to comprehensive Arab unity."

Tale: Arafat was a peacemaker.
Fact: Arafat ordered the most horrific acts of terrorism.
Photo: The bus that was burned by terrorists of Arafat's Fatah during the coastal road massacre, in which 38 Israeli civilians were killed, including 13 children. The commander Dalal Mughrabi is revered as a hero by the Palestinian Authority; schools and squares are named after her.

6. Archaeology

The Palestinian Tale: Israel uses archeology to oppress the Palestinians.

The Palestinians claim that the Israelis are looking only for Jewish historical remnants because they want to annoy them with extensive excavations.

However, there is hardly any other territory that is as rich in history and archeology as Israel, with remains from prehistoric times down to the modern day, and from a myriad of inhabitants: Jews, Canaanites, Philistines, Nabateans, Greeks, Romans, Crusaders, Byzantines and Arabs. And as anyone can see when looking at Israeli archaeological sites, they are all carefully excavated and examined, certainly not just recognizing Jewish history.

The irritation is caused in fact because archaeologists have indeed found many traces of Jewish history, something that the Palestinians do not like politically and which refutes another tale of theirs (see Tale: Jerusalem history).

As has been repeatedly shown, this is a case of Arab projection, in which Israel is blamed for behaviors that on the contrary are strikingly abundant in Arab countries: the disregard of (the remains of) other cultures. Well-known examples include the detonation of two giant sixth-century Buddha statues by Muslims in Afghanistan in 2001, the destruction of ancient mausoleums in Timbuktu in 2013 and the demolition of the temple in Palmyra (Syria) in 2015, all of which had been declared World Heritage monuments by UNESCO.

Palestinians collaborate wholeheartedly in this destruction. For example, Hamas bulldozers destroyed in April 2013 a portion of the ancient port of Anthedon in the Gaza Strip in order to build a military training ground. This port is more than 3,000 years old and originates from the Mycenaean period, but also mosaics and other remains from the Roman, Byzantine and Islamic periods were found on the site. The location was only a year earlier declared a World Cultural Heritage site by UNESCO.

Jewish archaeological items suffer the same fate. For example, on the Temple Mount the Palestinians undertook enormous excavations in the period 1996-1999 to dig out an underground mosque in the mountain. This was done despite the fact that the Temple Mount is also a designated World Heritage site – and one of the most important archaeological sites in the world. Bulldozers dug violently in the ground, after which 400 fully loaded trucks removed the debris. All that rubble, filled with archaeological remains, was dumped on a rubbish heap.

Israeli archaeologists are to this day busy carefully examining the material of the rubbish-heap. Obviously, important information is lost, because the exact locations of the findings are no longer known. But in the rubble thousands of important artifacts have been discovered, such as jewelry, signet rings, coins, arrowheads and floor tiles, comprising 3,000 years of Jerusalem history.

Tale: Israel uses archeology to oppress the Palestinians.
Fact: Archaeologists and volunteers have been working since 2004 to examine the Palestinian archaeological destruction of the Temple Mount historical site.

7. Atomic bomb

The Palestinian Tale: If Israel is allowed to develop a nuclear bomb, then Iran must have one too.

There are five reasons why this argument does not hold true, and why the possibility of Iran developing a nuclear weapon is an alarming and dangerous development.

First of all, Israel's survival has since its founding in 1948 been threatened by neighboring countries such as Egypt, Libya and Syria, which have much larger armies. Hence, Israel naturally desires deterrents like nuclear bombs. The nuclear deterrent is needed against countries like Iran, whose leaders repeatedly state that Israel must be completely destroyed.

Israel has never signed the international nuclear non-proliferation treaty (which aims to stop the spread of nuclear weapons), and so needs not adhere to it. However, Israel has expressly stated that it will never use nuclear weapons first, one of the requirements of the Convention.

On the other hand, Iran has signed the non-proliferation treaty. It thereby refrained voluntarily from developing nuclear weapons in exchange for a supply of nuclear knowledge for peaceful uses such as power generation. Iran must therefore allow inspections of its nuclear facilities by the International Atomic Energy Agency, which has concluded that regardless of the treaty Iran has been working on the development of nuclear weapons since 2003.

This means that Iran has not only violated the international non-proliferation treaty, to which it is a signatory, but it has deliberately lied to the world since 2003. This indicates that for Iran, the possession of nuclear weapons is more important than its international obligations. The knowledge transferred in breach of the agreements is misused for military purposes.

Israel's anxiety about its deterrence capabilities is fed by the aggressive nature of the Islamic government in Iran. Iran wants to be an important regional player and distribute the Shiite variant of Islam. As a result, Iran is involved in many conflicts in the Middle East. Remember the Iran-Iraq war in the 1980s, which caused approxi-mately 1 million deaths. Iran was and is involved in the violence in neighboring Syria, Iraq and Afghanistan. Iran furthermore finances, promotes and arms terrorist organizations such as the radical Islamic terrorist organization Hezbollah, which in 2006 pushed Lebanon into war with Israel.

Moreover, Iran is not a democracy but a religious Islamic dictatorship. Its actual power is in the hands of the ayatollahs, the Shiite spiritual leaders. These are extremists who hang gay men and stone adulterous women. Anti-Semitism is as widespread in Iran as it is in the Sunni world (see Tale: Arab anti-Semitism). Ayatollah Khomeini, who founded the Islamic dictatorship, wrote in his classic book *Hukumat-i Islami* (Islamic government) in 1970 about the *"miserable Jews"* and used Islamic history to depict Jews as the source of the Muslims' woes and therefore asked Allah to curse them.

Part of Shiite tradition is the belief in the coming of a Shiite messiah called Al-Mahdi during a time of global chaos. According to the tradition, nations will perish and a third of the world population will die during this global chaos. The former Iranian president, Mahmoud Ahmadinejad, is himself a member of the Hojjatieh movement, a group that believes that believers can and should actively accelerate the arrival of the Al-Mahdi. Ahmadinejad opened his speech to the United Nations in 2007 with the wish: *"Allah, accelerate the arrival of Imam al-Mahdi; grant him good health and victory."*

The ayatollahs are dangerous and should not get a finger near that red button. Not only is Israel threatened; Western Europe is also in reach of Iran's missiles. The world cannot risk ayatollahs, out of religious fervor, causing a nuclear Armageddon (the biblical end of times).

Tale: If Israel is allowed a nuclear bomb, Iran must have one too.
Fact: Iran kept nuclear sites hidden, in violation of international treaties.
Photo: Secret nuclear plant Natanz that Iran concealed until 2002.

8. Beasts (wild)

The Palestinian Tale: Animals in the wild are controlled by Israel.

Conspiracy theories (see Tale: Conspiracy theories) are popular in the Arab world, particularly those that claim Israel can manipulate animals.

Thus, the Palestinian newspaper *Al-Quds* in August 2015 reported that Hamas had caught a dolphin that the Israeli navy had purportedly used to attack members of Hamas's armed wing. According to the newspaper, Hamas fighters had seen a pod of dolphins making *"suspicious movements."* One dolphin was captured and was discovered to be equipped with a camera and a device to shoot arrows, according to Hamas. The animal could therewith have attacked Hamas frogmen.

The poor dolphin follows a long line of animals that were supposed to be manipulated by Israel to spy or attack Arabs, such as engineered mosquitoes, spying birds, eavesdropping squirrels and deadly jellyfish. Very spectacular was the story in 2011 about an Israeli radio-controlled shark developed to attack tourists in Egypt. As the newspapers reported at the time, the story was even spread by an Egyptian government spokesman: *"What is being said about the Mossad throwing the deadly shark to hit tourism in Egypt is not out of the question. But it needs time to confirm."*

Israel controls animals in nature. It's really too ridiculous for words, were it not for the fact that millions of Arabs would actually believe this kind of nonsense.

Tale: Animals in the wild are controlled by Israel.
Fact: Dolphins do not handle guns.

9. Blood libel

The Palestinian Tale: Israel is waging war in order to drink the blood of Palestinian children.

This assertion is based on the insane medieval blood libel that brought many Jews to the stake. The lie was spread that Jews have a religious duty to kill non-Jews to use their blood in Jewish rituals. But according to Jewish law, the consumption of blood is impermissible. Meat products prepared with blood are by definition counter to kosher dietary regulations, which require all blood from slaughtered animals to be removed through a process of rinsing and salting.

Nowadays this hateful tale is popular with Muslim fundamentalists. The blood libel, coming from Christian countries in the Middle Ages, is now alive in the Arab world, in countries like Egypt, Syria and Jordan. Below are two examples.

> *"One will kill the other and drink his blood, and thus attain eternal life. The Children of Israel had the holiday of Pesach, what is now called Passover. Every holiday, every group would look for a small child, kidnap and steal him, bring a barrel called the barrel of nails. ...*
> *They would put the small child in the barrel and his body would be pierced by these nails. In the bottom of the barrel they would put a faucet and pour the blood...*
> *The Devil or one of the big gods, demanded it of them as a condition for fulfilling their wishes, that they eat [matzah] bread kneaded with the blood of children."*
> – Sheikh Khaled Al-Mughrabi, who on behalf of the Palestinian Authority teaches twice weekly Islamic lessons in the Al-Aqsa Mosque on the Temple Mount in Jerusalem on May 29, 2015

"The targeting of Palestinian children has to do with faith. The Zionist entity subscribes to false biblical doctrines – especially today. This is manifest in the Koran, which quoted the Jews as saying: 'kill the sons of the believers' [Koran 40:25]. Thus, they subscribe to a principle of faith, which they must implement, and kill the sons of the believers.
In addition, they have beliefs which they have tried to conceal from the world. I am referring to the ancient biblical beliefs, which instructed [the Jews] to kill children and collect their blood, in order to knead it into the bread that is eaten on Passover."

– Hamas leader Salah Al-Bardawil on Hamas Al-Aqsa TV on November 26, 2015

This spokesman reveals here the root cause of the violence from Gaza, an area from which the Israeli army completely pulled out in 2005. That is the insane hatred of Muslim fundamentalist terror organizations such as Hamas and Islamic Jihad against people of other faiths in general and Jews in particular.

Tale: Jews drink the blood of non-Jews.
Fact: Medieval hogwash.
Photo: Death of Simon by Trent Michel Wolgemut and Wilhelm Pleydenwurff in Hartmann Schedel's *Nürnberger Weltchronik* (1493).

10. Borders

The Palestinian Tale: The borders of a Palestinian state are established.

What is usually referred to as the "1967 borders" or "green line" is actually a reference to the armistice line of 1949. A ceasefire line is not an official border.

The armistice agreement between Israel and Jordan in 1949 expressly states that the Green Line is an armistice line, which
> *"shall not be interpreted as prejudicing, in any sense, an ultimate political settlement between the Parties to this Agreement.*
> *The Armistice Demarcation Lines ... are agreed upon by the Parties without prejudice to future territorial settlements or boundary lines or to claims of either Party relating thereto."*

Jordan and the other Arab states have refused to recognize the Green Line as a border because of their unwillingness to accept the legitimacy of Israel, even within the Green Line.

By signing a peace agreement, Israel and Jordan have now mutually recognized that the ceasefire, and thereby the armistice lines, have been terminated. As a result, the Green Line is now not even an armistice line anymore and has no standing in international law in any way whatsoever. Jordan no longer claims the area west of the Jordan River, and the Jordan River now forms the western border of the state of Jordan.

The famous Resolution 242 of the Security Council in 1967 explicitly states that Israel is entitled to secure and recognized borders in exchange for a partial withdrawal from occupied territory. The resolution does not refer to the Green Line (see also the Tale: West Bank claims). The armistice line of 1949 does not form secure borders for Israel, as with these borders, Israel would be only 12 kilometers wide.
Yet, this tale claims that the temporary truce line must have the legal status of a permanent border.

"In the pre-1967 borders, Israel was barely ten miles wide at its narrowest point. The bulk of Israel's population lived within artillery range of hostile armies. I am not about to ask Israel to live that way again."
– The then American president Ronald Reagan in 1982

"Now they say we should go back to the '67 borders, but that's where we were so why was there a war?
And we had '47 borders [Partition Plan of the UN]. We didn't like them very much but we said yes to them. But there was still a war.
And after the '48 war they said we should go back to the '47 borders. But that's where we were. And that's where they wanted to get us out from.
They still nurture a hope that at some time we'll disappear."
– The then Israeli Prime Minister Golda Meir in the 1970s

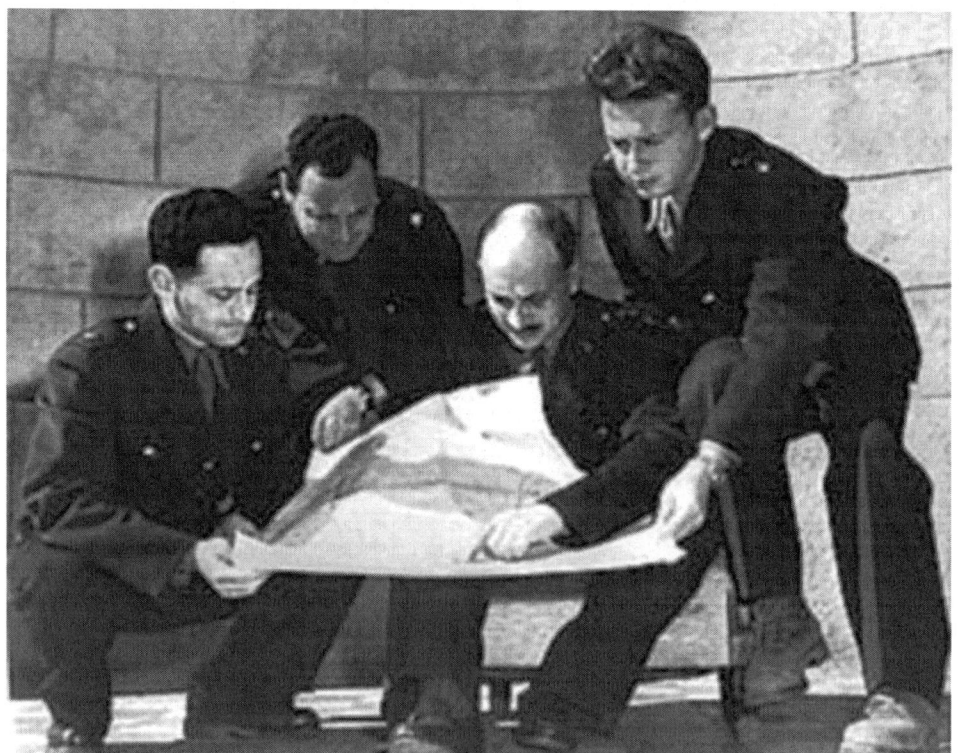

Tale: Israel and Palestine have recognized borders.
Fact: The Arab countries wanted only to establish ceasefire lines in 1949.
Photo: Israeli negotiating team in January 1949, with the future Prime Minister Yitzhak Rabin (right).

11. Boycott

The Palestinian Tale: A boycott of Israeli products will help bring peace.

The boycott movement against Israel (Boycott, Divest, Sanction, or BDS) purports to be for peace, but in reality its "peaceful solution" is the destruction of Israel. This is pointed out bluntly by BDS founder Omar Barghouti. Incidentally, and hypocritically, Barghouti studied at the University of Tel Aviv.

If you look at the boycotts, then it is clear how ignorant the boycotters are of what they are doing. Boycotts usually focus on agricultural products, while the major Israeli exports nowadays are high-tech products. For example there is no computer, tablet, laptop or smartphone which does not incorporate some Israeli technology (see Tale: Economy, Israeli).

BDS even calls for boycotts that will deprive the Palestinians of essential public facilities (see Tale: West Bank services). Another point of ignorance is that boycotts hit the Palestinian population harder than the Israelis. A significant portion of the income of the Palestinians in the West Bank is earned at Israeli companies (see Tale: Economy, Palestinian). When under pressure from BDS the Israeli company SodaStream moved its factory from the West Bank to the Negev, it cost 500 Palestinians their (well-paying) jobs. Their work is now done by Bedouins in the Negev. For good reason, it was found in a poll in 2010 that a large majority (60 percent) of Palestinians is against a boycott of Israeli products.

In 2014 the Palestinian Authority also became fed up with the boycotters. A spokesman in Ramallah said that the BDS movement creates an image that all Palestinians are radicals who prefer to damage Israel above all and are not interested in peace. This was on the occasion when boycotters disturbed the performance of an Indian dance group in Ramallah because the troupe had also performed in Israel, which made each participant guilty, in BDS's eyes, of *"normalization of relations with Israel."* However, the show was also attended by leaders of the Palestinian Authority, who were severely embarrassed by the riot.

Therefore – for the first time – four prominent boycott activists were arrested by the Palestinian Authority. They are being prosecuted for *"organizing riots and disturbing public order."*

And Israelis? They see that there are many calls to boycott the only Jewish state, but not Turkey, Morocco or China for their cruel occupations of respectively northern Cyprus, Western Sahara and Tibet. They also see that no one asks for separate labeling of products from other disputed territories, including the Crimea, which is occupied by Russia.

Therefore, they see boycotts only targeting Israel not as an incentive for peace, but as discrimination.

Boycotts of Israeli products are indeed condemned by French courts as anti-Semitic because they are based on discrimination. These rulings were appealed at the European Court of Human Rights in Strasbourg on the grounds that the anti-boycott verdict would violate freedom of speech. However, that appeal was rejected on July 23, 2009.

Similarly, individual U.S. states are taking legislative action against the BDS movement. For instance, South Carolina passed legislation that bars state agencies from contracting with any business that boycotts others *"based on race, color, religion, gender, or national origin."*

Tale: A boycott of Israeli products will help to bring peace.
Fact: Boycotts cost Palestinians their jobs.
Photo: Israeli industrial park Mishor Adumim in the West Bank, where the former SodaStream factory now stands deserted.

12. Caliphate

The Palestinian Tale: Palestinians are not interested in the pursuit of a Muslim caliphate.

According to various opinion polls, the majority of Palestinians support Hamas. Hamas won the majority vote in the last Palestinian elections (2006). The goal of Hamas, as stipulated in its charter, is to establish an Islamic empire (caliphate). This caliphate would cover all areas ever ruled by Muslims. Article 11 of the charter says:

> *"Palestine is an Islamic Waqf [an inalienable religious endowment in Islamic law, usually a plot of land] throughout all generations and to the Day of Resurrection. This is the status [of the land] in Islamic Sharia, and it is similar to all lands conquered by Islam by force, and made thereby Waqf lands upon their conquest, for all generations of Muslims until the Day of Resurrection."*

Hamas's objective is exactly the same as the objective held by the Islamic State (IS). It is not only "Palestine" – including Israel – that must be "recaptured," but also southern European countries like Spain, Greece, Croatia, Slovenia and Bulgaria.

In fact, Muslim fundamentalists believe that all this land is up for grabs. As the Lebanese cleric Amin Al-Kurdi stated on the television channel of Hamas on June 3, 2012:

> *"They [Gaza's inhabitants] are now talking about the liberation of Andalusia, because they consider the liberation of the Al-Aqsa Mosque and of Jerusalem to be a done deal, Allah willing. They know have their sights set on Andalusia, which the Muslims lost. They are convinced, because of their faith in Allah – and we are with them – that the liberation of the Al-Aqsa Mosque is a done deal. It will be liberated, and Jerusalem and Palestine in its entirety will be in the possession of the Muslims."*

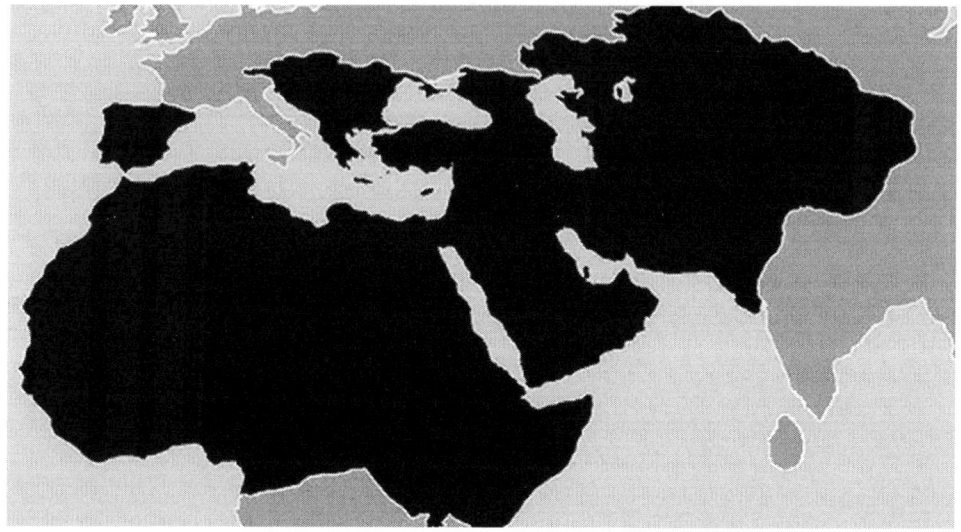

Tale: Palestinians are not interested in the pursuit of a caliphate.
Fact: Like the Islamic State, Hamas claims all land belonging, or that ever belonged to, Muslims.
Photo: The area claimed by Muslim fundamentalists for the caliphate.

13. Chosen people

The Palestinian Tale: Jews consider themselves superior as "the chosen people."

In the Torah, the Jewish people are repeatedly called "the chosen people."
In the Jewish tradition, however, this means that Judaism has a duty to speak of and teach about the one God and the need for compassion, as described in the Torah. Therefore, the Jewish people must live by high moral standards.
It puts therefore obligations on Jews; it does not imply that therefore Jews are privileged over other nations.

> *"He must be blind indeed who will assert that the Jews are not the chosen people – the people chosen for universal hatred."*
> – Leo Pinsker in 1882 in *Self-Emancipation*, the first book that argued for a modern Jewish state

Tale: Jews consider themselves superior.
Fact: Jews feel bound by such moral standards as the Ten Commandments (photo), which is precisely based on the equality of all people.

14. Christians

The Palestinian Tale: Christians are having a tough time in Israel.

On the contrary, Israeli Christians are a social success. For example, Christians score highest in Israeli education; in 2011, 64 percent of Christian students achieved the Israeli matriculation diploma giving access to higher education. Among Jews this number was 59 percent and among Muslims 48 percent.

The Christian community in Israel has grown considerably since the State of Israel was founded. In 1948, the number of Christians in Israel totaled approximately 30,000. In 2012 this number had increased five-fold to around 160,000. In addition, there is a large number of Christian foreign workers (mainly Filipinos).

This tale is another case of Arab projection, whereby Israel is criticized unjustly of persecution that in reality is happening in the Arab countries.

Christians in autonomous Palestinian territory – with Palestinian self-government – are having it difficult indeed, because of discrimination, intimidation, attempts at forced conversion and violence by Muslims.

For instance, in 1946, 80 percent of the population of Bethlehem was Christian. Their number has currently declined to 15 percent at most, a percentage that further decreases each year. The Gaza Strip has seen the number of Christians cut in half in the five years since the Hamas take-over in 2007. The pressure on Christians in the Gaza Strip to convert to an Islamic way of life continues to increase. With the current rate of emigration, in one or two generations there will be no more Christians living in the autonomous Palestinian territory. At the moment there are already more Palestinian Christians living in Chile than in the Palestinian territories.

This phenomenon occurs in all Islamic countries in the Middle East and North Africa. One hundred years ago, Christians were 20 percent of the population in the region; nowadays they make up only 5 percent of the population. In Turkey, the number of Christians declined in this period from 20 percent to 0.2 percent. In Iraq, only 5 percent of the population is Christian, but they constitute 40 percent of the Iraqis who fled abroad in recent years. And hundreds of thousands have been killed. In Sudan alone about 1.5 million Christians have been killed since 1984.

Israeli Greek Orthodox priest Gabriel Naddaf therefore said in 2014, in a speech to the UN Human Rights Council:

"Every year in the last decade, 100,000 Christians were killed throughout the Middle East, meaning that every five minutes a Christian was killed because of his faith ... those who could escape persecution by Muslim extremists fled, and those that remained are second- if not third-class citizens under Muslim rulers.

In the societies of the Middle East, there is one country where Christianity is not persecuted. Moreover, there is freedom of speech, worship and security warmly bestowed by Israel, the Jewish State.

Leaders, peace activists, end this witch hunt against the only free country in the region."

Tale: Christians are having a tough time in Israel.
Fact: Israel is the only country in the Middle East where Christians are safe.
Photo: Father Naddaf with his family.

15. Civilian Casualties

The Palestinian Tale: Israel is responsible for all Palestinian civilian casualties.

Islamic terrorist groups like Hamas by definition target their violence against innocent and defenseless civilians. That's a war crime (see Tale: War crimes, Hamas). Organizations such as the Taliban, Hamas and Islamic State also commit a second war crime at the same time: that is the hiding of their fighters, their weapons, explosives and missile installations behind and between their own citizens – even in homes, hospitals and mosques. This is the tactic of using "human shields." It is a horrible war crime, of course prohibited in the Geneva Convention of 1949. Although Israel does its best to target only fighters – and largely succeeds – it is because of this war crime that Palestinian civilian casualties are often caused in the conflict between Israel and Hamas. If Palestinian fighters would not hide among civilians, far fewer Palestinian civilians would be killed.

Moreover, it seems that many of the dead who – according to Hamas – were "civilians," were actually combatants. There are always few women among the victims, even though they make up half of the civilian population. This fact indicates that deaths recorded as "civilian" have in reality been members of terrorist organizations, as can often be determined from the victim's presence on social media. The same applies to many teenage boys that died (the reported casualties in 2014 included almost no girls), apparently used as child soldiers.

It is true that there are civilian casualties, however, these are largely the result of Hamas's call to act as human shields. While Israel issues air raid warnings to save civilian lives, Hamas issues messages to the Gaza population to ignore these notices. For instance in a directive from Hamas during the fights in 2014, it stated that the Israeli warnings
> *"are designed to weaken our resolve and to sow panic and fear among us, in light of the failures of our enemies. We call on Gaza residents not to pay attention to these messages and not to leave their homes."*

That's right. Hamas calls on the Palestinian citizens to deliberately put themselves in danger and therefore to sacrifice themselves. Hamas Member of Parliament Fathi Hammad is proud of this war crime. He declared on official Hamas TV:

"[The enemies of Allah] do not know that the Palestinian people has developed its [methods] of death and death-seeking. For the Palestinian people, death has become an industry, at which women excel, and so do all the people living on this land. The elderly excel at this, and so do the mujahedeen and the children. This is why they have formed human shields of the women, the children, the elderly, and the mujahedeen, in order to challenge the Zionist bombing machine. It is as if they were saying to the Zionist enemy: 'We desire death like you desire life.'"

The tale is therefore a case of Arab projection, in which Israel is blamed for something – in this case, civilian casualties – that is caused by the Arabs themselves. When terrorists fight from within the civilian population, they use a tactic called asymmetrical warfare that inevitably results in civilian deaths. It happens not only with Israel, but also for example with the Western armies in Afghanistan and Iraq. In Afghanistan many thousands if not tens of thousands of Afghan civilians have been killed by allied forces. Yet there was no call for a UN investigation or trial. Similarly, 5,239 people were killed and wounded in Yemen in the first half of 2015, of which 86 percent were civilians, according to a UN report. This civilian slaughter received almost zero news coverage.

These comparisons show that Israel is treated differently than other countries, while in fact no country does as much to avoid civilian casualties (see Tale: War crimes). The former commander of British forces in Afghanistan, Colonel Richard Kemp, testified before the United Nations about the 2014 war in Gaza:

"Innocent civilians were killed. War is chaos and full of mistakes. There have been mistakes by the British, American and other forces in Afghanistan and in Iraq, many of which can be put down to human error. But mistakes are not war crimes. More than anything, the civilian casualties were a consequence of Hamas's way of fighting. Hamas deliberately tried to sacrifice their own civilians.
And I say this again: the IDF did more to safeguard the rights of civilians in a combat zone than any other army in the history of warfare."

During the war in 2014 a Hamas spokesman called the method of human shields *"very successful."* What is that success, in the eyes of Hamas?

First, Muslim fundamentalists believe that anyone who "dies in the struggle against infidels" is an Islamic martyr. Each new death is a reason for Hamas to celebrate. Even the family of the victim is expected to be happy and proud. Mothers also often bear witness on Hamas television that they are very pleased with the death of their children (see Tale: Motherly love).

Secondly, Hamas knows that there are naïve people in the West who will always blame Israel for civilian deaths. Unfortunately, they are correct, because there are people who do not realize that Hamas bears the full guilt for both Israeli and Palestinian civilian casualties, because of their double war crime.

> *"If we accept the notion that terrorists will have immunity because as they fire on civilians they hide behind civilians, then this tactic will be legitimized and the terrorists will have their greatest victory."*
> – Israeli Prime Minister Benjamin Netanyahu

Tale: Israel is responsible for Palestinian civilian casualties.
Fact: Hamas provokes those casualties by using civilians and civilian buildings as cover.
Photo: Explosives in a mosque in Gaza.

16. Collaborators

The Palestinian Tale: It is logical that the Palestinians execute collaborators with Israel.

Those that the Palestinian regimes call collaborators (traitors) are largely Palestinians who give information about terrorists to Israel. The Palestinian Authority, which is obligated under the Oslo peace treaty to act against terrorists and to arrest them, rarely does so except occasionally under heavy American pressure, and even then the terrorists are thereafter quickly released. Because of these violations of the Oslo Accords, Israel itself is forced to act against Palestinian terrorists.

These so-called Palestinian "collaborators" act against violence and for peace because the Palestinian Authority fails to do so. More heinous is that these people are executed – often without due process.

Furthermore, the accusation of "collaborator" often turns out to be a front for Fatah and Hamas to murder political opponents. In retrospect, some victims turn out to be advocates of peace with Israel or opponents of the regime.

On November 20, 2012, six "collaborators" were murdered brutally and then dragged behind motorbikes in a public execution through the streets of Gaza City. The accusation of "espionage for Israel" by Hamas, which governs Gaza, turned out to be totally fabricated. One of the victims was even a member of a Muslim fundamentalist organization with ties to al-Qaeda, and therefore a "competitor" of Hamas. He was actually wanted by Israel because of his connection to a terrorist attack. And before he was killed, he had been incarcerated for many years in a Hamas prison, so spying for Israel was certainly out of the question.

In August 2014 around thirty "collaborators" were again killed in the streets of Gaza City. According to their relatives, these were people who had protested Hamas's senseless war against Israel. These killings are one of the many Palestinian violations of human rights and of the Oslo peace treaty.

Tale: It is logical that the Palestinians execute collaborators with Israel. The executed traitors are all spies for Israel.
Fact: The victims are often killed for other reasons, for example because they are political opponents.
Photo: A lynched "collaborator" in 1992.

17. Colonialism

The Palestinian Tale: Israel is fundamentally a European colonialist institution.

In 1922, the League of Nations, predecessor to the United Nations, decided unanimously that the Jews, after centuries of exile, persecution and discrimination, were entitled to a country. That country was the British Mandate for Palestine, which included present-day Israel, Jordan, the West Bank, Gaza and the Golan.

Twenty-two Arab countries in total were founded within the region of the former empire, one of them being a predominantly Christian country at the time (Lebanon).
What was more logical than granting self-determination to the oldest population of Middle East, the Jews, in their historical homeland? Moreover, the region destined to be the Jewish state was just a snippet of the whole area. In fact, the region on which the modern-day Arab countries were founded is 640 times the size of Israel.

As Winston Churchill wrote:
> *"It is manifestly right that the Jews, who are scattered all over the world, should have a national centre and a National Home. And where else could that be but in this land of Palestine, with which for more than 3,000 years they have been intimately and profoundly associated?*
> *We think it will be good for the World and good for the Jews. But we also think it will be good for the Arabs."*

The same was true for the famous "Lawrence of Arabia"; the Arabist and lifelong friend of Arab nationalism. In 1917 and 1918, he helped as an officer in the British Army to support the Arab revolt against the Turks. After that, he was an advisor of several Arab rulers. He saw Jewish immigration to the British Mandate as highly beneficial to the Arabs: *"The sooner the Jews farm it, all the better: Their colonies are bright spots in a desert."*

In 1920, he wrote an article stating that:

> *"The colonists will take back with them to the land which they occupied for some centuries before the Christian era samples of all the knowledge and technique of Europe.*
>
> *The success of their [Zionist] scheme will involve inevitably the raising of the present Arab population to their own material level, only a little after themselves in point of time, and the consequences might be of the highest importance for the future of the Arab world. It might well prove a source of technical supply rendering them independent of industrial Europe, and in that case the new confederation might become a formidable element of world power."*

The later king of Iraq, Faisal I, son of the Sharif of Mecca and descendant of Muhammad, wrote in 1919:

> *"We feel that the Arabs and Jews are cousins in having suffered similar oppressions at the hands of powers stronger than themselves, and by a happy coincidence have been able to take the first step towards the attainment of their national ideals together.*
>
> ***The Arabs, especially the educated among us, look with the deepest sympathy on the Zionist movement.***
>
> *Our deputation here in Paris is fully acquainted with the proposals submitted yesterday by the Zionist Organization to the Peace Conference, and we regard them as moderate and proper. We will do our best, in so far as we are concerned, to help them through: we will wish the Jews a most hearty welcome home. The Jewish movement is national and not imperialist. Our movement is national and not imperialist, **and there is room in Syria for us both.**"*

In 1919, Faisal even signed a treaty with the Zionists in which he openly supported the founding of the Jewish state on the condition that the Arabs would gain their independence as well. England did not allow this at the time. Perhaps surprisingly, even the majority of Israeli Arabs believe that the Jews have a legitimate claim to the area. In a survey held in January 2016, 57 percent of Israeli Arabs expressed that the Jews have equally large or even larger historical, religious and cultural ties with the country than do the Palestinians. Only 27 percent believed that the Palestinian ties are greater.

Anthropologist José R. Martínez-Cobo designed a checklist to assess whether a people is indigenous. This anthropologist was also the Special Rapporteur of the Subcommittee on Prevention of Discrimination and Protection of Minorities of the United Nations. The checklist includes primarily living on ancestral land (or at least a part of it) and having common ancestry with the original inhabitants of the country. Secondly, it is the culture – including religion, community shape, clothing, livelihood, lifestyle and so on – and, moreover, that the language and religion are connected to the ancestral land. When applied to the Jewish people, the checklist clearly indicates that the Jews have a longer-lasting and more intensive relationship with the land than the Arabs claim to have had.

The Arabs arrived in the Mediterranean 2,000 years after the Jews and, until recently, have oppressed resident populations, such as Copts, Yazidis, Kurds and Berbers.
Of the Jewish population in Israel, the majority was born in an Arab country or has at least one ancestor from an Arab country (see Tale: Origin).

Israel has stronger claims to exist than Suriname or Australia, and yet, no one calls for their elimination.
In fact, Israel is the oldest country in the world with the same name, the same language and the same faith – after 3,000 years!

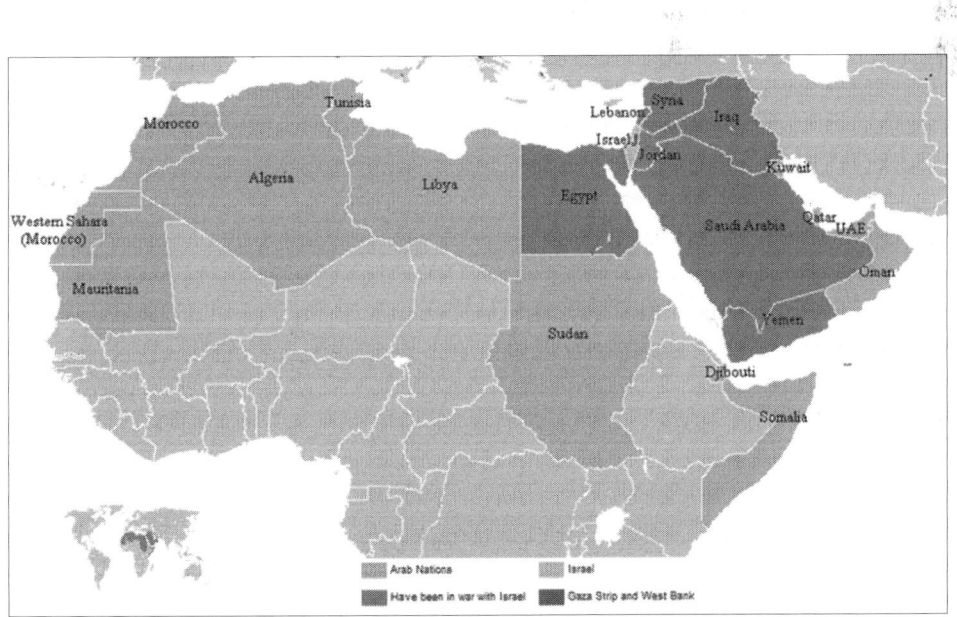

Tale: Israel is an artificial invention.
Fact: Almost all Arab countries were newly created after the breakup of the Ottoman Empire.

18. Conflict

The Palestinian Tale: If the Arab-Israeli conflict were resolved, there would be peace all over the Middle East.

There are huge problems in the Arab world, which Arabs themselves are causing and which have no relationship with current or past Western interference. The Arabs like to blame all ills on the West, due to their victim culture (see Tale: Victim culture). But this blame game itself is a problem; it results in a lack of taking responsibility. The big problems of the Arab world, like oppressive regimes, lack of human rights, conflicts between Sunnis and Shiites, Islamism and Jihadism, oppression of minorities and women, poor education, weak economic structure and so on, have nothing or little to do with the world outside the Middle East. These are problems caused by the culture of the Middle East itself.

There is a lot of attention focused on the conflict between the Arabs and Israel. On the one hand this is due to the victim role, making it possible for Arabs to blame all their problems on Israel. Arab leaders do so gladly – to divert attention from their own failures. On the other hand it is because Jews attract much interest – "Jews are news."

This means that the conflict is greatly overexposed in the media. In a list of numbers of deaths in conflicts since 1945, this conflict reaches only the 48th place (based on a list compiled by Professor Gunnar Heinshon in 1999) with 40,000 Arab and 22,000 Jewish dead. In that same period, 11 million Muslims were killed in other conflicts. More than 90 percent of these were slain by fellow Muslims. So there were about 250 times more Muslims slain by Islamic violence than in the conflict with Israel.

For example: In the 1990s, just in the Algerian civil war against Islamists there were in ten years more than twice as many Arab deaths as in 100 years of the Arab-Israeli conflict. The same applies to the civil war in Tajikistan during the 1990s, where more than a million Muslims had to flee their homes.

Conflicts involving many more deaths, millions even, as in Sudan and the Congo, garner not a fraction of the attention that is given to the Arab-Israeli conflict. In the Syrian civil war, the number of victims was in a few years a large multiple of the total number of deaths in the Arab-Israeli conflict during the past hundred years. The Syrian civil war and the dozens of other conflicts across the Middle East will certainly not stop just because peace is reached between Israel and the Arabs.

Which brings us to the most important point in this tale: at this time, you have to be blind to facts not to see that it is Muslim hatred of and bloodlust against people of other faiths that enflames the entire Middle East and North Africa.

Consider terrorist groups such as Hamas, Islamic State, Boko Haram, al-Shabaab, al-Qaeda, al-Nusra, Taliban, and the terrible massacres these and other terror groups have carried out in Afghanistan, Algeria, Egypt, Iraq, Yemen, Lebanon, Libya, Mali, Somalia, Syria, and so on.

If the origin of these conflicts disappears, Israel will know peace.

> *"It turns out that even when a British Muslim beheads a British Christian there will always be someone willing to blame the Jew."*
> – Israeli Minister of Economy Naftali Bennett, in response to the remark that Israel would have caused the rise of Islamic State

> *"The situation in Iraq and Syria and Libya should cure anybody of the illusion that the Arab-Israeli conflict is the main source of problems in the region. For far too long, that's been used as an excuse to distract people from problems at home."*
> - US President Barack Obama in a speech to the United Nations, September 24, 2014

> *"That thinking – I am not saying 'religion' but 'thinking' – that corpus of texts and ideas that we have sacralized over the years, to the point that departing from them has become almost impossible, is antagonizing the entire world. It's antagonizing the entire world!"*
> – Egyptian President Sisi, on December 28, 2014, in a call to reform Islam

Tale: When the Arab-Israeli conflict is resolved, there will be peace in the Middle East.
Fact: All over the Middle East and North Africa there is Muslim fundamentalist violence.
Photo: IS fighters in Iraq.

19. Conspiracy theories

The Palestinian Tale: Arabs don't let themselves get carried away by conspiracy theories.

Unfortunately, the examples of Arab conspiracy theories about Jews are almost infinite. Jews are named the cause of homosexuality, drug trafficking, earthquakes, sexual misconduct – basically everything that is considered evil by radical Muslims.

The craziest, most laughable conspiracy theories make the rounds. Pepsi is a Jewish conspiracy; it is supposed to be an abbreviation of *"Pay Every Penny to Save Israel."* The cartoon *Tom and Jerry* is a Jewish conspiracy; The Iranian professor Hasan Bolkhari claimed on Iranian television on February 19, 2006, deadly serious, that Tom and Jerry were invented by the Jews to enhance the image of the mouse (which is considered a bad animal in *Sharia* law):

> *"The mouse [Tom] is very clever and smart. Everything he does is so cute. He kicks the poor cat's ass. Yet this cruelty does not make you despise the mouse. He looks so nice, and he is so clever. This is exactly why some say it was meant to erase this [negative] image of mice from the minds of European children, and to show that the mouse is not dirty and has these traits. No ethnic group or people operate in such a clandestine manner as the Jews."*

In addition to Islamic university professors, the political top of the Islamic world is also heavily involved in a range of conspiracy theories. As Malaysia's Islamic Prime Minister Dr. Mahathir bin Mohammad said in 2003 to the Conference of the Organization of Islamic Countries:

> *"Today the Jews rule the world by proxy. They get others to fight and die for them. The Jews invented socialism, communism, human rights and democracy so that persecuting them would appear to be wrong, so that they can enjoy equal rights with others."*

The other participants at this conference expressed their support for this statement. The foreign minister of Yemen said that he completely agreed, and he added, *"Israelis and Jews control most of the economy and the media in the world."* The Egyptian foreign minister called bin Mohammad's *"a very, very wise assessment."*

How is it possible that this kind of nonsense is commonly believed in the Islamic world? It stems from a feeling of Islamic superiority: Islam is the best religion. Allah Akbar – Allah is the greatest. The Koran says: *"You are the best nation produced as an example for mankind."* So if Muslims are not doing well, but the Christians and Jews are, it must be because of the conspiracies they have perpetrated against the Muslims – especially in regard to the Jews, who didn't want to follow the Islamic prophet Muhammad and therefore were persecuted by him.

And of course, in the autonomous Palestinian territory it is handy for the dictatorial Palestinian regimes of Fatah and Hamas to portray Israel as external enemy, blaming it for everything that goes wrong under their jurisdiction so that they don't have themselves to blame. These conspiracy theories thrive greatly because of the lack of free press in the Arab world.

And it works. For example, an opinion poll taken after the Charlie Hebdo attacks in Paris in 2015 showed that as many as 84.4 percent of Palestinians believed that the attacks *"were probably committed by Israel."* In contrast, only 8.7 percent of Palestinians believed that Islamic extremists perpetrated the attacks.

So it is a tale that Arabs do not believe in conspiracies. Everything that goes wrong in Arab countries is caused by the West, the Jews (see also Tale: Arab anti-Semitism), Christians, Americans, or a combination of all of them. Simply because the Arab-Islamic culture can't be wrong (see also Tale: Victim culture).

Tale: Arabs don't let themselves get carried away by conspiracy theories.
Fact: Conspiracy theories are rife in the Arab world, like the attacks of 9/11 were perpetrated by the CIA or the Jews, notwithstanding that responsibility was claimed by Osama bin Laden.
Photo: The attack on the twin towers of the World Trade Center on September 11, 2001 (see Palestinian Tale: Victim culture).

20. Criticism of Israel

The Palestinian Tale: Jews call all criticism of Israel anti-Semitic.

Critiquing the State of Israel is not automatically and directly anti-Semitic. However, much of the recent criticism targeted at Israel contains anti-Semitic streaks. The definition and categorization of what is anti-Semitic is agreed upon by the International Holocaust Remembrance Alliance. As such, it is supported by the governments of 31 countries, including Canada, the Netherlands, the United Kingdom and the United States.

This definition raises the following examples to recognize anti-Semitism in criticisms of Israel:

- Denying the Jewish people their right to self-determination, e.g., by claiming that the existence of a state of Israel is a racist endeavor.
- Using the symbols and images associated with classic anti-Semitism (e.g., claims of Jews killing Jesus or the blood libel) to characterize Israel or Israelis.
- Drawing comparisons of contemporary Israeli policy to that of the Nazis.
- Holding Jews collectively responsible for actions of the state of Israel.
- Applying double standards by requiring of Israel a behavior not expected or demanded of any other democratic nation.

All of these examples are regularly found in critical reflections on Israel. One can often detect a double standard; enough of a double standard to amount to discrimination. The outrage over the real or alleged misdeeds of Israel is far bigger and receives more criticism than over the offences of other countries. For example:

- On the list concerning the greatest political conflicts, the Arab-Israeli conflict is in 48th place with more than 60,000 deaths (see Tale: Conflict). About 50,000 deaths in Mexico in recent years were due to drug violence, but you hear less about those from the media. The African country of Congo went through a civil war with over 4 million deaths since 1998, about which the media seldom mentions anything. One also hears very little about the thousands of Christians killed by Muslims in Nigeria.
- According to Wikipedia, there are approximately 100 disputed territories in the world. The West Bank, however, gets more attention than all others combined.
- The call to launch a boycott against Israel is unique to this conflict. When did you hear a call to boycott China because of their occupation of Tibet, against

Russia because of the illegal annexation of Crimea, against Morocco because of its – according to the International Court – illegal occupation of Western Sahara, or against Turkey because of the illegal occupation of North Cyprus?

"From 1821 to 1922, 5 million Muslims were expelled from Europe, mostly to Turkey. In the 1990's Yugoslavia broke apart, leading to 100,000 people killed and about 3 million displaced.
And as we speak today, Yazidis, Bahai, Kurds, Christians and even Muslims are being killed and expelled at a rate of 1,000 people per month, following the rise of radical Islam. The chances of any of those groups to return to their homes is almost non-existent.
So why is it then, that the tragedies of the Serbs, the European Muslims, the Polish refugees or the Iraqi Christians are not commemorated? How come the displacement of the Jews from the Arab world was completely forgotten, while the tragedy of the Palestinians, the Nakba, is still alive in today's politics?"
   – George Deek, the Israeli consul in Norway (and Israeli Arab), 2014

"In the end, we will remember not the words of our enemies, but the silence of our friends."
   – Martin Luther King

Tale: Jews label all criticism of Israel anti-Semitic.
Fact: anti-Israel statements are often inspired by anti-Semitism.
Photo: Israel compared with Nazis at an anti-Israel demonstration in Amsterdam, July, 20, 2014. That is anti-Semitic, according to the relevant definition.

21. Death cult

The Palestinian Tale: Palestinians fear death, like Westerners do.

Islamic fundamentalist organizations such as Hamas impress on followers that death is most important and desirable for a Muslim. The majority of Palestinians support Hamas. The motto of the Muslim Brotherhood, of which Hamas is the Palestinian branch, is:

"Allah is our objective. The Prophet is our leader. The Koran is our law. Jihad is our way.
Dying in the way of Allah is our highest hope."

This belief is inculcated in the Palestinian population. Dying in the struggle against "the infidels" is the highest ideal. Those that die martyrs will go to paradise and will have the privilege of designating 70 family members who (after death) also will be admitted directly to paradise.

Thus spoke the Hamas MP Fathi Hammad on Hamas television on February 29, 2008:

"We use women and children as human shields. [The enemies of Allah] do not know that the Palestinian people has developed its [methods] of death and death-seeking. Death is our way. This is why we use the elderly, women and children. They are doing a great job. We love death so much, like Zionists love live."

Gaza's population is told that they should be happy with the number of casualties in the wars against Israel. Thus spoke the leader of the Muslim Brotherhood on Hamas television on August 1, 2014:

"Without a doubt, the blood being spilled [in Gaza] is dear. But the advantage is: Those killed from our side are in Paradise, and those killed from their side in Hell.
We are not afraid of Martyrdom. Not long ago, you cried out loud: 'Death for Allah is our most exalted wish!' You received the death you wanted. We have no problem with death. We are not like the children of Israel."

This Islamic fundamentalism is the only thing the residents hear since the takeover by Hamas in 2006, hence the rhetoric's widespread effect on the population. An Israeli TV journalist asked a young mother from Gaza, whose son's life was saved by heart surgery in Israel, whether she still wanted her son to die as a "martyr." The answer:

> "We feel that life is nothing. Life isn't worth a thing. That's why we have suicide bombers. They're not afraid to die. It's natural. None of us fear death. Even our children. It's natural to us."

That is the Muslim fundamentalist organization Hamas. But even the so-called "moderate" and "secular" Fatah of Palestinian president Abbas promotes this death cult also. Below are two examples.

A mother whose son died in anti-Israeli violence conveyed on the official Palestinian Authority television on September 12, 2014, that she had never been so happy:

> "This is the first time I see joy in my heart.
> This is the first time I see such joy.
> Thank Allah for giving him Martyrdom."

And the Palestinian Religious Affairs Minister Mahmoud Al-Habbash said on the official Palestinian television on December 20, 2013:

> "After prophecy and righteousness there is no status Allah has exalted more than Shahada (Martyrdom): 'And think not of those who have been killed in Allah's way as dead. Nay, they are alive (and) are provided sustenance from their Lord.'
> Allah forbade us to consider them [the Shahids (Martyrs)] as dead or to speak of them as being dead. They went smiling to their deaths. The Shahid has merit with Allah, a merit that no one else has.
> The Shahid – his sins are forgiven with the first gush of his blood from his wound. The Shahid advocates on behalf of 70 members of his family, and saves them all from hell.
> We will never reach the level of the prophets. We won't. So let us reach the level of the Shahids. I say to you, brothers, as the Prophet [Muhammad] said: 'He who honestly seeks Shahada, Allah will give him the status of the Shahids, even if he dies in his bed.'
> Brothers, Allah willing, only one of the two best things will happen to us – victory or Martyrdom (Shahada) – and what a good fate this is, what a good level is this – victory or Martyrdom."

Tale: Palestinians fear death, like Westerners do.
Fact: Perpetrators of suicide attacks are considered heroes.
Photo: Poster of Palestinian terrorist Alasmar.

22. Democracy, Israel

The Palestinian Tale: Israel is not a real democracy.

Each year, the international human rights organization Freedom House conducts a worldwide study on democracy. The survey measures the following factors in each country: freedom of elections, multi-party system, the system of government, freedom of speech, the right to organize, the legal system and the rights of the individual. Each year, the organization notes that only a tiny 2 percent of the population of the entire Middle East lives in complete freedom, in just one country: Israel.

The highest possible score in their investigation is 1. Israel has for many years received the second highest score, 1.5. Thereby the country is equivalent, for example, to Japan. In total, 90 countries are considered completely free (with a score between 1 and 3). Israel is the only country in the Middle East to reach this group.

The Israeli Declaration of Independence states that Israel *"will ensure complete equality of social and political rights to all its inhabitants irrespective of religion, race or sex"* and guarantees to its people *"freedom of religion, conscience, language, education and culture."*

Israel is indeed, as Freedom House's yearly study shows, a real vital democracy with equal rights for minorities, an independent judiciary and free press – quite an achievement for a country that has existed in a state of war since its founding in 1948. That freedom is shown clearly in the simple fact that much of the criticism of Israel comes from Israeli organizations that can express their criticism freely and instigate many legal proceedings against the Israeli state, sometimes successfully.

The Palestinians realize this too. In annual polls held among Palestinians between 1996 and 2002, it was asked what political system the Palestinians admired the most. Israel came out on top every time, sometimes with more than 80 percent appreciation. It was only then followed by countries like the United States and France.

This tale is a case of Arab projection, whereby Israel is accused of abuses that occur not in Israel but in all Arab countries.

Because it is the Arabs in the West Bank and Gaza Strip that by Freedom House are classified as "not free" – both the Palestinians under the control of Fatah as well as under Hamas.

That lack of freedom obviously applies to many Muslim dictatorships; it is Sudan, Syria, Gaza and Saudi Arabia that are dangling at the bottom of the list, with the least freedom for their citizens.

Tale: Israel is not a real democracy.
Fact: In the 2015 Israeli elections 16 Arab MPs were elected, including Ahmed Tibi (photo), who complained in 2015 how much he missed Arafat.

23. Democracy, Palestinians

The Palestinian Tale: The Palestinian government is democratically elected.

To start, the participation of Hamas in the Gaza elections in 2006 was contrary to the internationally guaranteed peace agreements concluded with Israel. The peace treaty Oslo-2 explicitly forbids the *"the nomination of any candidates, parties, or coalitions that commit or advocate racism"* or *"pursue the implementation of their aims by unlawful or non-democratic means."* All this applies to Hamas, as evidenced by their Charter.

Also, the peace treaties determine that Palestinians must disarm all terrorist organizations. That also has not happened in the case of Hamas – or with any other of the Palestinian terrorist organizations.

The regulations of Oslo-2 are there for a reason. It is a general international principle that parties who wish to participate in elections always should lay down their weapons and endorse democratic principles first. This applies to Eastern Europe and to Northern Ireland. That is the painful lesson of Nazi Germany; otherwise the gun will eventually rule, as inevitably happened in Gaza. Nowhere in the world are anti-democratic, racist and/or terrorist parties allowed to join in elections.

Actually Hamas is all three. Anti-democratic, because the elections were purely used to come to power. No elections were held thereafter. Muslim fundamentalism and democracy are fundamentally incompatible, if only because the *Sharia* law grants fewer rights to women and non-Muslims. Furthermore, Fatah opposition in the Strip was completely silenced soon after the elections by the murder of its leaders and supporters. Hamas is racist, because its central goals as stated in its charter are the destruction of Israel and the murder of Jews. Also, Hamas is a terrorist organization because it seeks to achieve its goals through violence against civilians: *"Jihad is the only solution"* (Article 13 of the Hamas Charter). See also Tale: Hamas.

> *"Any kind of Islamism wants Sharia, instead of the constitution."*
> – Nadia Ait Zai, professor at the Faculty of Law of the University of Algiers

Yet Hamas was allowed to participate in the elections in 2006 and won the majority of parliamentary seats. Choosing an anti-democratic party meant – just like for Germany – the end of democracy: these elections were the first and also the last Palestinian parliamentary elections. All terms of the elected persons have long ago expired.

Moreover, now, because of internal disagreement, there are now two Palestinian governments: the West Bank is controlled by Fatah and Hamas controls the Gaza Strip. So the authority of President Mahmoud Abbas is also based on expired election results and thus contrary to law. The Palestinian presidential elections were held on January 9, 2005, and Mahmoud Abbas was elected for a term of four years. A decade later he was still there.

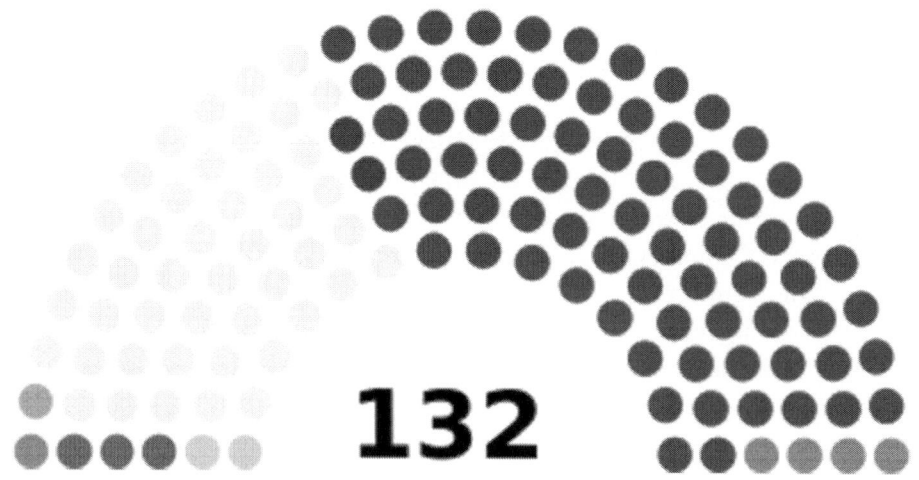

Tale: The Palestinians have democratic elections.
Fact: The majority of seats – 74 out of 132 – went to an undemocratic party (Hamas), which according to international law should never have been allowed to participate. Furthermore, elections have not been held since 2006.

24. **Destruction of Israel**

The Palestinian Tale: The Palestinians have abandoned their wish to destroy Israel.

On the contrary, the terrorist organization Hamas keeps repeating again and again the necessity to exterminate the Jews. Based on the ideology of Muslim fundamentalism, peace can never be obtained (see Tale: Hamas). At best the Palestinians may agree to a temporary truce with Israel. In a television interview in 2014 a Hamas spokesman and MP, Mushir al-Masri, confirmed that a long-term truce with Hamas will never be possible:

"It is all Zionist nonsense. Their dream is to live in peace and security for ten years, but we will continue to give the Zionists nightmares, until the very last Zionist leaves our Palestinian land – all of Palestine, from the [Jordan] River to the [Mediterranean] Sea.
Any armistice will be temporary, for a set period of time. We are not talking about a long-term truce or about a peace agreement. In the lexicon of the Jihad, the word armistice means preparation for the battles to come.
Our resistance will continue to develop, produce and expand its arsenal of weapons. It will produce new surprises for the battles to come, until the Zionist enemy leaves our land in its entirety, Allah willing."

Hamas is supported by Iran, where Khamenei is the "Supreme Leader." In 2015 he published a book called *Palestine*. In it he explains how Israel must be destroyed: by incessant terror, continuing until the Jews will emigrate out of desperation.

Less well known is that the other major Palestinian movement, Fatah, led today by President Abbas, adopted the *Plan for the phased destruction of Israel* in 1974 (see Tale: Arafat).

Statements made by Fatah leaders indicate that the plan is still in effect. Three examples:

"Even the most extreme among us, Hamas, or the fighting forces, want a state within the '67 borders. Afterwards, we [will] have something to say, because this inspiring thought (the ultimate goal) cannot be achieved all at once but in stages."
   – The spokesman for Abbas, Abbas Zaki, on Syrian satellite TV on December 23, 2013

"The accord should be based upon the borders of June 4, 1967. When we say that the accord should be based upon these borders, President [Abbas] understands, we understand, and everybody knows that the great goal cannot be accomplished in one go. If Israel withdraws from Jerusalem, evacuates the 650,000 settlers, and dismantles the wall – what will be left of Israel?
It will come to an end. If I say that I want to finish with Israel – and that would be wonderful, wonderful – but it is difficult. It is not an official policy. You cannot speak to the world like that. You can only tell it to yourself."
   – The spokesman of Abbas, Abbas Zaki, on Al Jazeera on September 23, 2011

"I wished we could see the black banners of Khorasan marching towards Jerusalem, as foretold by our Prophet Muhammad, and that we could celebrate the victory same as we ended other tragedies throughout our long history. ...
We would like to see the demise and the shattering of this alien entity.
I would like to express again my gratitude to the Islamic Republic of Iran for the training, financing, and weapons it has provided us, as well as for its political and diplomatic positions regarding Palestine. Iran has helped us to attain our great victory.
I am not saying that Palestine will be liberated tomorrow, but we have made real strides on the path to liberation. A missile with a 200-kilogram warhead will carry a warhead of 100 tons in the future, because weapons change as men change. We just need to cross the scientific threshold to get to our goal."
   – Palestinian ambassador to Iran, Salah al-Zawawi, on Iranian television on September 16, 2014

And the Palestinian population supports it, as is shown in the results of a poll published on June 25, 2014. The solution for the conflict, as indicated by a clear majority of Palestinians (60 percent) should be *"recovering the whole of historic Palestine, from the river to the sea."* This refers to the Jordan River and the Mediterranean Sea, so it means the destruction of Israel. Only 27 percent supported the two-state solution, and another 10 percent the one-state solution of Jews and Arabs living together.

Another poll, conducted by the Palestine Center for Public Opinion in 2015, showed that of Palestinians in the West Bank, 81 percent favor the battle for the whole of historic Palestine, as *"Palestinian territory where Jews have no right to."* In Gaza, the percentage is even higher, being 88 percent.

At first glance, the support for a two-state solution has increased. But that is because Palestinians are willing only to accept it as a step in the plan of the phased destruction of Israel. Sixty-four percent says that once the two-state solution is achieved *"we must continue to fight until all of Palestine will be free."*

Tale: The Palestinians have abandoned their wish to destroy Israel.
Fact: The Hamas emblem (photo) is based on the destruction of Israel.

25. Development aid

The Palestinian Tale: Development aid for Palestinians is well spent.

The United States and Europe pay huge sums of "development aid" to the Palestinians, who per capita receive about as much assistance as all other worldwide groups of refugees put together. In the past 70 years, Palestinians received one-third of all UN refugee funds!

Viewed another way: Palestinians have received 25 times as much as Europeans received under the Marshall Plan after World War II (converted to current purchasing power). Foreign countries – particularly European – pay about one third of the Palestinian budget.

Is that money well spent? Not really.

First, funds are used to keep millions of Palestinians locked up in camps. They are not allowed to live outside; they have to live on welfare paid from foreign aid (see Tale: Refugee problem). At the schools in the camps, students are taught to hate Jews - in lessons paid for with "development aid."

Second, this money is used to pay the salaries of the absurdly large number of officials employed by the Palestinian Authority. A report by ECA, the European Court of Auditors of the European Union, in 2013 showed that many Palestinian officials received salaries despite never working.
In 2015, the media reported that Dutch development aid is used to pay Israeli fines imposed on Palestinian farmers. Palestinians are thus encouraged to violate the law and are even rewarded for doing so.

Third, because the Palestinian Authority is very corrupt, a lot of aid money disappears into the pockets of the Palestinian leadership (see Tale: Palestinian leaders). Yasser Arafat was born poor, but he died a billionaire without ever starting or selling a business during his lifetime: all his money he obtained by rummaging in Palestinian funds, paid each year by international taxpayers.

Fourth, it is not only the Palestinian Authority that gets huge amounts of development aid. Hamas also receives hundreds of millions in development aid. Hamas uses the money mainly for the purchase of missiles and materials for building war tunnels.

Fifth, much European tax money is given to organizations that incite hatred against Israel, both in Europe and the Middle East, in the form of grants. In Europe, for example, organizations like Oxfam and Church-in-action are involved in campaigns to boycott Israeli products (see also Tale: Human rights oganiza-tions). Palestinian organizations such as Addameer and Al-Haq also receive subsidies. Several leaders of Addameer have ties with terrorist organizations like the Popular Front for the Liberation of Palestine (PFLP), which is on the EU's list of extremely dangerous terrorist organizations. For example, members of the PFLP committed the infamous murder of the Fogel family in 2011, in which even the three-month-old baby had its throat slit and was decapitated.

The aforementioned Al-Haq organization calls Israel racist, opposes the peace process, supports Palestinian terrorism against Israeli civilians and calls for a total boycott of Israel. Al-Haq played a critical role in the action against Dutch public water company Vitens, which led to the company's withdrawal from cooperation with Israel.

Sixth, European tax money is used to pay top salaries and huge bonuses to Palestinian murderers (because they are revered as heroes, see Tale: Terrorists). Approximately 6 percent of the Palestinian budget is spent on terrorist bonuses. The Palestinian Authority even built a mausoleum to pay homage to Palestinian terrorists who attacked a hotel in Tel Aviv, in which a Dutch tourist was killed – a fifteen-year-old boy from Amsterdam.

By the way, the last three items are breaches of international law. UN Resolution 1373, passed by the UN Security Council in 2001, prohibits the financing of terrorism or terrorists by member states. Member states should:
"prohibit their nationals or any persons and entities within their territories from making any funds, financial assets or economic resources or financial or other related services available, directly or indirectly, for the benefit of persons who commit or attempt to commit or facilitate or participate in the commission of terrorist acts, of entities owned or controlled, directly or indirectly, by such persons and of persons and entities acting on behalf of or at the direction of such persons."

Other humanitarian organizations find the huge sums that go to the Palestinians abnormal and disproportionate to their humanitarian needs. In a report, the Norwegian branch of MSF (Doctors without Borders) noted that the health situation in the Palestinian Territories is relatively good. For example, the life expectancy of Palestinians is equal to that of Hungarians. A child in Chad is more than six times more likely to die before the age of five than a Palestinian child. Yet Palestine received 3.5 percent of Norway's total humanitarian aid in 2012, against Chad's 0.00022 percent.

The hundreds of millions of euros spent by Europe on Palestinians and Palestinian terrorist organizations can really be spent much better.

Tale: Development aid for Palestinians is well spent.
Fact: Development aid from the international community is spent to confine generations of Palestinians to refugee camps.
Photo: Balata camp in the West Bank.

26. Economy, Israeli

The Palestinian Tale: The cost of "occupation" and "settlements" is ruining the Israeli economy.

Israel initially had a centralized socialist economy, organized by the Labor Party, which headed the Israeli government continuously from 1948 to 1977. There was a large bureaucracy and a powerful trade union, which had tremendous power until around 1980; it was even the largest employer in Israel. In the 1980s this resulted in a deep economic crisis: the Israeli economy shrank and inflation was sky high.

The many economic reforms, liberalization and privatization by subsequent Likud governments have since created a dynamic economy in Israel. How much so became apparent during the long years of global decline around 2010. When all Western economies were stagnant or shrank, the Israeli economy continued to grow by 3 to 5 percent per year. Unemployment in Israel was the lowest in three decades in 2013, while just at that time in Europe it reached historically record levels.

Israelis therefore in 2011 surpassed the level of wealth per capita of the Italians and Spaniards. Japan was overtaken in this measure in 2014 and now the more prosperous European countries have come into Israel's sight.

What makes the Israeli economy do so well? It is partly because the Israeli economy is concentrated in modern growth sectors: computer technology, software, medical technology, pharmaceuticals, renewable energy and water technology (recycling and purification). All these sectors are fueled by a huge range of scientific innovations. Israel spends the highest amount per capita in the world on scientific research. High-tech currently drives 35 percent of Israel's exports. Seventy percent of Israel's economic growth originates from high-tech enterprises.

Israel with its 8 million inhabitants has more companies listed on the technology stock exchange in New York NASDAQ than the whole of Europe – although Europe has nearly a hundred times as many people. In the words of former president Shimon Peres:
> *"In Israel, a land lacking in natural resources, we learned to appreciate our greatest national advantage: our minds. Through creativity and innovation, we*

transformed barren deserts into flourishing fields and pioneered new frontiers in science and technology."

All the technology giants, from Apple to Intel, Microsoft and Google, have major research and manufacturing facilities in Israel and invest massively in Israel and Israeli high-tech companies.

Europe is now trying to attract Israeli companies. For example, a Dutch province pays up to 2.5 million Euros for each Israeli company willing to relocate there.

So the story that by maintaining "settlements" the Israeli economy is hard hit is in short nothing more than a tale. For decades no Western economy has done as well as Israel's.

"Israel is the leading, largest and most promising investment hub outside the United States. The number-one country is Israel, which is far ahead of larger and richer countries.

I'm not Jewish, but Israel reminds me of the United States after its birth. The determination, motivation, intelligence and initiative of its people are remarkable and extraordinary. I'm a big believer in Israel's economy."

– The world's greatest investor, Warren Buffett, the third-richest man in the world

"Israel is, by many measures, the country, relative to its population, that's done the most to contribute to the technology revolution."

– Bill Gates, founder and chief executive of Microsoft, and the richest man in the world

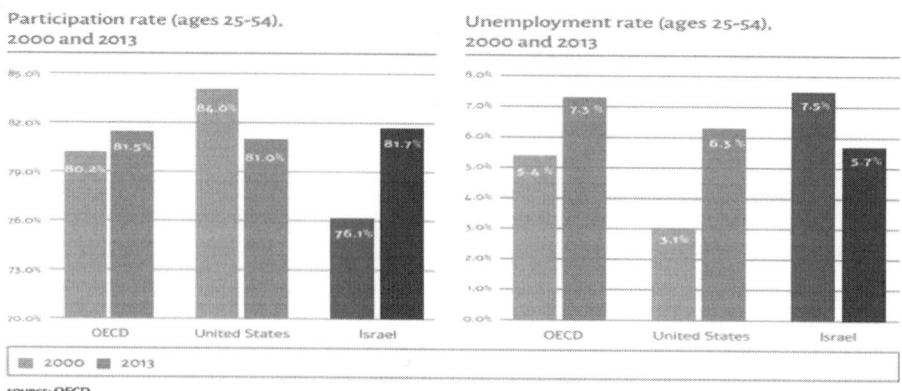

Tale: The "occupation" ruins Israel's economy.
Fact: Israel has one of the best performing Western economies.

27. Economy, Palestinian

The Palestinian Tale: The Palestinian economy is negatively affected by Israel.

To the contrary, in reality the Palestinian economy profits from Israel. The wealth and well-being of Palestinians is higher than that of Arabs in most Arab countries (excluding most oil states, where incomes are much higher because of huge oil revenues).

The British Peel Commission noted way back in 1937 that the Arabs in Palestine substantially benefited from Jewish know-how, capital and employment:
"The Arab population shows a remarkable increase since 1920, and it has had some share in the increased prosperity of Palestine. Many Arab landowners have benefited from the sale of land and the profitable investment of the purchase money. The fellaheen [poor farmers] are better off on the whole than they were in 1920. This Arab progress has been partly due to the import of Jewish capital into Palestine and other factors associated with the growth of the [Jewish] National Home. In particular, the Arabs have benefited from social services which could not have been provided on the existing scale without the revenue obtained from the Jews."

The Palestinians continued to benefit (see Tale: Suffering of the Palestinians).

Unfortunately, in the Arab countries (and the Palestinian territories are no exception) there are several factors that fundamentally limit economic growth, making the Middle East and North Africa likely to be among the most economically lagging areas of the world. Some notable facts:
- Spain, with 47 million inhabitants, translates more books in one year than the Arab world (with its total of 365 million people) has in all of history.
- Israel, with 8 million inhabitants, registered 16,805 patents in 2010, compared to the 836 patents registered in all 22 Arab countries combined.
- Finland, with 5.5 million people, exports more than all Arab countries combined (excluding oil).

There are certain objective causes such as limited education, women's low employment rates, high corruption and lack of support for private initiative. The underlying causes are cultural factors: the victim culture (see Tale: Victim culture), the clan culture and Islamist extremism.

Most Muslim countries have not existed for long and were created quite arbitrarily. Therefore, more important than national team spirit and identity is faith and the clan.

For instance 94 percent of Pakistanis see themselves primarily as Muslims – as compared to only 3 percent who see themselves primarily as Pakistani. The Muslim-Arab identification comes with some significant cultural burdens that can inhibit economic growth. In the schema of relative cultural values developed by the prominent Dutch sociologist Geert Hofstede, Arab societies generally loathe initiative, are particularly conscious of hierarchical structures and are focused not on the individual but on the group.

Furthermore, adherents to the conventional Islamic tradition are focused on the literal truth of the Koran. In education, therefore, the emphasis is rote learning, not on stimulating discussion or creativity. This is strongly inhibitive on innovation, whether for business, scientific or social progress. The same applies to Islam's enormous fatalism; everything happens only by the will of Allah, without the exertion of individual free will. When nearly 1,000 pilgrims were killed by trampling in Mecca in 2015, the highest religious authority in Saudi Arabia responded, *"As for the things that humans cannot control, you are not blamed for them. Fate and destiny are inevitable."*

Because women mostly have a subordinate role, 50 percent of the workforce is under-used or not used at all. This is all quite apart from the violence perpetrated in the name of Islam.

Another factor is, as mentioned, the clan culture. Therein, one's own tribe is completely trusted. The clan takes care of you, and you take care of the other clan members. It provides a social safety net. This positive aspect of the clan culture in close groups, however, goes awry in a modern economy. It does not bring the best person to a job, but rather a fellow clan member. And someone who is successful is expected to share his wealth with the entire clan, which obstructs private initiative. Because in a clan culture the state is less important, there is also much less attention to good governance. Corruption, arbitrariness, abuse of power and repression are often the result.

This tale is again a case of projection, whereby Israel is accused of something the Arabs are doing themselves. Contrary to the tale, it is not just in the past that the Palestinians benefited from Israel. The report by the Palestinian Central Bureau of Statistics for the first quarter of 2015 shows that more than 110,000 Arab residents of the West Bank work in Israeli companies. Of these, 20,000 work for companies in the "settlements." The average salary for these companies is about double the salary paid by the average Palestinian employer.

An article in the Palestinian newspaper *Al-Hayat Al-Jadida* of September 21, 2014, discloses that Palestinian workers in Israeli companies always receive their salaries (except sometimes when a Palestinian mediator sits in between!), that they get paid twice the salary as Palestinians working for Palestinians, and that other working conditions are good. The latter involves, for example, transport to work, health insurance and a pension.

Also evident from the data of the Palestinian Bureau of Statistics is that approximately 25 percent of the income of Arabs in the West Bank comes from Israeli employers, of which 5 percent are located in "settlements."

As a result, more than 100,000 Palestinians and their families derive their income from Israeli jobs, with pay more than twice the Palestinian average. These incomes contribute a 25 percent share to the Palestinian economy in the West Bank, where these earnings are spent in Palestinian shops, service providers and so on – generating more work for Palestinians.

Tale: The Palestinian economy is negatively affected by Israel.
Fact: Palestinians are economically better off than Arabs in neighboring countries.
Photo: Ramallah, the West Bank.

28. Emigration

The Palestinian Tale: Israelis are unhappy and are fleeing from Israel.

This tale surfaces regularly, even in major news magazines and newspapers. But it is not true. Emigration from Israel is among the lowest rates of any country in the developed world. Emigration from Israel consists of about two people per thousand inhabitants per year. In the Netherlands this number is five per thousand – two-and-a-half times as great. The Republic of Ireland has 16 leavers per thousand inhabitants.

The number of people who want to settle in Israel is much greater – even nearly twice as large as the rate of emigration. It is expected that immigration into Israel will remain high due to the growing anti-Semitism in Europe.

Tale: Israelis are unhappy and therefore are fleeing from Israel.
Fact: Immigration to Israel is much higher than emigration.
Photo: New immigrants.

29. European Union

The Palestinian Tale: The EU is not doing enough to stop the Israeli "occupation."

There are about a hundred disputed territories in the world, according to Wikipedia. No disputed territory gets as much attention from the European Union as the West Bank. This happens while a large part of the population of the West Bank already has self-government, in contrast to many other disputed territories. As many as 96 percent of the Arab population in the West Bank lives under self-government, which employs its own civil servants, levies taxes and performs all other functions of government.

In addition, Israel has strong legal claims to (part of) the West Bank (see Tale: Occupation West Bank) and governs on the basis of the Oslo agreements, which, please note, are guaranteed by the European Union.

The European Union exposes its double standards in other ways. When Russia occupied Crimea, for example, the European Union was indignant but did not ask for special labels on goods from "occupied Ukrainian territory," something they increasingly demand of Israeli products from the West Bank.

Interesting is the comparison with two occupations by Muslim countries: the Western Sahara and Northern Cyprus. The European Union will not conclude treaties with Israel if they would also cover Israeli companies based in the West Bank. When they do business with Morocco, however, this distinction is no problem. Indeed, the EU has concluded fisheries agreements with Morocco at the direct expense of the indigenous population of the Western Sahara. European fishermen are allowed by these treaties to help rob the fish from the waters of the occupied Western Sahara.

The occupation of (European) Northern Cyprus by Turkey is very brutal. A third of the indigenous population is displaced. The United Nations noted many human rights violations in a 2011 report. There is a nearly 200-kilometer border with high fences across the region. Tens of thousands of Turkish settlers came to live there, replacing the original Greek inhabitants. Greek Cypriot heritage is destroyed deliberately.

What is the European Union doing about it? Nothing. Or rather, it supports and finances the occupation; various projects in occupied Northern Cyprus, such as road construction, are eligible for funding from the European Union.

Not to mention how Europe ignores the call for autonomy of its own peoples, such as the Basques, the Catalans, the Corsicans and many more.

Another striking example of Europe's double standard was that when Israel killed the leader of Hamas, a terrorist organization – designated by Europe as such – it was condemned by Europe; when the United States killed al-Qaeda leader Osama bin Laden, Europe offered congratulations.

The then Dutch foreign minister Frans Timmermans admitted, during his visit to Israel in 2013, that the European Union treats Israel differently: *"Europe uses other standards for Israel than with other countries in the region,"* he said. Europe thus discriminates. Europe, which throughout history already has initiated so many boycotts of Jewish individuals and companies, now has the Jewish state first in the crosshairs to boycott.

> *"I think that there are many common challenges that we face, and in this regard I find it perplexing that some in Europe are still possessed by the anti-Israeli obsession.*
> *Hundreds of thousands are being slaughtered in the Middle East, millions are being displaced, but some in Europe believe the only thing they have to do is to press, boycott and vilify the Middle East's only true democracy, Israel, the only vanguard of liberty, the only country where human rights are respected, where there is a free press and where the values that we share with Europe serve as our map and our compass and our way of life.*
> *I find this inexplicable but I find it also to the detriment of Europe. We are the guardians of civilization here in the heart of the Middle East against this new barbarism."*
> – Israeli Prime Minister Benjamin Netanyahu, in 2015

How is this possible? Anti-Semitism certainly plays a role with some Europeans, but that is only a part of the explanation. There are also major economic interests in play, because there are 57 Islamic countries in the world. Of course this includes major oil countries. Canada, Japan, the Netherlands, the United Kingdom and the United States know everything about this, because of its Arab oil boycott of 1973. Moreover, many European countries have fast growing Muslim communities that exert political pressure.

Even so, the Anglo-Dutch writer Ian Buruma finds the indignation of many European intellectuals against Israel and the United States strange in a world where so many dictators oppress and slaughter their own people. He explains it with feelings of "guilt and fear."

European history, and certainly the two world wars caused by Europe, resulted in such terrible massacres that Europeans now have an aversion to military force and colonialism. Forgoing these, goes the logic, should lead to lasting peace. It is an imaginary world, for peace was maintained thanks to the protection of the United States, the only Western democracy that was still willing to maintain power politics. The fear in Europe is that military power could drag Europe into a new war, and so awaken her from this dream world.

Regarding Israel, guilt prevails. Israel was forced by Arab aggression to use methods that remind Europe of its colonial past.

In addition, there is of course also residual European guilt about the Holocaust, in which Nazis killed 6 million Jews without compassion simply because they were Jewish. It is convenient, then, to have the Jews look "bad" because then the perpetrators and bystanders of these past atrocities can relinquish some of that guilt. This is called "blaming the victim," as sometimes also happens in cases of sexual assault. The United States and Israel remind Europe of its guilt, of its own very violent past, and that raises reluctance among Europeans to embrace them.

> *"I am often asked whether there is a future for Jews in Europe. My answer to them is to ask whether there is a future for Europeans in Europe."*
> – Former Soviet dissident and former Israeli Minister Nathan Sharansky

> *"Since 1945, I was not so afraid as I am now. I am afraid because anti-Semitism, which I had thought belonged to the past, has somehow survived. I was convinced in '45 that anti-Semitism had died with its Jewish victims at Auschwitz and Treblinka, but I see, no, the Jews perished, but anti-Semitism in some parts of the world is flourishing."*
> – Elie Wiesel, Nobel Peace Prize winner, in 2011

Tale: The European Union is not doing enough against the Israeli "occupation."
Fact: Israel's actions get infinitely more attention than, for instance, the occupation of Northern Cyprus by Turkey (photo).

30. Expulsion now

The Palestinian Tale: There are Israeli parties who want to expel the Arabs.

This refers to the Israeli party *Israel Beiteinu* of Israeli minister Avigdor Lieberman. However, he has never proposed expulsion. What he has suggested is that in a final peace agreement there could be an exchange of territories, in which Israeli territory that almost exclusively is inhabited by Arabs would become under Palestinian rule. This, of course, has nothing to do with expulsion, because the Arabs would continue to live in their own homes. The only difference would be that they would come under Arab rule.

The tale that Arabs are at the moment being expelled from the West Bank or Jerusalem is already refuted in the tale "Jerusalem, Judaization."

However, when Israel withdrew from parts of the West Bank and the entire Gaza Strip, all of the Jews living in the affected territory were forced to leave. And the Palestinian leadership has made it clear that further withdrawals should also result in cleansing of the Jews living in those territories.

Again, the Arabs unjustly accuse the Jews of an act that, in reality, is being done by the Arabs.

Tale: There are Israeli parties who want to expel the Palestinians
Fact: Avigdor Lieberman (pictured) never said such a thing.

31. Expulsion 1948

The Palestinian Tale: Israel expelled the Palestinians in 1948.

This is a case of Arab projection, whereby Israel is blamed for something that the Arabs themselves did, or wanted to do. It is obvious that the Arabs at that time strove for the expulsion – and even the extermination – of the Jews of Palestine. The day after the proclamation of the State of Israel in 1948, the president of the Arab League, Azzam Pasha said:
> *"It will be a war of extermination a momentous massacre which will be spoken of like the Mongolian massacre and the Crusades."*

The Jews were thus confronted with a threat of a new Holocaust – only three years after the end of World War II. This time it was in a war started by the Arab nations (see Tale: War of Independence in 1948).

It is a fact that approximately 600,000 Palestinian Arabs fled. Efraim Karsh, professor at the University of London, has determined exact population figures. He arrives at a number between 583,000 and 609,000.
His book *Palestine Betrayed* (2010) contains much new information from recently opened archives.

Professor Karsh contends that the vast majority of Palestinian Arabs were not expelled but fled without immediate cause. Approximately 100,000 Arabs had already fled even before the Jews started to counter-attack in March 1948. About half of all the refugees, approximately 300,000, had already left before the declaration of the State of Israel in May 1948.
As reported by Alan Cunningham, the British High Commissioner, in December 1947:
> *"Arabs are leaving the country with their families in considerable numbers, and there is an exodus from the mixed towns to the rural Arab centers."*

And one month later:
> *"The panic of the middle class persists and there is a steady exodus of those who can afford to leave the country."*

There was no plan for an (systematic) expulsion of Arabs by Jews in 1948. However, indeed, some 10 percent of the refugees were given instruction to leave their living places. This stemmed from concerns in the heat of battle. It happened in order to limit the number of civilian casualties or to keep Arab fighters from certain places where there were no Jewish forces ready for the defense. So the reasons were military rather than political.

The only – and much publicized – example of a displacement of an urban population happened in the Arab town of Lydda and neighboring Ramla. The mayor and notables of Lydda had surrendered to the Jews in July 1948. But after the surrender, Arab fighters in the town killed the mayor and resumed to fight from within the civilian population, causing many casualties. That made it militarily necessary to evacuate the civilian population.

Ismayil Safwat, commander of the Arab factions, was even surprised by this, writing on March 23, 1948: *"The Jews have not attacked any Arab village, unless attacked first."*

Much larger was the number of cases where the Arabs fled following Arab orders, often even against the wish of the Jews. The largest and best-known example is Haifa, where tens of thousands of Arabs were ordered and even forced to leave the city by the Arab leadership. The motivation was to paralyze the country's main port. There were intensive attempts by the Jews to persuade the Arabs to stay. For example, in a report by the Arab Higher Committee of Haifa to the Arab League countries:

> *"The military and civil (Israeli) authorities expressed their profound regret at this grave decision (taken by the Arab military delegates of Haifa and the Acting Chair of the Palestine Arab Higher Committee) to evacuate Haifa despite the Israeli offer of a truce.*
> ***The Jewish mayor of Haifa made a passionate appeal to the delegation of Arab military leaders to reconsider its decision."***

However, as the British magazine *The Economist* reported in 1948:

> *"Of the 62,000 Arabs formerly living in Haifa not more than 5,000 or 6,000 remained. Various factors influenced their decision to seek safety in flight. There is little doubt about that the most strong weighting of the factors were the announcements made over the air by the Higher Arab Executive, urging the Arabs to quit.*
> ***It was clearly threatened that the Arabs who remained in Haifa and accepted Jewish protection would be regarded as traitors."***

In Tiberias also, 6,000 Arabs were forced to flee by their own leaders, against the wishes of the local Jews. And in Jaffa, the largest Arab city, the Arab council organized the evacuation of thousands of residents by land and by sea. In Jerusalem, the Arab leadership ordered women and children to leave. Moreover, local Arab gang leaders drove residents away from several quarters during the fighting. The same happened with thousands of Arab villagers.

The mass expulsion is a Tale, and the same goes for stories about massacres committed. The Palestinians will always recount the tragic story of the village of Deir Yassin. However, this was a legitimate military target because Iraqi soldiers and Arab fighters from this hilltop village fired constantly on the lower-lying road Tel Aviv – Jerusalem. The civilian population was called upon to leave and part of them obeyed. During the fight, Arab fighters hid in between the remaining civilian population and this caused civilian casualties. (The same as happened more recently in Gaza. Not much has changed, even after all this time.)

This story, the number of victims etc. was afterwards very much exaggerated, mainly through the Arab radio stations. The goal was to incite the masses to take up the arms in revenge.

There exists many more stories of "massacres" but those were completely fabricated, as when the mayor of Jaffa invented a story according to which "hundreds of Arabs were killed." It is just a total fantasy.

The effect of it all turned out to be the opposite of what was intended; the Arabs did not take up arms but were seized by fear and fled massively.

And it is another case of Arab projection, because massacres of Jews by Arabs did happen. For instance, there was an attack on a medical convoy to Hadassah Hospital in Jerusalem, in which 78 Jews were killed, mostly doctors, nurses and patients. The 127 male inhabitants of Kfar Etzion had surrendered but were still thereafter massacred by the Arabs.

The Arab violence started immediately after the adoption of the Partition Plan by the UN in November 1947 (see Tale: War of Independence in 1948). The US consul general in Jerusalem, Robert Macatee, wrote about Arab violence against Jews in December 1947:

> *"Innocent and harmless people, going about their daily business are picked off while riding in buses, walking along the streets, and stray shots even find them while asleep in their beds. A Jewish woman, mother of five children, was shot in Jerusalem while hanging out clothes on the roof. The ambulance rushing her to the hospital was machine-gunned, and finally the mourners following her to the funeral were attacked and one of them stabbed to death."*

No wonder, then, that at the time few of the Palestinian refugees blamed the Jews for their flight and the loss of their property. Sir John Troutbeck – the head of the British Office for the Middle East in Cairo and certainly no friend of Israel or the Jews – was amazed in 1949 to find that the refugees

"express no bitterness against the Jews (or for that matter against the Americans or ourselves); they speak with the utmost bitterness of the Egyptians and other Arab states.
'We know who our enemies are,' they will say, and they are referring to their Arab brothers who, they declare, persuaded them unnecessarily to leave their homes. I even heard it said that many of the refugees would welcome the Israelis if they were to come and take the district over."

The Palestinians know that, of course, as was for instance expressed by a Palestinian on the official television of the Palestinian Authority on July 7, 2009:

"The radio stations of the Arab regimes kept repeating to us: 'Get away from the frontline. It's a matter of ten days or at most two weeks, and we'll bring you back to Ein-Kerem.'
And we said to ourselves, 'That's a very long time. Two weeks is too much.'
That's what we thought. And now 50 years have gone by."

In this context, it is interesting to have a look at the personal histories of the first and second presidents of the Palestinian Authority. The first President Yasser Arafat said he was born in Jerusalem. In reality, he was born in Cairo and grew up there. The second President Mahmoud Abbas also lied about his family history. When speaking to the United Nations on September 26, 2013, he said:

"I am personally one of the victims of Al-Nakba, among the hundreds of thousands of my people uprooted in 1948 from our beautiful world and thrown into exile."

However, on his government's own Palestinian television station, Abbas had stated on January 1, 2013, less than a year earlier, what had really happened. His family was not "uprooted," but fled without any Jewish involvement whatsoever:

"The [Arab] Liberation Army retreated from the city [Safed in 1948], causing the [Arab] people to begin emigrating. The 1929 massacre was most severe in Safed and Hebron. In Safed, just like Hebron, people were afraid that the Jews would take revenge for the [Arab] massacre [of Jews] in 1929.
The people were overcome with fear, and it caused the people to leave the city in a disorderly way."

So, the family Abbas was, like almost all the refugees, not expelled, not attacked nor even threatened, but fled of their own accord, without tangible force. No harm found the Palestinian Arabs that remained; they simply became Israeli citizens and now form 20 percent of the population. They have rights akin to that of every Israeli. For instance, the northern Israeli town of Nazareth has had Arab mayors since 1948.

The tale of the expulsion is another case of Arab projection, accusing the Jews of something which was the doing of the Arabs themselves. In reality it is just the other way around: 100 percent of the Jews were expelled in 1948 from the territories that were conquered by the Arabs: the West Bank, Gaza and East Jerusalem.

"For the first time in 1,000 years not a single Jew remains in the Jewish Quarter. Not a single building remains intact. This makes the Jews' return here impossible."

Tale: The Arabs were expelled in 1948.
Fact: Arabs could continue living West Jerusalem, but the Arabs expelled all the Jews from East Jerusalem, including the centuries-old Jewish quarter (photo).

32. Fatah

The Palestinian Tale: Fatah and its leader Abbas are moderate and reject all violence.

Fatah has a long history of terror (see Tale: Arafat). The same applies to Mahmoud Abbas, Arafat's successor as Palestinian president. Abbas was one of the organizers of the attack at the Munich Olympics in 1972, in which eleven Israeli athletes were killed.

Until this day, Fatah continues to promote terror through its terrorist affiliate, the Al-Aqsa Martyrs Brigades. During the Gaza war in 2014 it reported proudly that it had also fired rockets at Israeli civilians.

Fatah's most recent charter, signed in 2009, still assumes a "Palestinian right of terror," a total nonsensical right to war crimes (see Tale: Terror, right to):
"Fatah launched the armed struggle for liberating the homeland. This method, and other methods of legitimate resistance, is the right of the Palestinian people, recognized by international law."

This violence is constantly promoted, as on Palestinian television:
"Yesterday in Hebron, they escorted 17 Martyrs to burial. This is of course a source of pride for all of us. I say that whoever carried out individual acts of heroism, we in the Fatah movement bless and encourage them. We consider them heroes and a crown on the head of every Palestinian. At this point, when there is weakening and frustration, there is a group of people, beginning with our brother Muhannad Halabi [terrorist who murdered two people] and ending with the last Martyr.
There is a competition between individuals. This is one of the issues we need to address – are we for or against it? I say that we in the [Fatah] Central Committee have discussed this matter, and we are in favor."
  – Jibril Rajoub, the adjunct-secretary of the Central Committee (board) of Fatah, on Palestinian television, January 2, 2016

"First of all, allow me to say that we kiss every forehead, every hand and even every foot that carries out Ribat [war over land claimed to be Islamic] at the Al-Aqsa Mosque and in Jerusalem. We are behind them.

A few days ago, President [Mahmoud Abbas] greeted them, reinforced them and requested more Ribat from them."

– Mahmoud Al-Habbash, the top Palestinian Islamic judge and personal advisor to President Abbas, on official Palestinian television on November 5, 2014. The reference to "foot" means the foot on the accelerators of cars that were used in ramming attacks against Israelis waiting at bus and train stops

"We bless you, we bless the Islamic fighters.
We bless every drop of blood that has been spilled for Jerusalem, which is clean and pure blood, blood spilled for Allah, Allah willing. Every Martyr will reach Paradise, and everyone wounded will be rewarded by Allah.
The Al-Aqsa [Mosque] is ours, the Church of the Holy Sepulcher is ours.
They have no right to defile it with their filthy feet.
We will not allow them to, and we will do everything in our power to protect Jerusalem."

– Palestinian President Abbas in a speech on September 16, 2015, on official Palestinian television

Tale: Fatah rejects violence.
Fact: The Fatah logo is based on the destruction of Israel.
Photo: Child with the Fatah flag on the 48th anniversary of Fatah in 2013.

33. Gaza blockade

The Palestinian Tale: The blockade of Gaza is illegal.

There is no general blockade by Egypt and Israel against the Gaza Strip. The only blockade is an arms blockade, which exists legally. The legal committee of the United Nations (named after its chairman, professor of law Geoffrey Palmer) concluded in 2011:

> *"The fundamental principle of the freedom of navigation on the high seas is subject only to certain limited exceptions under international law. Israel faces a real threat to its security from militant groups in Gaza. The naval blockade was imposed as a legitimate security measure in order to prevent weapons from entering Gaza by sea and its implementation complied with the requirements of international law."*

According to international law, the boarding of ships that are breaking a legal blockade, even in international waters, which happened in 2010 with the Turkish ship the *Mavi Marmara*, is legal as well.

Those who are against this legal arms blockade are actually in favor of arming Hamas. Hamas, which is regarded internationally as a terrorist organization, would continue to use these weapons to commit war crimes by attacking Israeli civilians with rockets.

The mainstream media has framed the arms blockade of Gaza as a terrible injustice. Newspapers have labeled it the "Strangling Blockade." So, what exactly is the target of this arms blockade? Not food, not medicine; unlimited amounts of these resources are let into Gaza at a rate of hundreds of trucks a day.

Only the following items are stopped:
- Category A: weapons and ammunition.
- Category B: dual-use materials that can be turned into weapons by terrorists. This list is based on the international *Wassenaar Arrangement on export controls for arms and dual-use* in 2008. Fiber-reinforced materials and objects, as well as chemicals that can be used to make rockets and rocket fuel, fall under this category. But is there really a "strangling" blockade just because Epoxy and Vinyl Ester resins, accelerators for Vinyl Esters, hydroxyl-terminated polybutadiene and Toluene diisocyanate cannot be imported?

- Category C: Building materials, especially concrete and steel and accessories. These may only be imported if their use is monitored by international organizations such as the UN.

The entire B and C categories list only 34 goods. That's it. Anything else can be imported on an unrestricted, unlimited basis.

Those who state that Israel is the cause of the blockade confuse cause and effect. The blockade is a response to rocket fire, not vice versa. Israel is here accused of something the rulers of Gaza have initiated themselves.

Tale: Israel subjects Gaza to an inhumane blockade.
Fact: Every month, 6,000 trucks cross the border into Gaza.

34. Gaza densely populated

The Palestinian Tale: Gaza is one of the most densely populated areas in the world.

Areas like Macau, Monaco, Singapore and Hong Kong are considerably more densely populated than Gaza (the first two almost five and four times as much, respectively). Gaza City does not appear on Wikipedia's list of the 80 most populated cities in the world, nor does the Gaza Strip appear on its list of 25 most densely populated areas.

Palestinians use this tale as an underlying argument for another tale: because of the dense population, you see, terrorist groups in Gaza have to shoot their rockets out of residential areas. They endanger their own citizens under the tale *"there is no other place to shoot rockets from."*

However, anyone with access to Google Earth can establish that Gaza has large open spaces and green, unpopulated areas.

Tale: There are no open spaces in Gaza, so rocket launchers have to be placed between buildings and in residential areas.

Fact: Much of Gaza is made up of open spaces.

35. Gaza hunger

The Palestinian Tale: There is hunger in Gaza because of the blockade.

The Gaza Strip has access to an unlimited amount of imported food (see Tale: Gaza blockade). About 80 percent of Palestinians in the Gaza Strip are completely taken care of with food, housing, education, medical care, laptops for students and so on – by the UN, because they are descendants of Palestinian refugees from 1948.

The problem in Gaza is not starvation. In fact, a disproportionate amount of the population is overweight.

A survey of mothers aged 18 to 50 in the Gaza Strip, published in *BMC Obesity* on April 22, 2014, concluded that much of the population is overweight. Fifty-seven percent of women living in cities, 67 percent in the refugee camps and 68 percent in rural areas of Gaza, are overweight. The main cause of obesity in the Gaza Strip, along with many other territories, is a combination of the traditional Arab cuisine of high fat and sugar with contemporary Western unhealthy fast foods.

Hunger is not an epidemic in Gaza.

Tale: There is hunger in Gaza because of the blockade.
Fact: There is food in abundance; in fact, many residents struggle with weight problems.

36. Gaza open-air prison

The Palestinian Tale: Israel has made Gaza into an open-air prison or concentration camp.

To begin with, it is internationally agreed upon that oversight for the bulk of Gaza's passenger traffic falls to Egypt. As part of this agreement, Israel only allows foreigners and Palestinians to cross the Gaza border when they need to be in Israel: for example, if people who live in Gaza want to visit Jerusalem for the Muslim Sacrifice Feast, or if they seek medical care in Israel.

Israeli doctors treat everyone without discrimination. For example, the daughter of Gaza's Prime Minister (Ismail Haniyeh, a senior political leader of Hamas) was treated in an Israeli hospital despite her father's continuing calls for the destruction of Israel.

The international agreement stipulates that the border between Egypt and Gaza is supposed to be monitored by Palestinian Authority officials and by international observers. However, after the coup by Hamas in 2007, both groups of observers are prevented from monitoring. Moreover, Hamas supports Muslim fundamentalist attacks against the Egyptian army and police in the Sinai desert. Thus, Egypt's trade with Gaza is limited and the border is regularly closed.

The Gaza Strip is not a prison, but is an area that is difficult to access because of the war it is waging against its two neighbors, Egypt and Israel. Since when can 15,000 rockets be launched from inside a "prison"?

And Hamas is capable of changing this situation any time.
The leadership of Hamas only has to meet three conditions set by the United States, Russia, the European Union and the United Nations in order for border restrictions to cease. These three conditions are to renounce violence, to recognize Israel, and to honor the signed peace treaties. Both Egypt and Israel have promised that they will then lift the border restrictions.

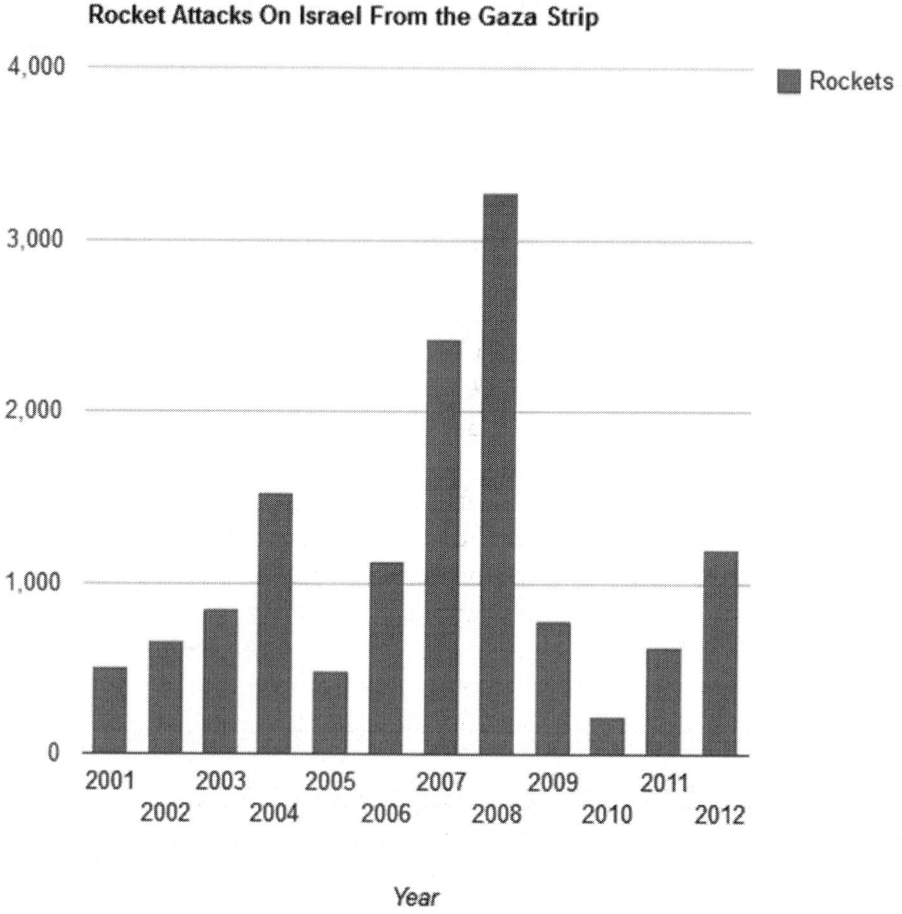

Rocket Attacks On Israel From the Gaza Strip

Tale: Gaza is an open-air prison.
Fact: From this "prison," more than fifteen thousand rockets were fired at Israel, as well as terrorist attacks perpetrated in the Egyptian Sinai desert.

37. Genocide

The Palestinian Tale: Israel has committed and is committing genocide against Palestinians.

This is a grotesque accusation. Although there is no denying that regular Palestinian deaths occur when violence flares, these deaths are not organized systematically, but rather result from Israeli self-defense. When Palestinians initiate violence against Israel, Israel responds legitimately in self-defense, under international law.

Israel targets rocket launchers and combat tunnels. Israel never willfully fires at random at the Palestinian population. The vast majority of the Palestinians who are killed in these incidents are people who opted themselves for violence. If Israel really wanted to commit genocide, it would not warn Palestinian people about upcoming attacks by phone, text message and flyers. Civilian casualties are caused by terrorists' intensive use of civilians as human shields (see Tale: Civilian casualties).

Since 1945, more than 40,000 Arabs (most of whom were soldiers in wars) and 22,000 Jews have died in the Arab-Israeli conflict. That is far too many deaths, but not enough to be considered genocide. As described in the tale "Conflict," around 10 million Muslims were killed in the region by Muslims themselves during the same period. This is 250 times as many deaths in inter-Arab wars then with the Jewish state. There seems to be far less of a mainstream media focus on these inter-Arab casualties. For example, the deaths of 3,000 Palestinian civilians who were recently killed in the Syrian civil war did not make headlines.

Rapid Palestinian population growth also refutes the nonsensical allegation of genocide. Despite the number of deaths caused by the conflict, the Palestinian population is one of the fastest growing populations in the world.

Israel assisted in this population growth. Since 1967, when Israel took over the administrations of the West Bank and the Gaza Strip, Israel has invested heavily into facilities that improve the living conditions of the Palestinians. Israel has built many clinics and hospitals, and has given the majority of Palestinian homes access to water and sanitation. Therefore, the infant mortality rate has decreased sharply, and life expectancies have risen (see Tale: Suffering of the Palestinians).

None of this progress occurred under Arab administration in the period between 1948 and 1967 when Egypt and Jordan held the Gaza Strip and the West Bank. The population of the Gaza Strip has approximately quadrupled since 1967. That's more like a reverse genocide! Ultimately, Israel is being blamed for something while in fact the opposite has happened.

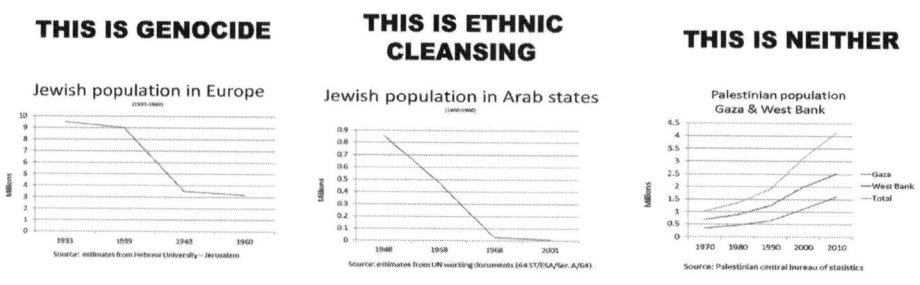

Tale: Israel commits genocide against the Palestinians.
Fact: The Palestinians are one of the fastest growing populations in recent world history.

38. Greater Israel

The Palestinian Tale: Israel aims to expand territory for a Greater Israel.

On the contrary, Israel has in its history ceded a lot of land to her (former) enemies; land that was conquered after acts of aggression from neighboring countries.

Israel has already ceded the Sinai desert twice (1956 and 1982), parts of Egypt and Syria conquered in the Yom Kippur War (1973), Gaza (2005), Southern Lebanon (1983 and 2000) and the densely populated parts of the West Bank (1990s).

Israel has thus ceded territory approximately seven times its own area, hoping to establish peace with its Arab neighbors. This is unique in world history.

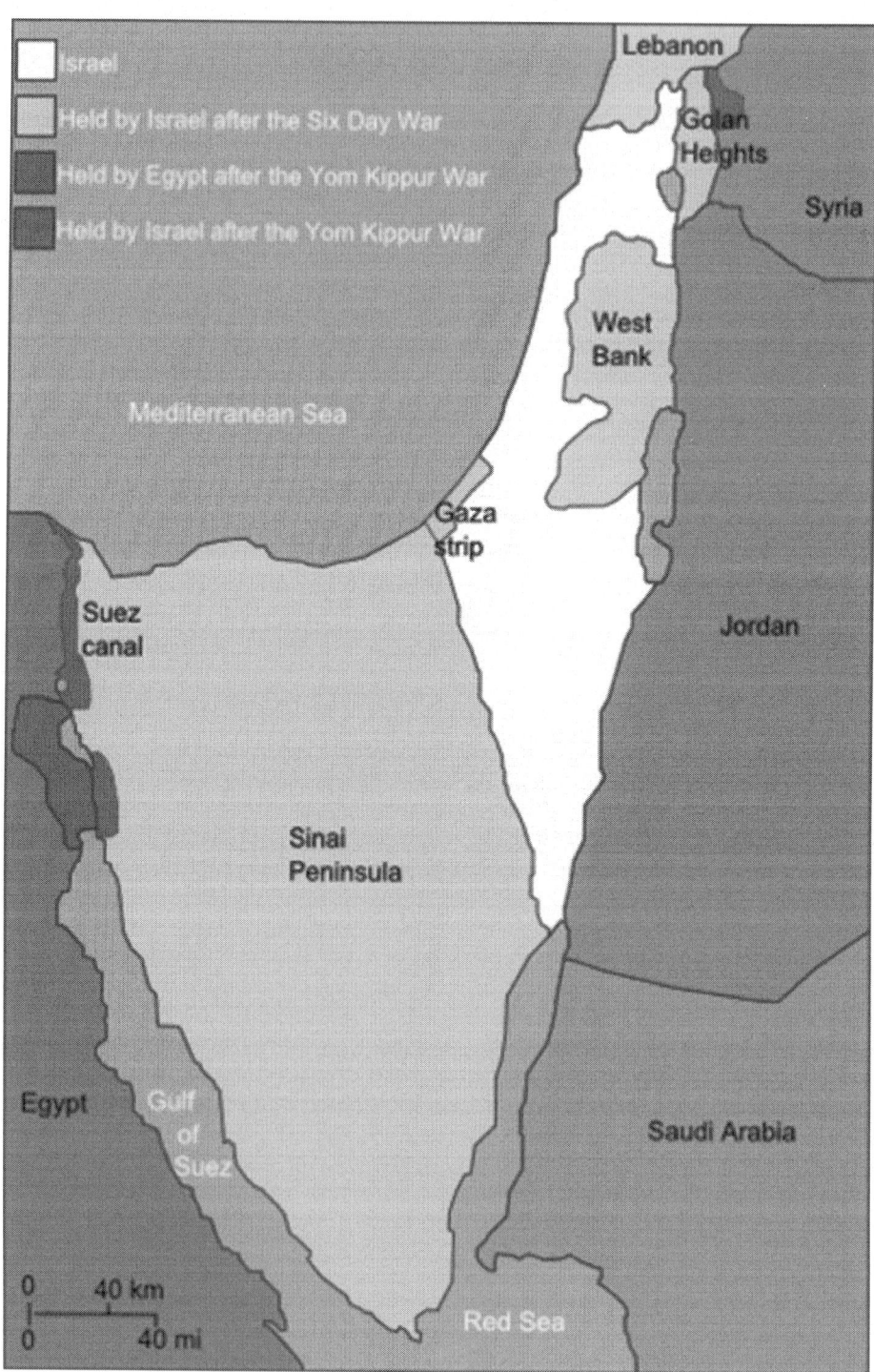

Tale: Israel strives for a greater Israel.
Fact: For peace, Israel ceded to Egypt the Sinai, about three times the size of Israel.

39. Hamas

The Palestinian Tale: Hamas is committed to a political solution of the conflict.

This is the Big Lie. Hamas's own charter states in many places that the only solution will be the destruction of Israel. Some examples:

> *"The control of the land and the land itself ought to be endowed as a Waqf for all generations of Muslims until the Day of Resurrection. The ownership of the land by its owners is only one of usufruct, and this Waqf will endure as long as Heaven and earth last. Any demarche in violation of this law of Islam, with regard to Palestine, is baseless and reflects on its perpetrators."* – article 11

> *"[Peace] initiatives, the so-called peaceful solutions, and the international conferences to resolve the Palestinian problem, are all contrary to the beliefs of the Islamic Resistance Movement. The initiatives, proposals and International Conferences are but a waste of time, an exercise in futility. The Palestinian people are too noble to have their future, their right and their destiny submitted to a vain game. For renouncing any part of Palestine means renouncing part of the religion. There is no solution to the Palestinian problem except by Jihad."* – article 13

> *"When our enemies usurp some Islamic lands, Jihad becomes a duty binding on all Muslims. In order to face the usurpation of Palestine by the Jews, we have no escape from raising the banner of Jihad."* – article 15

> *"Leaving the circle of conflict with Israel is a major act of treason and it will bring curse on its perpetrators."* – article 32

The fact that Israel is not ruled by (religious) Muslims upsets Hamas. Even worse for them is that its rulers are Jews.
Some interpretations of Islam are open to other faiths, such as the Sufi, who are very respectful of the Jewish religion. Iran ruthlessly oppresses the Sufi minority in its country and like Hamas promotes a very anti-Jewish interpretation of Islam. So is Saudi Arabia, whose rulers pay for anti-Israel propaganda in the West.

The Belgian professor Elchardus stresses that much Islamic Jew-hatred is "theologically inspired." He sees a direct link between Muslim faith and nurturing anti-Semitic feelings.

More religious often means more anti-Semitic, according to a survey by the University of Potsdam among French Muslims in May 2015. Thus, 30 percent of French people of Muslim origin think that there exists a "worldwide Zionist conspiracy." Among moderately religious Muslims that view was held by 42 percent of respondents and among actively practicing Muslims by 56 percent.

This prejudice is reflected in the Charter of Hamas, which is full of anti-Semitism. Again, some examples:

> *"The prophet, prayer and peace be upon him, said: 'The time will not come until Muslims will fight the Jews (and kill them); until the Jews hide behind rocks and trees, which will cry: O Muslim! There is a Jew hiding behind me, come on and kill him! This will not apply to the Gharqad, which is a Jewish tree.'"* – article 7

> *"They stood behind the French and the Communist Revolutions and behind most of the revolutions we hear about here and there. They also used the money to establish clandestine organizations which are spreading around the world, in order to destroy societies and carry out Zionist interests.*
> *As regards local and world wars, it has come to pass and no one objects, that they stood behind World War I, so as to wipe out the Islamic Caliphate.*
> *They also stood behind World War II, where they collected immense benefits from trading with war materials and prepared for the establishment of their state.*
> *'As often as they light a fire for war, Allah extinguishes it. Their efforts are for corruption in the land and Allah loves not corrupters. [Koran, Sura V (Al-Ma'ida – the Table spread), verse 64]"* – article 22

> *"The Zionist invasion is a mischievous one. It does not hesitate to take any road, or to pursue all despicable and repulsive means to fulfill its desires.*
> *Zionism strives to demolish societies, to destroy values, to wreck answerableness, to disturb virtues and to wipe out Islam. It stands behind the diffusion of drugs and toxics of all kinds in order to facilitate its control and expansion.*
> *Israel, by virtue of its being Jewish and of having a Jewish population, defies Islam and the Muslims.*
> *'Let the eyes of the cowards not fall asleep.'"* – article 28

Incidentally, it was well understood in Europe that talking with terrorists only makes sense if they first lay down their arms. Only under these conditions would Europe negotiate with European terrorist movements such as the Northern Irish IRA and the Basque ETA. Hamas is unwilling to meet these conditions, as is clear from many programs on the Hamas TV station.

MP for Hamas Yunis Al-Astal on Hamas television on May 11, 2011:
"The Jews are brought in droves to Palestine so that the Palestinians – and the Islamic nation behind them – will have the honor of annihilating the evil of this gang."

Hamas Prime Minister Ismail Haniyeh on Hamas television on March 23, 2014:
"Allah Akbar. Praised be Allah. Continue on the path. Continue on the path, Hamas. Hamas is the canon and we are the ammunition. My dear Izz ad-Din Al-Qassam Brigades, strike, strike Tel Aviv!
Resistance and martyrdom are the way to liberate Palestine and to restore Jerusalem and Al-Aqsa.
The tunnels inaugurate a new strategy to fight against the enemy – the tunnel strategy.
I say again and again: We will not, we will not, we will not recognize Israel!"

A children's television program on Hamas TV on May 2, 2014, featured a young child who wanted to join the police when she grew up:
Child host: *"OK, so what does a policeman do?"*
Little girl: *"He catches thieves and people who make trouble."*
Child host: *"And shoots Jews. Right?"*
Little girl: *"Yes."*
Child host: *"You want to be like him?"*
[Little girl nods]
Child host: *"Allah willing, when you grow up."*
Little girl: *"So that I can shoot Jews."*
Child host: *"All the Jews? All of them?"*
Little girl: *"Yes."*
Child host: *"Good."*

As long as the Palestinians adhere to this ideology, the conflict will continue.

Tale: Hamas is committed to a political solution.
Fact: Hamas wants the land from the Mediterranean to the Jordan River.
Photo: Election poster in Ramallah.

40. Hamas founding

The Palestinian Tale: Hamas was created by Israel.

The Islamist organization Muslim Brotherhood was founded in 1928. Hamas is the Palestinian branch of the Brotherhood. The first Palestinian leader, the Grand Mufti of Jerusalem Al-Husseini, was a fanatical supporter of the Brotherhood in the 1920s (see Tale: Nazism) and the movement has been active among Palestinians since that time.

What then is the origin of this tale? The Muslim Brotherhood in Egypt and the Palestinian branch, Hamas, both grew rapidly during the 1980s. In those years, support for Islamic fundamentalism in the Muslim world increased rapidly as a result of the millions of oil dollars pumped in by the Arab oil states as subsidies. Hamas was at first only active in religious welfare, and built mosques, youth centers, schools and hospitals. Obviously this type of activity was not obstructed by Israel, and even encouraged. Of course all support by Israel stopped when Hamas in 1989 committed its first terror attack and founded a terrorism branch in 1992, the Izz ad-Din al-Qassam Brigades.

Tale: Hamas was created by Israel.
Fact: Of course, Israel does not support any organization that aims to murder its citizens.
Photo: Destruction by a Hamas rocket.

41. Hebron

The Palestinian Tale: Jews have no connection to Hebron.

Often when seeing reports on the relatively small Jewish community of 500 people in the city of Hebron, one wonders why it is there, amidst a much larger and hostile Arab population. However, after Jerusalem, Hebron is historically and religiously the most important Jewish city. According to the Bible, almost all patriarchs and matriarchs of the Jewish people are buried there.

Because of its Jewish historical importance, the city always had a Jewish community, well into the twentieth century. However, 67 Jews were brutally murdered during a pogrom in Hebron in 1929. Some of the dead appeared to have been tortured or raped. The remaining 400 Jews of Hebron managed to flee. Two years later, 160 Jews dared to return. In 1936, however, it became again so unsafe that they fled a second time – except for one family that had been living in Hebron for eight generations.

Even the non-religious, socialist Prime Minister of Israel, David Ben Gurion, wrote in 1970:

> *"Hebrew history begins in Hebron. Don't forget: the beginnings of Israel's greatest king were in Hebron, the city to which came the first Hebrew about eight hundred years before King David, and we will make a great and awful mistake if we fail to settle Hebron, neighbor and predecessor of Jerusalem, with a large Jewish settlement, constantly growing and expanding, very soon. Hebron is worthy to be Jerusalem's sister."*

The problem is not the small Jewish community in Hebron; the problem is the Arab hostility against that community.

Tale: Jews have no connection to Hebron.
Fact: There was an ancient Jewish community in Hebron.
Photo: The destruction of the synagogue in Hebron pogrom in 1929.

42. Herzl

The Palestinian Tale: The desire for expulsion of the Arabs was part of Zionism from the beginning; it was already propagated by its founder, Theodor Herzl.

This tale is always based on one quote. For example, this tale appears in the 2012 book *Law and Justice* by Naim Ateek, a Christian Palestinian and founder of the anti-Israel organization Sabeel:

"Herzl wrote in his diary on June 12, 1895: 'When we occupy the land... we must expropriate gently the private property on the estates assigned to us' and 'we shall try to spirit the penniless population discreetly across the border.'"

This quote is always cited in support of the accusation that Zionism always envisioned an expulsion of the Arabs living in the land of Israel. Here it is again twisted. The full translation appears below. Regarding this quote:
- Other similar quotations are not found in Herzl's writings.
- On the contrary, the entire oeuvre of Herzl creates an image of an ideal society in the Jewish state, where everyone works together to build a country where racism is eliminated.
- Herzl was very opposed to racism, given his own experiences with anti-Semitism.

Whoever reads the actual and complete text of the diary page understands what Herzl intended. He wanted to encourage property purchases and payments for poor, underprivileged Arabs to leave the country. Forced displacement was out of the question:

"When we occupy the land, we shall bring immediate benefits to the state that receives us. We must expropriate gently the private property on the estates assigned to us. We shall try to spirit the penniless population across the border by procuring employment for it in the transit countries, while denying it any employment in our own country. The property-owners will come over to our side...

It goes without saying that we shall respectfully tolerate persons of other faiths and protect their property, their honor, and their freedom with the harshest means of coercion. This is another area in which we shall set the entire old world a wonderful example...

If this offer [to buy property] is not accepted, no harm will be done... We shall simply leave them there."

Herzl was thus, according to this subsequent text on that page of his diary, precisely a sworn opponent of expulsion. Again, only by maiming the quote can one accuse him falsely of racism.

The later Zionist leaders acted in the tradition of Herzl, saying repeatedly that the Arab minority should have equal rights (see Tale: Jewish state creation).

> *"My testament for the Jewish people: So build your state that a stranger will feel contented among you."*
> – Theodor Herzl in his diary on August 6, 1899

This is a case of Arab projection, whereby Israel is falsely blamed for actions that were taken in the Arab countries. Because the Jews were in fact expelled from Arab countries; of the 1 million Jews in Arab countries in 1948, now only a few thousand remain. The rest fled, mostly to Israel or to the United States. Saudi Arabia and Jordan have racist legislation barring Jews from living in those countries. The Palestinian Authority wants the same legislation.

Altneuland

Roman

von

Theodor Herzl

Wenn Ihr wollt,
Ist es kein Märchen

Leipzig
Hermann Seemann Nachfolger.

Tale: Herzl wanted to expel the Arabs.
Fact: In his novel *Altneuland* (photo), Herzl envisions peaceful coexistence of Arabs and Jews in a future Jewish state.

43. Holocaust

The Palestinian Tale: Israel was created out of a sense of guilt caused by the Holocaust.

Palestinians often claim that they are victims of the Holocaust because Europeans agreed with the founding of the State of Israel only out of feelings of guilt over the genocide. This tale is aimed at people who lack historical knowledge. Already in 1922 the British Palestine Mandate (by the way, including Jordan and the Golan) was awarded by unanimous vote to a future Jewish state by the League of Nations (the predecessor of the UN).

Everyone thought it was logical that in addition to the 22 Arab states created from the breakup of the giant Turkish Ottoman Empire, one state would also be formed for Jews. Obviously, this was to be in the historic homeland of the Jews, where they had lived continuously for more than 3,000 years.

Israel was founded in 1948, but long before that there already functioned a Jewish democratic state in the British Mandate area with its own language (Hebrew), culture, agriculture, universities, newspapers and military force.

> *"It is hard to see how the Arab world, still less the Arabs of Palestine, will suffer from what is mere recognition of accomplished fact – the presence in Palestine of a compact, well organized, and virtually autonomous Jewish community."*
> – London Times editorial, December 1, 1947

In 1947, the United Nations proposed a partition plan, which was rejected by the Arab world. But Israel would anyway have proclaimed its independence.

The Jewish state had long been in the works before World War II and would have come about anyway, even without the war and the Holocaust. And the Jewish population would actually have been much larger without the Holocaust.

> *"There are those who say that if the Holocaust had not occurred, the State of Israel would never have been established. But I say that if the State of Israel would have been established earlier, the Holocaust would not have occurred."*
> – Israeli Prime Minister Benjamin Netanyahu

Tale: Israel was created out of a sense of guilt about the Holocaust.
Fact: The Jews were already building their state long before World War II.
Photo: The foundation of Tel Aviv in 1909, on barren dunes.

44. Holocaust denial

The Palestinian Tale: Palestinians recognize the horrors of the Holocaust.

On the contrary, total or partial Holocaust denial is rather common among Palestinians. A reporter on Hamas television on October 22, 2012, spoke about the Holocaust:

> "It is a Zionist lie spread throughout the world by the Zionist enemy, as if the Nazi regime in Germany killed millions of Zionists...
> The world is punished by the spreading of the lie."

Or it is said that the Holocaust was justified. As suggested by Hamas MP Marwan Abu Ras on Hamas television on January 23, 2015:

> "Were the Jews burned for no fault of their own? Their conspiracies and treachery are what led to their being burned."

The thesis that Palestinian President Abbas submitted for his PhD at a Russian university in Moscow set out to establish that the events of the Holocaust were exaggerated. It was published in 1984 as a book entitled *The downside: The secret relationship between Nazism and Zionism*.

This thesis is very popular as a textbook in Palestinian schools.

Abbas's book states that the number of Jewish victims of the Holocaust was probably less than 1 million, and accuses Zionist leaders of encouraging the persecution of Jews. It also denies that the gas chambers were used to murder Jews. Some quotes from the book:

> "It seems that the interest of the Zionist movement, however, is to inflate this figure [of Holocaust deaths] so that their gains will be greater. This led them to emphasize this figure [6 million] in order to gain the solidarity of international public opinion with Zionism. Many scholars have debated the figure of 6 million and reached stunning conclusions – fixing the number of Jewish victims at only a few hundred thousand.
>
> A partnership was established between Hitler's Nazis and the leadership of the Zionist movement... [the Zionists] gave permission to every racist in the world,

led by Hitler and the Nazis, to treat Jews as they wish, so long as it guaranteed immigration to Palestine.

All of this wasn't enough – the Zionist movement led a broad campaign of incitement against the Jews living under Nazi rule to arouse the government's hatred of them, to fuel vengeance against them and to expand the mass extermination.

Having more victims meant greater rights and stronger privilege to join the negotiation table for dividing the spoils of war once it was over. However, since Zionism was not a fighting partner – suffering victims in a battle – it had no escape but to offer up human beings, under any name, to raise the number of victims, which they could then boast of at the moment of accounting."

So this is the vision of the Palestinian President Abbas on the subject. What is remarkable is that many Palestinians who deny the Holocaust took place, themselves call for a second Holocaust.

"The [Jews] are brought in droves to Palestine so that the Palestinians – and the Islamic nation behind them – will have the honor of annihilating the evil of this gang."
   – Hamas MP Yunis Al-Astal on Hamas television, May 11, 2011

"I swear that if we had a nuke, we'd have used it this very morning."
   – Jibril Rajoub, member of the Central Committee (board) of Fatah and chairman of the Palestinian Olympic Committee, on Al-Mayadeen television, April 30, 2013

Tale: Palestinians recognize the horrors of the Holocaust.
Fact: The Palestinian leadership was involved in the Holocaust (see Tale: Nazism).
Photo: The first Palestinian leader Al-Husseini shaking hands with SS leader Heinrich Himmler.

45. Holy places, access

The Palestinian Tale: Jews have open access to Jewish holy sites.

As described in the tale "Holy places, respect," unlimited access for Jews is just very difficult. The tomb of Joseph, a Jewish holy site under the control of the Palestinian Authority, can only under very difficult and dangerous circumstances be visited by Jews.

The Israeli army controls access for Jews to two Jewish sacred places in areas transferred to the Palestinian Authority. These are the cave of Machpelah in Hebron and Rachel's Tomb in Bethlehem (the two major Jewish holy sites, after the Temple Mount). Without the presence of the Israeli army, Jews may not visit these two places as it would be too dangerous. This is evident from the violence that Jewish pilgrims often suffer, such as stone throwing.

During the occupation of the West Bank by Jordan between 1948 and 1967 (an occupation that was deemed illegal by both the Arab League and the UN), it was impossible for Jews to visit these two holy Jewish sites.

During that illegal occupation it was also completely impossible for Jews to visit their most sacred site, the Temple Mount and the adjacent Wailing Wall in East Jerusalem. No Israeli was admitted to this area between 1948 and 1967. On top of that, all the synagogues in the pre-1948 predominantly Jewish neighborhoods in eastern Jerusalem – 57 in number! – were completely destroyed by Jordan. Gravestones from Jewish cemeteries, some 3,000 years old, were used as building material, including for urinals, or were destroyed to be used in the construction of the road to a massive hotel on the Mount of Olives.

Even today there are constant tensions when Jews visit the Temple Mount. Thus spoke President Abbas on October 17, 2014, on Palestinian television, regarding the Al-Aqsa Mosque on the Temple Mount:
> "We have to prevent them, in any way whatsoever, from entering the Sanctuary. This is our Sanctuary, our Al-Aqsa and our Church [of the Holy Sepulcher]. They have no right to enter it. They have no right to defile it."

Forbidding access for Jews to their most holy site is a violation of human rights. While 3 million Muslims visit the Temple Mount each year, only 12,000 Jews are allowed. These figures also refute the tale that Muslims cannot easily visit the Temple Mount.

But it is not only the Temple Mount the Palestinians want to see rid of Jews. They would even like to restrict Jewish access to the adjacent Wailing Wall. In a speech on official Palestinian Authority television on February 21, 2014, Palestinian Minister of Religious Affairs Mahmoud Al-Habbash expressed:

"The right to pray at the blessed Al-Aqsa Mosque belongs exclusively to Muslims, exclusively to Muslims. The Al-Aqsa Mosque with its courtyards, its colonnades, its stone benches, its domes, its trees, its walls, includes the Al-Buraq Wall [the Western Wall of the Temple Mount], especially the Al-Buraq Wall."

On October 29, 2014, there was a murder attempt on Rabbi Judah Glick, who was severely wounded but survived. The attack was committed because this rabbi has argued for the right of Jews and Muslims to be allowed to pray on the Temple Mount. Palestinian President Abbas expressed his sympathy, not with the victim, but the perpetrator, Ibrahim Hijazi. The latter died in a gunfight after he fired at the Israeli police team that wanted to arrest him. Abbas wrote in a letter:

"With anger, we have received the news of the vicious assassination crime committed by the terrorists of the Israeli occupation army against [your] son Mu'taz Ibrahim Khalil Hijazi, who will go to heaven as a martyr defending the rights of our people and its holy places."

Prohibiting access for Jews to the Temple Mount and the Wailing Wall is obviously contrary to all international conventions and declarations on human rights covering freedom of religion. It's a big tale that Palestinians award free and safe access to the Jews to their holy places – something Israel does indeed offer to Muslims.

Tale: Palestinians offer Jews open access to Jewish holy sites.
Fact: The Tiferet synagogue in East Jerusalem was deliberately destroyed in 1948 (pictured) – as well as 56 other synagogues in Jerusalem. The same destruction happened in 2000 to Joseph's Tomb in the West Bank after its transfer to the Palestinians.

46. Holy places, respect

The Palestinian Tale: The Palestinians have respect for Jewish holy places.

Many times Muslims have claimed holy places of other faiths. Not only have Jews experienced this, but also, for example, Hindus.
The true origins of the holiness of places sacred to other faiths is ignored or even denied. The best-known Jewish examples are the two holiest places in Judaism, the Temple Mount in Jerusalem and the Cave of Machpelah in Hebron (the burial site of most biblical patriarchs and matriarchs). On top of these two places, mosques were built. A synagogue has stood over the grave of Jewish matriarch Rachel in Bethlehem for centuries, but the Palestinians claim now that this is actually a mosque.

It is questionable whether those places are in fact so important to Islam. The word Jerusalem does not even appear in the Koran. The Koran says that Muhammad after death went to heaven *"at the farthest mosque,"* and this is said to refer to Jerusalem. But Jerusalem at the time of Muhammad's death was not yet conquered by the Arabs. So there was no mosque at all; the first mosque in Jerusalem was built only about 50 years later.

That mosque, the Al-Aqsa, was built because the caliph (Islamic ruler) in Damascus lost control of Mecca to rebels. He therefore needed an alternative mosque as a Muslim pilgrimage site, for which he built the mosque on the Temple Mount. After his conquest of Mecca, Jerusalem again became unimportant.

Thereafter, the Islamic importance of Jerusalem throughout history was only highlighted at the moment that other faiths were engaged with it, such as the Christians during the Crusades, and now Israel. From historical photos it can be seen that the mosque on the Temple Mount was in great neglect 100 years ago. The building was damaged, the paint had peeled off and the square around it was overgrown by vegetation; it apparently received barely any visitors.

But even now it appears the Al-Aqsa Mosque on the Temple Mount is hardly relevant or even well-known to Muslims. While in the media it is constantly presented as the third holiest place of Islam, in a survey of 6,000 students in Jordan in January 2016 over 60 percent did not know what that meant.

Also there is even now sometimes little evidence of holiness. Muslim rioters hide stocks of stones and Molotov cocktails at the Al-Aqsa mosque, to throw against Jews on the Temple Mount. Youth regularly play football on the Temple Mount. Non-Jews visiting the Temple Mount are haunted by loudly shouting Muslim women. We never see Jews acting that way at their holy places, like the Wailing Wall, or Catholics in St. Peter's Square.

Another example is the tomb of the biblical Joseph, in the city of Nablus. Following the Oslo peace treaties, it was transferred to the Palestinian Authority by Israel in 1995.
The Palestinian Authority had given guarantees for the protection of the site and free access for Jews. How those guarantees worked out, Israel subsequently found out. In 2000, the tomb was massively attacked by Palestinians. An Israeli policeman was slain, and the holy place and the Jewish religious school (yeshiva) above it were burned to the ground. The tombstone was destroyed.

The remaining ruin was then painted green, indicating that it would be a mosque from then on. Under great international pressure, the shrine was again painted white.
Visiting this holy place remains problematic for Jews. In 2011, Jewish pilgrims were shot by Palestinian police, who killed one and wounded three. In October 2015 the holy site was attacked again and set on fire by Palestinians.
This is the only Jewish holy site that Israel handed over to the Palestinian Authority in a quest for peace. From its fate, one can learn how little respect there is among Palestinians for Jewish holy places. The fate of Joseph's tomb shows that it is a tale that Palestinians have respect for the holy places of other faiths.

Tale: The Palestinians have respect for Jewish holy places.
Fact: Before Israel was founded, the Temple Mount – Judaism's holiest site – was completely neglected.
Photo: The mosque on the Temple Mount had very few visitors in 1912, evidenced by the large amount of grass growing between the tiles.

47. Human rights organizations

The Palestinian Tale: Human rights groups have neutral attitudes toward Israel.

Unfortunately, many major human rights organizations have been hijacked by extreme leftists and therefore have a far-left political agenda. Israel, as a symbol of the West, cannot do anything right, while much less attention is given to abuses by radical Islamists in the region. However, Israel is the only democracy in the region (see the Tale: Democracy Israel), and in the Human Rights Indicator country ranking it scores better than 140 other countries.

The best-known example of human rights groups with biased political agendas is Oxfam International, led both in the Netherlands and in Belgium by former members of left-wing terrorist organizations. The director in the Netherlands, Farah Karimi, was active in the extreme left-wing Iranian terrorist organization Mujahidin Khalq. When she realized authorities were on her trail, she fled and received asylum in Germany on the basis of a made-up refugee story. She went to work for a branch of Mujahidin Khalq in Paris, where she invented asylum stories for other members of the group. A special forgery group substantiated these stories with counterfeit documents. In Karimi's book she writes that in the year she lived in Paris she invented an estimated 150 asylum stories out of extreme-left motives.

The president of the Belgian Oxfam, Guido Van Hecken, was also active as a terrorist. He assisted in a mega-terror car bomb assault in South Africa, in which 19 people were killed and 217 wounded.

So it is not surprising that Oxfam Novib, according to the Israeli human rights organization Shurat HaDin, subsidizes two umbrella organizations of the Palestinian terrorist organization PFLP. The PFLP (the Popular Front for the Liberation of Palestine), inter alia, committed the infamous murder of the Fogel family in 2011 and is designated a terrorist organization by the US and the EU.

Anyhow, it is strange that an organization that states its goal as "alleviating poverty" subsidizes a series of anti-Israeli organizations. All kinds of groups that actively deny Israel's right to exist have received subsidies, without any relation to fighting poverty. Even the organization *Stop the occupation* of the well-known Dutch anti-Semite Gretta Duisenberg has received subsidies from Oxfam. How a subsidy to this very wealthy widow of a Central Bank president helps combat poverty remains a mystery.

Many of these organizations – like Oxfam – advocate a boycott of Israeli products. Since Oxfam does not promote boycotts for any other country in the world, no matter what their human rights record, this is a clear case of discrimination of the Jewish state (see Tale: Boycott).

Human rights organizations also often exhibit unhealthy ties with extremist Palestinian organizations. In 2016 Israel publicized evidence that the director of the NGO World Vision in Gaza had funneled millions of dollars to the Hamas terror group.

Another example is Amnesty International. That organization was founded to support political prisoners held in dictatorships, but it now increasingly focuses its criticism on democracies. A low in that regard were its protests against the ban on burqas in Belgium and France. Those protests were directed against democratic decisions taken in these open Western democracies that were aimed at the emancipation of Muslim women.

Several Amnesty leaders appear to be associated with terrorist organizations. As revealed by the *London Times* in 2015, the international director of Amnesty's Human Rights Department, Yasmin Hussein, has ties with the Muslim Brotherhood, and his wife has ties to Hamas.

Amnesty regularly accuses Israel of "war crimes." As described in the relevant Tale, that is an unproven allegation without a very thorough investigation that relies on more than self-proclaimed eyewitnesses. Amnesty's leading researcher, Donatella Rovera, herself admitted that witness statements often are misleading, sometimes deliberately, in an article of April 28, 2014:
"In Gaza, I received partial or inaccurate information by relatives of civilians accidentally killed in accidental explosions or by rockets launched by Palestinian armed groups towards Israel that had malfunctioned and of civilians killed by Israeli strikes on nearby Palestinian armed groups' positions.
When confronted with other evidence obtained separately, some said they feared reprisals by the armed groups."

When Saudi Arabia carpet bombed Yemen in 2015, Amnesty was much more reticent. Then, it only mentioned the "possibility" of war crimes that should be investigated further.

A final example is the organization Human Rights Watch. That group is nowadays partly funded by Saudi Arabia, one of the worst human rights violators in the world. This new dependence is reflected in this organization's reports on the Middle East. For instance, Human Rights Watch condemned the demolition by Israel of the home of a Palestinian terrorist in December 2014 as "a war crime." But the act of the same terrorist was not condemned; he had intentionally run over civilians at a light-rail station, killing a young woman and a baby.

Because of this kind of bias, the founder of Human Rights Watch, Robert Bernstein, no longer wants to have anything to do with the organization. He stated in 2009, in an article in *The New York Times*:

"As the founder of Human Rights Watch, its active chairman for 20 years and now founding chairman emeritus, I must do something that I never anticipated: I must publicly join the group's critics.

The [Middle East] region is populated by authoritarian regimes with appalling human rights records. Yet in recent years Human Rights Watch has written far more condemnations of Israel for violations of international law than of any other country in the region.

The Arab and Iranian regimes rule over some 350 million people, and most remain brutal, closed and autocratic, permitting little or no internal dissent. The plight of their citizens who would most benefit from the kind of attention a large and well-financed international human rights organization can provide is being ignored as Human Rights Watch's Middle East division prepares report after report on Israel."

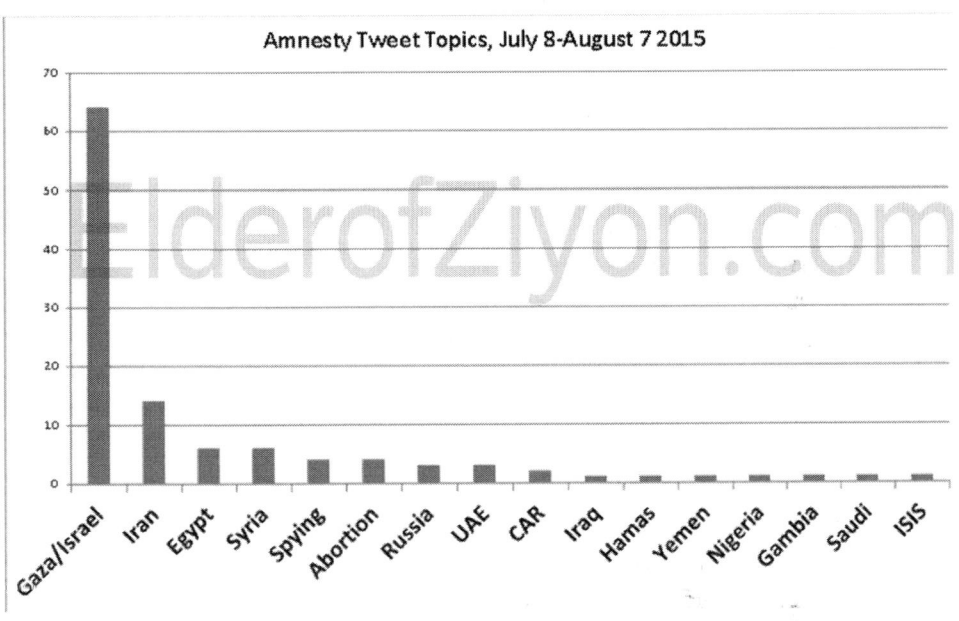

Tale: Human rights groups have neutral attitudes towards Israel.
Fact: Human rights organizations expend excessive negative attention on Israel.
Photo: Amnesty's tweets during one month in 2015. At that time there were wars underway in Yemen, Syria and Iraq, but more than half of Amnesty's tweets concerned Israel.

48. Islam

The Palestinian Tale: The Arab-Israeli conflict is a conflict over land and has nothing to do with Islam or Jew-hatred.

The Palestinian-Israeli conflict was started by the Palestinian leader Mufti Amin al-Husseini in the 1920s. The Grand Mufti of Jerusalem was a fanatical supporter of the Islamic fundamentalist group Muslim Brotherhood. His movement spread leaflets, for instance, with the following text:
> "O Arab! Remember that the Jew is your strongest enemy and the enemy of your ancestors since oldest Times. Do not be misled by his tricks for it is he who tortured Christ, peace be upon him, and poisoned Muhammad, peace and worship be with him. It is he who now endeavors to slaughter you as he did yesterday."

The conflict had therefore at the outset a strong religious base.

In 2006, Hamas won the Palestinian elections and the majority of the parliamentary seats. Hamas is the Palestinian branch of the Muslim Brotherhood and likewise operate s on the basis of religious beliefs. As its charter states in Article 8: "*Allah is its goal, the Prophet its model, the Koran its Constitution, Jihad its path and death for the case of Allah its most sublime belief.*" Article 28 states: "*Israel, by virtue of its being Jewish and of having a Jewish population, defies Islam and the Muslims.*"

The nominally secular Fatah is actively anti-Semitic. On January 9, 2012, Mufti Mohammed Hussein spoke to a crowd on the occasion of Fatah's 47th anniversary. The mufti is appointed by the Palestinian Authority as the top Islamic cleric in the West Bank, and his speech was broadcast on official Palestinian television:
> "The time will not come until Muslims will fight the Jews [and kill them]; until the Jews hide behind rocks and trees, which will cry: O Muslim! There is a Jew hiding behind me, come on and kill him."

This message is broadcast throughout the Arab world (see Tale: Arab anti-Semitism). The problem is that the Koran contains certain passages that are anti-Jewish, although it also contains passages with more positive messages about Jews. In the chaotic struggle when Islam was founded, some Jewish clans supported Mohammed's army and others supported his enemies. It is historically just as accurate to say that Jews saved Mohammed's life as it is to state that *"Jews tried to kill Mohammed"* (Guess which of these two statements is more popular today.)

At that time, there was a large Jewish population in Arabia. For example, they accounted for about half of the population of Muslim holy city of Medina. The Jews, however, were expelled from the Arabian Peninsula by Muhammad and his successors.

For Muslim fundamentalists, hatred of Jews is part of their faith. As the Dutch newspaper *NRC* reported on July 19, 2014:

"Professor Elchardus, who led the Belgian study [on anti-Semitism among Belgian Muslims], emphasized that this Jew-hatred is not caused by the Israeli-Palestinian conflict, socio-economic disadvantage and educational attainment, but 'anti-Semitism theologically inspired in Muslim students. There is a direct link between being Muslim and the nurturing of anti-Semitic feelings.'"

It is difficult for moderate Muslims to change these perceptions because the hatred of the Jews and the duty of Jihad are laid down in the Islamist tradition, which is considered sacred. They also risk of being seen as heretics by Islamists – a crime that carries the death penalty.

> *"Oh armies of the Islamic nation, we are about to enter the month of blessing and victories [Ramadan]. This is your hour. Oh armies of the Islamic nation, either you die while obeying Allah and for His sake, in support of your religion, of your Lord and of the free men among Muslims.*
> *Oh Allah, protect the Al-Aqsa mosque from the filth of the Jews. Oh Allah, annihilate all the Jews! Oh Allah, enable us to kill them!"*
>   – Palestinian preacher Sheikh Ali Abu Ahmad in a sermon delivered at the Al-Aqsa Mosque on the Temple Mount on May 20, 2016

Tale: The conflict has nothing to do with Islam or Jew-hatred.
Fact: The Palestinian leader who started the conflict, Al-Husseini, relied on Islam to spread hatred of Jews.
Photo: Al-Husseini inspecting Muslim recruits of Hitler's Waffen-SS.

49. Islamic State (IS)

The Palestinian Tale: Islamic State was founded by the Zionists.

This tale was spread, for instance, by top Dutch official Yasmina Haifi, who tweeted on August 12, 2014: *"ISIS has nothing to do with Islam – is deliberate plan by Zionists who knowingly want to blacken the reputation of Islam."*

This nonsense is also spread by Palestinian leaders. Fatah Central Committee member Sultan Abu Al-Einein said on Lebanese television on February 5, 2015, that he sees IS as *"an extension of the Zionist enterprise."*

Of course, IS is thoroughly Islamic: The organization calls itself "Islamic State." The organization gets money from Muslims and Muslim countries. All its members are Muslims. The members live strictly according to *Sharia* law. The members are willing to sacrifice their lives for Islam, according to Islamic tradition, to enter the Islamic paradise as Islamic martyrs, where they will be rewarded with 72 virgins, according to Islamic tradition. Moreover, Muslim martyrs may designate 70 family members to also inherit Islamic paradise. Members of IS get their inspiration from the Koran. The organization is recommended by some Islamic clergy. The organization aims for a Caliphate (Islamic Empire), which it seeks to attain through Jihad, Islamic holy war. On that basis the organization fights against non-Muslims, including civilians, who are permitted to be slain. Members are recruited by Muslims. Members constantly call "Allah Akbar" (Allah is the greatest).

And therefore Muslims come flocking to IS from around the world. They want, as Muslims, to fight for IS and give their lives for it. A poll conducted by the Arab broadcasting network Al-Jazeera in 2015 found that 81.3 percent of the visitors of their website support the goals of IS.

How can people then still send the message to the world that IS has nothing to do with Islam and was created the "Zionists"? This blatant lie is hard to explain for people in the West. This lie is partly due the Arab culture of shame: Arabs cannot do anything wrong, therefore accusations are flatly denied. Also, since Islam is the best religion, if Muslims are not doing well, conspiracies must be to blame (see Tale: Conspiracy theories).

It is sad – and worrying – that even a seemingly well-integrated Muslim with an important function, as the above mentioned official Yasmina Haifi, is not able to escape from this culture. Also, this is another clear case of Arab projection, where Israel is falsely blamed of something which the Arabs themselves are guilty of.

Tale: IS was founded by the Zionists.
Fact: IS was founded by al-Baghdadi (pictured), a fundamentalist Muslim, who graduated in Islamic studies from the Islamic University of Baghdad.

50. Jerusalem, capital

The Palestinian Tale: Tel Aviv is the capital of Israel.

Jerusalem has been the capital of Israel since 1949. It is true that many countries do not recognize this. They do not want to offend Arab countries before the final borders of Israel are established. Israel is the only country in the world without a universally recognized capital.

That does not alter the fact that each country can decide which city is its capital. Israel can have only one capital.

As the first president of Israel, Chaim Weizmann, remarked early in the twentieth century to then British Foreign Secretary, Lord Balfour: *"Jerusalem was already our capital when London was still a swamp."*

> *"A capital is the municipality enjoying primary status in a country, usually as its seat of government."*
> – Wikipedia

Tale: Tel Aviv is the capital of Israel.
Fact: The Knesset (Israeli parliament; photo) and other government buildings are in Jerusalem.

51. Jerusalem, East

The Palestinian Tale: Jews are invaders in eastern Jerusalem.

Anyone who knows the facts understands how calling the Jews invaders is humbug.

Jerusalem was already 3,000 years ago the highly developed capital of the people of Israel, 1,700 years before the Arabs arrived there. Jews have always lived in Jerusalem, even following the destruction of the Holy Temple by the Romans; since the year 1600 the Jews have (again) become the largest population group in Jerusalem.

The Jews were the first to settle eastwards outside the medieval city walls of Jerusalem, around 1860.

In what is now called East Jerusalem lies the ancient Jewish quarter – next to the Wailing Wall and the Temple Mount, the holiest site of Judaism. The only time in history that no Jews lived in that quarter was between 1948 and 1967, as a result of the ethnic cleansing by the Jordanian army in 1948. The 57 (!) synagogues in the Jewish Quarter were all destroyed, blown up with dynamite.

The same applies to the area of Gush Etzion, south of Jerusalem. Jews bought land in this area in the 1920s and four Jewish villages were established there. Those villages were conquered by Arab armies during the Arab attack on Israel in 1948. The inhabitants of one of the villages, Kfar Etzion, surrendered, but all male inhabitants (127 people) were nevertheless massacred by the Arabs. The villages were destroyed and the remaining inhabitants were expelled. Israel recaptured the area in 1967 after it was attacked by Jordan. Jews from East Jerusalem and Gush Etzion went back to their homes.

As agreed in the Oslo Accords, East Jerusalem and parts of the West Bank remain under Israeli control. The final borders would be determined in a final peace treaty (see Tale: West Bank claims). However, the Palestinians have refused to negotiate this point seriously for the past 20 years. By the way, Clinton's proposed compromise for peace in the years 2000 and 2001 placed the Jewish neighborhoods in and around Jerusalem in Israeli hands – logically so, because of the Jewish majorities there.

Jews buying homes in East Jerusalem is labeled by many as a shameful act. The remarkable thing is that if people would say that Jews should not be allowed to buy houses in eastern New York, they would be called horrible racists, and rightly so. Just as someone who would say that Muslims should not be allowed to buy houses there. But then why this is allowed to be said about Jews in East Jerusalem?

On official Palestinian television on November 14, 2014, this racism was even further extended by PLO Central Council member Yaakub Qureish. He openly called for the total ethnic cleansing of Jews from Jerusalem, both east and west:
"I say this without hesitation, and I speak for the entire Palestinian people and the entire Arab and Islamic nation. I am thereby representing what [our] leader, Mahmoud Abbas, said in his speech ten minutes ago: There will not be a single Jew or Israeli in Jerusalem. Not a single one."

Prime Minister Netanyahu responded indignantly to the criticism that no Jews should be allowed to buy houses in East Jerusalem:
"Arabs in Jerusalem are free to purchase apartments in the western [part of the] city and no one is arguing against it. I have no intention of telling Jews they can't buy apartments in east Jerusalem. This is private property and an individual right. There cannot be discrimination – not against Jews and not against Arabs.
If you said to me that in some city in the United States or in Mexico, or anywhere else, Jews cannot buy apartments, there would be an uproar. You know, there's not only the freedom of property, but the right of every individual to live where they want, as long as they purchase the apartment legally."

Tale: Jews are invaders in East Jerusalem.
Fact: The Jewish neighborhood of Silwan in East Jerusalem existed already in 1870 (photo).

52. Jerusalem, history

The Palestinian Tale: Jerusalem has no Jewish history.

This is probably one of the most absurd tales debunked in this book.
After all, the evidence that Jerusalem has an – intensive, 3,000-year long – Jewish history is overwhelming: historical documents, historians from ancient times, many mentions of Jerusalem in the Jewish Bible, archeology, scientific dating of Jewish artifacts, and so on.

And yet all this is denied by many Arabs. It shows how they deal with unpleasant facts. Some examples:

A news broadcast on official Palestinian Authority television proclaimed on October 25, 2012:
> "Deep underground beneath the Al-Aqsa Mosque, there's [an Israeli] race against the clock to complete the excavations in search of [Jerusalem's] Temple that exists only in the minds of radical organizations... They falsify historical facts by linking them to Jewish history, the traces of which don't exist in our land."

The former official mufti of the Palestinian Authority, Sheikh Ikrima Sabri, said the same on Al-Arabiya TV on May 11, 2012:
> Interviewer: *"So in your opinion, today there are no places whatsoever in Jerusalem that are holy to the Jews?"*
> Ikrima Sabri: *"No, none. They build new synagogues, but there are no archaeological remains [pertaining to the Jews]. For many years, they have been digging for archaeological remains, but they haven't found anything. How can we acknowledge something when they themselves admit that they have found nothing?"*

Shamekh Alawneh, a lecturer in modern history at Al-Quds Open University, denied on official Palestinian television on August 11, 2009, that there was historicity to the Wailing Wall:
> *"It has no historical roots. This is political terminology to win the hearts and the support of the Zionists in Europe, so they would emigrate and come to Palestine. Nothing more!"*

Likewise, a lecturer on Islam at Al al-Bayt University in Jordan, Bahjat Habashneh, declared on official Palestinian television on June 21, 2016:

> *"According to the Jews, the holiest place in the world is the [Foundation] Stone [i.e., on the Temple Mount]. But the question arises: Since Allah didn't bestow it with holiness, where did the holiness come from? There is no text, not in the Talmud, not in the Jewish Bible, not in the Apocrypha, and not in any of the Jewish writings that gives holiness to Jerusalem. The source of the sanctity and purity of Jerusalem, and the existence of a mosque in it, are in the Islamic texts."*

Note: Jerusalem is mentioned 669 times in the Jewish Bible, and Zion (another name often used for Jerusalem) appears 154 times, for a total of 823 references. With zero mention of Jerusalem in the Koran (or perhaps one time: "the furthest mosque").

But this is what students learn in Arab universities!

During the peace negotiations in 2000, Palestinian leader Yasser Arafat also claimed this view, to a completely bewildered US President Clinton: there had never been a Jewish temple in Jerusalem. The current Palestinian President Mahmoud Abbas is also spreading this nonsense.

How absurd this is, is shown by the fact that older Arabic and Islamic books and writings confirm the existence of a Jewish temple in Jerusalem, even in the Koran. Additionally, the Supreme Moslem Council of Jerusalem in 1925 declared: *"Its [Temple Mount] identity with the site of Solomon's Temple is beyond dispute."*

But now truth is taboo for Arabs.

> *"In my office in Jerusalem, there's an ancient seal. It's a signet ring of a Jewish official from the time of the Bible. The seal was found right next to the Western Wall, and it dates back 2,700 years, to the time of King Hezekiah. Now, there's a name of the Jewish official inscribed on the ring in Hebrew. His name was Netanyahu."*
> – Israeli Prime Minister Benjamin Netanyahu

Tale: Jerusalem has no Jewish history.
Fact: Romans conquered Jerusalem in the year 70 (which had then already been the Jewish capital for about a thousand years) destroyed the temple and seized the temple's treasures.
Photo: Detail of the Titus arch on the Roman Forum in Rome.

53. Jerusalem, Judaization

The Palestinian Tale: Israel constantly makes Jerusalem more Jewish and expels Palestinians.

This tale is propagated by the Palestinian President Abbas. He said in a broadcast on official Palestinian television on January 17, 2014:

"The occupation authorities are continuing their efforts to achieve their final goal of Judaizing Jerusalem. First, these include their attempt to change Jerusalem's landscape in every detail, and replace it with a different landscape whose purpose is to serve delusional tales and the arrogance of power.

They imagine that by brute force they can invent a [Jewish] history, establish claims and erase solid religious and historical facts."

In reality, Jerusalem's population has become more Arabic since Israel broke down the fence that had divided the city, between 1948 and 1967, into an eastern and western part.

Anyone can investigate this, for instance on Wikipedia. The Muslim population has not decreased at all since 1967. In fact, it has grown tremendously. There was an immense five-fold increase; the growth occurred at a whopping 411 percent rate. This outpaces the growth in the number of Jewish inhabitants by a large factor: Jewish population increased by only 154 percent. Thus, under Israeli sovereignty, the number of Palestinian residents in Jerusalem increased more than twice as fast as the number of Jews.

This applies just as much to recent developments: the population of Jerusalem has grown between 2008 and 2012, from 759,700 to 815,300 persons. Most of the growth was in the Arab neighborhoods, which grew by 32,200 inhabitants in that period. The Jewish population increased far less both in absolute and relative terms, with only 23,400 new residents.

So this is another case of Arab projection, in which Israel is accused is of something that Arabs are guilty of themselves. Because the Jews indeed were fully expelled from East Jerusalem in 1948. By the way, the Christian population was treated similarly: when East Jerusalem was under Jordanian rule, from 1949 to 1967, the Christian population shrunk by half as a result of Arab oppression. Nowadays too, many Palestinians want all Jews expelled from Jerusalem (see Tale: Jerusalem East).

The enormous growth of the Arab population thus refutes another Palestinian tale, that of the "bullying" of Arabs out of Jerusalem. The occasional demolition of Palestinian homes is used to support this allegation. However, demolition happens to all houses built without planning permits, the same as anywhere in the world. Religion plays no role whatsoever in these decisions, which is evident by the fact that more of the illegal houses demolished in Jerusalem belong to Jews rather than Arabs.

The enormous population growth refutes yet another tale, which says that Arabs suffer from terrible living conditions in Jerusalem under Israeli rule. As shown by the population figures, Arabs are pouring in. Evidently, they want to live under Israeli rule. Thus, the residents of the predominantly Arab neighborhood of Jabel Mukaber petitioned the Israeli Supreme Court to have the route of the security fence changed in such a way that their quarter would be on the Israeli side.

It was also a surprising finding when the Arabs in East Jerusalem were asked in 2010 how they would feel if their neighborhood would be included in a Palestinian state. Forty percent said they would consider moving to another neighborhood in order to remain under Israeli rule, rather than Palestinian. Another poll in 2015 showed that a majority (52 percent) even prefer Israeli citizenship over Palestinian (42 percent).

That preference is not hard to understand. First, there is an economic motive; Arabs prefer to opt for Israeli jobs, schools, health and social benefits rather than a life with the abuse of power and corruption of the Palestinian autonomous administration. Further, a majority of these polled Arabs are either women, gay or Christian. These groups know very well that the Arab-Islamic society for them means a reduction in rights. Their nationalism is not strong enough to give up their civil rights.

So why not hold a referendum to hear directly from the inhabitants of Jerusalem, whether they prefer to Israel or be part of an autonomous Palestinian territory? Such a referendum was proposed in the 1947 Partition Plan (see Tale: Partition Plan) of the United Nations: it called for a referendum of inhabitants within ten years over the future status of Jerusalem.

> *"I often hear them accuse Israel of Judaizing Jerusalem. That's like accusing America of Americanizing Washington, or the British of Anglicizing London. You know*

why we're called 'Jews'? Because we come from Judea [the region that has Jerusalem at its center]."

– Israeli Prime Minister Benjamin Netanyahu at the 66th session of the General Assembly in the United Nations headquarters, September 23, 2011

Tale: Israel constantly makes Jerusalem more Jewish and expels Palestinians.
Fact: The number of Arabs in Jerusalem is growing faster than the number of Jews.
Photo: Arab neighborhood in the Old City.

54. Jesus

The Palestinian Tale: Jesus was a Palestinian.

Every Jew and Christian, even with little knowledge of the Bible, knows that Jesus was a Jew, like all prophets in the Torah (the Old Testament) were Jews. However, according to Islam, they were all Muslims. They call even Jesus the first Muslim martyr – someone who died in the struggle to defend Islam – despite the fact that Islam was only founded 600 years after Christ.

Palestinians go a step further and call Jesus a Palestinian, though the Romans only named the region Palestine about a hundred years after the death of Jesus.

Here are a few examples from the Palestinian media.

Dr. Omar Ja'ara, lecturer at Al-Najah University in Nablus, on official Palestinian television on February 15, 2012:
> "The Muslims of the Children of Israel went out of Egypt under the leadership of Moses, and unfortunately, many researchers deny the Exodus of those oppressed people who were liberated by a great leader, like Moses the Muslim, the believing leader, the great Muslim."

The Palestinian daily *Al-Hayat Al-Jadida* – under the control of Palestinian President Abbas – stated on November 30, 2012:
> "Jesus is a Palestinian; the self-sacrificing Yasser Arafat is a Palestinian; Mahmoud Abbas, the messenger of peace on earth, is a Palestinian. How great is this nation of the holy Trinity!"

Issa Karake, the minister of prison affairs of the Palestinian Authority, declared on official Palestinian television on May 4, 2012:
> "Jesus, the Palestinian, was the first prisoner and the first Shahid [Islamic martyr] in history."

Sheikh Mohammed Hussein, the mufti (highest Muslim cleric) of the Palestinian Authority, together with the top Muslim cleric in the West Bank, preached on Palestinian television on April 12, 2009:

"Jesus was born in this land; he took his first steps in this land and spread his teachings in this land. He and his mother, we may say, were Palestinians par excellence."

Tale: Jesus was a Palestinian.
Fact: Jesus was a Jew. The Romans only named the region Palestine about a hundred years after the death of Jesus.
Photo: Jesus in the Temple, painting by Giovanni Paolo Panini.

55. Jewish lobby

The Palestinian Tale: American support for Israel is a result of the Jewish lobby.

There is indeed relatively large support for Israel in the United States. However, this is not so because of the Jews; they form only about 2 percent of the population, about the same percentage as Muslims. The decisive factor is the largely pro-Israel attitude of the general population in the US: about 65 percent of Americans are pro-Israel, compared to approximately 15 percent that support the Palestinians.

There is not only a pro-Israel lobby; there exists also a very active and powerful Arab lobby, as there are a thousand different interest groups in America. These Arab lobbyists have much more money at their disposal than the pro-Israel lobby, thanks to petrodollars. And the number of embassies of Muslim countries in the US is 57, compared with the one Jewish state's embassy – so the US State Department frequently tilts pro-Arab.

Moreover, the Arab countries are very important for the US arms industry, the oil industry and the oil supply. Until 1967, US policy was downright anti-Israel: Israel was discredited, among other reasons, because of its socialist society.

For these reasons, the Arab lobby is at least as strong as the Jewish lobby. Just think about how cautiously the United States handles Saudi Arabia, although it is a major financier of Islamic fundamentalism – 15 of the 19 September 11 hijackers were from Saudi Arabia.

Among the amounts countries spent in 2013 on their American lobby organizations, Israel finished in last (83rd) place with a paltry $1,250. The top countries were the UAE ($14.2 million), Germany ($12 million), Canada ($11.2 million) and Saudi Arabia ($11.1 million).

Nobody has ever mentioned the great leverage of the Islamic lobby. The Palestinian Authority itself hired a top American firm in 2015 for its lobbying – at the rate of $600,000 per year.

Anyhow, it is strange that anyone could think that about 15 million Jews have more world power than the 1.5 billion Muslims, outnumbering Jews by a factor of 100.

But there is so much emphasis on the imagined power of the Jews that, according to a 2015 survey by the Anti-Defamation League, 40 percent of Americans thought that Jews make up more than 10 percent of world population. Twenty-four percent even thought Jews constituted more than 20 percent of world population! This latter figure is approximately a hundred times greater than the reality, which is 0.2 percent.

The tale of the power of the Jewish lobby is the modern packaging of the Nazi tale that *"the Jews are out to obtain world domination."* This is unadulterated anti-Semitism.

> *"A third of the world does not recognize Israel – 57 nations of the United Nations do not recognize Israel, a third of the world – their international relationships can't be all that good. More countries recognize North Korea than Israel."*
> – King Abdallah II of Jordan

Tale: American support for Israel is a result of the Jewish lobby.
Fact: Israel has broad support among the general US population.
Photo: Pro-Israel demonstration in Florida.

56. Jewish refugees

The Palestinian Tale: The Jews did not need to flee to Israel from neighboring Arab countries.

Before 1948, there were more than one million Jews living in Muslim countries. Those communities had often been there for thousands of years and were systematically discriminated against and attacked (See Tale: Jews in Arab countries). Arab pogroms increased in frequency in the 1920s and 1930s. This new wave of violent anti-Semitism was the result of two growing anti-Semitic movements: Nazism and Islamic fundamentalism. For example, in 1941, at least 600 Jews were murdered in a pogrom in Baghdad (Iraq). Furthermore, about a 1,000 Jewish shops and homes were looted, demolished and set on fire. When the United Nations proposed to create a Jewish and an Arab state in the British Mandate of Palestine at the end of November 1947 (a proposal in accordance with the goal of the British Mandate), the aggression against the Jewish communities increased even more.

Even before the vote concerning this proposed partition of Palestine took place, Arab countries stated that they would make the Jews living in the British Mandate and in Arab countries suffer if a Jewish state were to be founded.

> *"The United Nations should not lose sight of the fact that the proposed solution might endanger a million Jews living in the Moslem countries. Partition of Palestine might create in those countries an anti-Semitism even more difficult to root out than the anti-Semitism which the Allies were trying to eradicate in Germany. If the United Nations decides to partition Palestine, it might be responsible for the massacre of a large number of Jews.*
> *No force on earth could prevent blood from flowing there. Jewish blood will necessarily be shed elsewhere in the Arab world."*
> – Muhammad Hussein Heykal Pasha, head of the Egyptian delegation to the UN

Following the announcement of the vote, great unrest broke out in the Arab world: Arab countries instituted anti-Jewish laws, and there was a large number of riots between Arabs and Jews. The situation intensified when the State of Israel came into being six months later, in May 1948. Eighty Jews were killed in Yemen, more than 70 in Cairo, 44 in Morocco and 72 in Syria as a result of anti-Jewish violence following the creation of the State of Israel.

On May 16, 1948, *The New York Times* headlined: *"Jews in grave danger in all Moslem lands."*

The article mentions the creation of a law drafted by the Arab League that
"...intended to govern the legal status of Jewish residents in all Arab League countries. Their bank accounts will be frozen and used to finance resistance against the 'Zionist ambitions in Palestine.' Jews believed to be active Zionists were to be imprisoned and have their assets confiscated."

The hostile climate within the Muslim countries caused a massive exodus of the Jewish communities.

The exodus of Egyptian Jews, for example, had started slowly following a pogrom in Cairo in 1945. After the establishment of Israel, the violence intensified further. In June 1948, a bomb exploded in the Jewish quarter of Cairo, causing 22 Jewish casualties. In July 1948, Jewish shops and synagogues in Cairo were attacked, which resulted in the death of 19 Jews. Hundreds of Jews were arrested and had all of their possessions confiscated. Due to anti-Jewish measures and violence, almost 40 percent of the Jewish population of Egypt, had left within two years following the creation of the State of Israel. Eventually, all Egyptian Jews left Egypt, ending their 3,000 years of continuous presence.

Mass departures of Jews, as was happening in Egypt, took place in all Muslim countries. Large numbers of Jews fled, and most of them were forced to leave behind all their belongings. Today, only a few thousand Jews live in Arab countries. Before the exodus, there were 140,000 Jews living in Iraq. Today, only a few are left. Similarly, there used to be 140,000 Jews living in Algeria. Today, only ten still do.

After the creation of Israel, Jews in the West Bank were driven out completely. All of the approximately 10,000 Jews in the West Bank were forcibly evicted by the Arab-Jordanian army, which had conquered the area. The same happened to the approximately 5,000 Jews in East Jerusalem. According to Jordanian law, no Jews were permitted to live in Jordan. This discriminatory legislation is still in force today.

The ancient Jewish quarter in East Jerusalem was completely burned down and demolished in 1948. The 57 (often ancient) synagogues located there were utterly destroyed.

Of the more than one million Jewish refugees from Arab countries, the vast majority (850,000) went to Israel. Many of these refugees lived in squalid refugee camps during their first years in the country but gradually managed to integrate into Israeli society with no foreign aid or help from the United Nations.

Jewish refugees vastly outnumber Arab ones by a factor of two-to-one, according to a study completed in 2008. Moreover, Jewish refugees lost far more of their possessions/property. Palestinian Arab refugees lost property with an estimated worth of 450 million dollars (currently valued at around $3.9 billion) while the Jewish refugees lost property worth 700 million dollars (about $6 billion today).

Tale: The Jews did not have to flee from the Islamic countries.
Fact: Most Jews fled, as a result of state-sponsored violence.
Photo: Arab looting of East Jerusalem after the flight of the Jews.

57. Jewish state

The Palestinian Tale: A Jewish state is an absurd idea; it is discriminatory.

This is a curious argument, because you rarely hear this about other countries. For there exist 18 officially Christian countries. The flags of England, Finland, Greece, Sweden and Switzerland depict a cross. The kings of England, Denmark and Norway, are automatically the heads of their national churches. The constitution of Denmark says: *"The Evangelical Lutheran Church shall be the Established Church of Denmark, and, as such, it shall be supported by the State. The King shall be a member of the Evangelical Lutheran Church."*

Almost a third of all countries have a religious symbol on their national flag: 31 Christian and 21 Muslim symbols. There are 26 officially Islamic states, in which ethnic and/or religious minorities often have reduced civil rights. Of these, there are even four that have a religious reference in the name of their countries: the Islamic Republics of Afghanistan, Iran, Pakistan and Mauritania.

The Jordanian constitution says: *"Islam is the religion of the State. No person shall ascend the Throne unless he is a Moslem – of Moslem parents."*

In Afghanistan the constitution declares: *"The sacred religion of Islam is the religion of the Islamic Republic of Afghanistan. No law shall contravene the tenets and provisions of the holy religion of Islam in Afghanistan."* The president must be a Muslim.

The constitution of Malaysia states: *"Islam is the religion."* Believers of other religions are faced with many restrictions. This while only approximately 60 percent of the population is Muslim.

The Saudis go one step further, refusing even to have a constitution: *"The Kingdom of Saudi Arabia is a sovereign Arab Islamic state with Islam as its religion; God's Book and the Sunnah of His Prophet, God's prayers and peace be upon him, are its constitution."* The Saudi flag consists of the Islamic statement of faith above a sword.

In December 2015, the Gambia declared itself an Islamic republic and obliged women to wear a headscarf in public. There was no international outrage.

Also, the autonomous Palestinian areas are Islamic, so declared by the Palestinian Authority. Thus, in the constitution, Islam is the official religion and Islamic *Sharia* law is the basis for the legal system, which is discriminatory against non-Muslims, women and gay men. And speaking of discrimination: Palestinian President Abbas has often stated that no Jews will be allowed to live in a future Palestinian state. Selling real estate to a Jew earns a Palestinian the death penalty.

It is not all that unusual for a state to have a connection to a religion (with America being the famous exception, carefully separating state and religion). The influence of Judaism on Israeli society (see Tale: Orthodox Jewish power) turns out to be less than the religious influence in many Christian or Muslim countries.

This again shows Arab projection, in which Israel is blamed for something that is common in Arab countries. In many Arab countries, Islam is a state religion – which results in very discriminatory laws – not so with Judaism in Israel.

Tale: The concept of a Jewish state is absurd and discriminatory.
Fact: Anyone can freely express his or her faith in Israel, while in Saudi Arabia, as an exclusively Islamic state, the practice of other faiths is forbidden.
Photo: The flag of Saudi Arabia contains the text of the Islamic statement of faith and a sword.

58. Jewish state, creation

The Palestinian Tale: The Palestinians had good reasons to oppose the creation of a Jewish state.

After the end of World War I, the Ottoman Empire collapsed. A mere 0.5 percent of the vast amount of land which previously belonged to the Empire was intended for the Jews, while the other 99.5 percent of lands was given to Arabs. A total of 22 modern-day Arab states were founded on their share.

In contrast to all the Arab nations, the Jews posited that, in their state, minorities would have equal rights. Politicians from both the left and the right side of Jewish politics agreed on this principle. The leader of right-wing Zionism and ideological father of the Israeli Likud Party, Ze'ev Jabotinsky, wrote in 1923 that he was prepared
> *"to take an oath binding ourselves and our descendants that we shall never do anything contrary to the principle of equal rights, and that we shall never try to eject anyone."*

Eleven years later, Jabotinsky was in charge of writing a constitution for a Jewish state. According to its articles, Arabs and Jews would share rights and obligations of the state equally, including military service as well as civil service. Hebrew and Arabic were to have the same legal status. Furthermore, Jabotinsky stated that *"in every government cabinet with a Jewish Prime Minister, the position of deputy Prime Minister will be offered to an Arab and vice versa."*

In 1936, leaders of the Alawite (Shia) in Syria, including the grandfather of Syrian dictator Bashar Assad, pointed out that the intransigence of Sunni Muslims was to blame for preventing harmony within the Middle East:
> *"The situation of the Jews in Palestine being the strongest and most concrete proof of the importance of the religious problem among the Muslim Arabs toward anyone who does not belong to Islam.*
> *Those well-meaning Jews, who have brought civilization and peace to Muslim Arabs and have spread wealth and prosperity in the land of Palestine, have not hurt anyone and have not taken anything by force. Nevertheless, these Muslims have declared a holy war against the Jewish and have not hesitated to slaughter their women and children."*

In order to reduce objections against a Jewish state, the 99.5 percent share for Arabs of previous Ottoman land was increased. As a result, Sunni Arabs were given 78 percent of the mandated territory of Palestine in 1922. This part of the land would later become the state of Jordan. According to the United Nations's 1947 Partition Plan, Sunni Arabs would receive another 45 percent of the remaining part of the mandated territory. Just a little over 10 percent of that area remained to be allocated to the Jews.

Despite their disappointment, the Jews chose to accept this unjust partition plan (see Tale: Partition Plan). However, many Sunni Arabs believed that the Jews did not even deserve 10 percent of the mandate area, and turned down the proposed distribution.

Today, Hamas agrees with this belief, which becomes clear in Article 11 of its charter:

"The Islamic Resistance Movement believes that the land of Palestine has been an Islamic Waqf throughout the generations and until the Day of Resurrection.
No one can renounce it or part of it, or abandon it or part of it.
No Arab country nor the aggregate of all Arab countries, and no Arab King or President nor all of them in the aggregate, have that right, nor has that right any organization or the aggregate of all organizations, be they Palestinian or Arab, because Palestine is an Islamic Waqf throughout all generations and to the Day of Resurrection.
This is the status [of the land] in Islamic Sharia, and it is similar to all lands conquered by Islam by force, and made thereby Waqf lands upon their conquest, for all generations of Muslims until the Day of Resurrection."

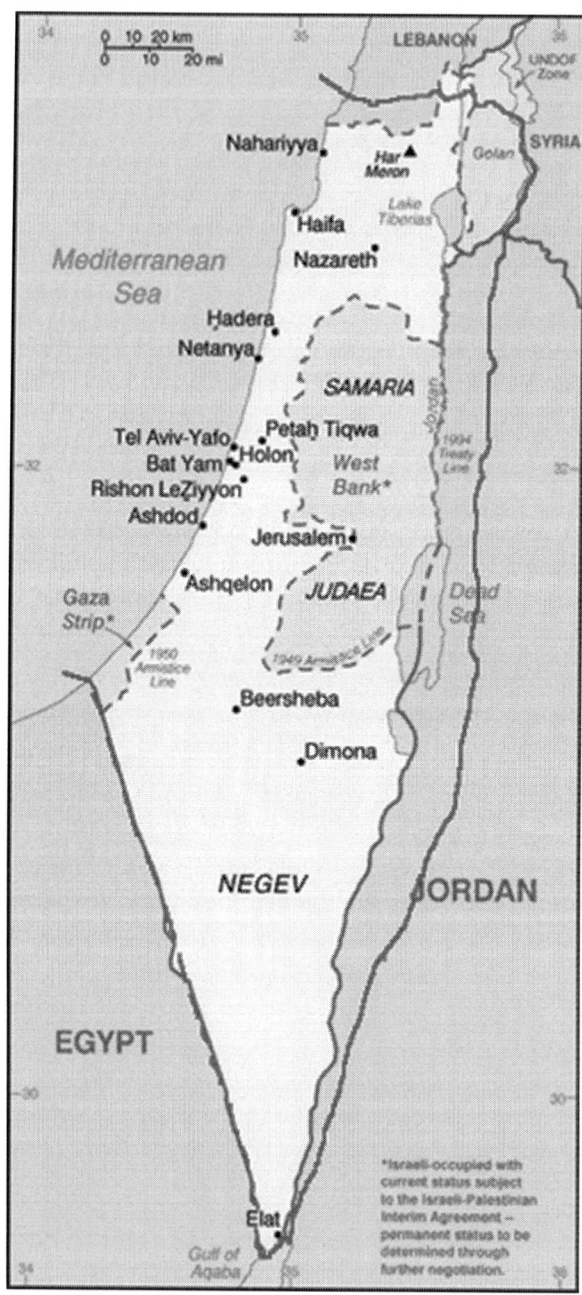

Tale: Palestinians have valid historical reasons to oppose the creation of a Jewish state.
Fact: Arab leader Emir Faisal signed a treaty in which he accepted a Jewish state in 1919 (see Tale: Colonialism).
Photo: Map of the treaty. The dark line indicates the border of the Jewish state.

59. Jewish terror

The Palestinian Tale: Like the Arabs, Jews committed massive terror in their struggle for independence.

In the 1930s, the Jews founded several militias in order to defend themselves against increasing Arab violence influenced by Islamism and Nazism (see Tale: Nazism).

Although these militias existed primarily to defend Jewish civilians, they committed a number of reprisals against the Arab population following attacks on Jews. After World War II, the British (who were in charge of the region at the time) did not act in accordance with the agreements that were intended to be the foundation of creating and upholding a Jewish state. The militia grew frustrated with the passivity of the British and began to target British military objectives in turn. The militia intended to cause only material damage, not to harm British soldiers. That intention changed after the British executed a number of captured Jewish fighters.

Anti-Israel opponents typically raise the example of the militia's attack on the King David Hotel in Jerusalem in the context of Jewish violence. However, the King David Hotel was the British military command headquarters at the time.
So it was strictly a prime military target, not at all a civilian target.

Furthermore, it was not the militia's intention to cause any casualties, only to blow up British military intelligence files. The intention not to cause any casualties is evidenced by the telephone calls made right before the bombing. These calls warned the British that a bomb had been placed in the hotel. Unfortunately, the British ignored this warning up to three times. All deaths resulting from the bombing had thus been completely avoidable.

However, the fact that Arab terrorists blew up the Ben Yehuda Hotel (used to rent out rooms to civilian tourists) a year and a half later, is never mentioned.

Thus, with the exception of occasional retaliations against Arab attacks in the 1930s, the militia focused purely on self-defense and (British) military targets. In contrast to strategic military attacks, the attacks of Palestinian Arab terrorists were almost exclusively directed at civilians and civilian targets, as they still are today.

Tale: The Jews committed terrorist attacks against civilians.
Fact: In all but a few exceptional cases, the Jews only intended to use violence in self-defense. The need for self-defense can be implied from the photo above: every Jewish village could be attacked by Arab terrorists and thus needed a watchtower in order to spot attackers from afar.
Photo: Jewish Ain Geb settlement at the Sea of Galilee in the 1930s.

60. Jews in Arab countries

The Palestinian Tale: Jews always enjoyed a good life in the Islamic world.

The situation, of course, was not the same everywhere, in a region stretching from Morocco to Iran and a period spanning over 1,400 years.

But overall, the Jews were not treated well in the Islamic world. Oppression of and discrimination against non-Muslims was almost universal, also affecting Christians. There were regularly pogroms – violent outbursts – against Jews, with many persons killed.

Discrimination against Jews and Christians originates in the Koran. The Koran says that Jews and Christians are "dhimmies": second-class citizens, with fewer rights. For example, in verse 9:29:
> *"Fight against those People of the Book [Jews and Christians] who have no faith in God or the Day of Judgment, who do not consider unlawful what God and His Messenger have made unlawful, and who do not believe in the true religion, until they humbly pay tax with their own hands."*

Therefore Jews (and Christians) had to pay additional taxes (which have been reintroduced by the Islamic State). They were not allowed to testify against a Muslim in court and were often bound by dress codes so they could be distinguished from the Muslims. For example, Jews were forced, in Baghdad in the 9th century, to wear a yellow badge.

In 1818, the Italian Filippo Pananti visited Algiers, now the capital of Algeria. He described the life of the Jews there as follows:
> *"There is no species of outrage or vexation to which they are not exposed. They are prohibited from writing or speaking Arabic, to prevent their being able to read the divine Koran. They cannot ride on horseback, but are obliged to go on mules and asses; the first being too noble an animal for them. When passing a mosque, they are obliged to go bare-footed.*
> *Their clothing is obliged to be black; which color is held in contempt by the Moors. The Jewish women are only permitted to veil a part of their features. The indolent Moor, with a pipe in his mouth and his legs crossed, calls any Jew who is passing, and makes him perform the offices of a servant. Others amuse themselves by smearing*

the hands, visage, hair, and clothes of the Jewish boys, with paint or mud; while the Turkish soldiers often enter their houses, insulting the females.
It is the business of Jews to execute all criminals, and afterwards bury their bodies. They are also employed to carry the Moors on their shoulders, when disembarking in shoal water. They feed the animals of the sequestered living quarters used by wives and concubines, and are incessantly exposed to the scoffing and derision of the young Moors, without the possibility of resenting it. Frequently beaten by their persecutors, if they lift a hand in their own defense, agreeable to the lex talionis [principle of retaliation] of the Moors, it is taken off."

Many descriptions like this have been preserved, including of the situation in Palestine. As Karl Marx wrote in 1854 regarding the situation of the Jews of Jerusalem, despite the fact that the Jews were already in the majority:
"Nothing equals the misery and the sufferings of the Jews in Jerusalem, inhabiting the most filthy quarter of the town, called hareth-el-yahoud, the quarter of dirt, between the [Mounts] Zion and the Moriah, where their synagogues are situated – the constant objects of Mussulman oppression and intolerance."

The list of pogroms in the Islamic world is long. Frequently the Jews were victims of very violent rapes and killings, often organized or tacitly permitted by the Islamic government. These occurred from Morocco to Iran; sometimes thousands of Jews were murdered.

This also happened in the area that is now Israel. The town of Safed in northern Israel was the site of several pogroms, including in 1517 and 1660. In 1834 there was a pogrom that lasted no less than 33 days. The number of deaths is not known, but most of the 4,000 Jewish inhabitants (the majority of Safed's population at the time) managed to flee. Their possessions were stolen and their 13 synagogues destroyed.

In 1929 there were many pogroms throughout the land of Israel. In Hebron alone, 67 Jews were brutally murdered: men, women and children (see Tale: Hebron).

The British high commissioner in the Mandate area, Sir John Chancellor, declared in 1929:
"I have learned with horror of the atrocious acts committed by bodies of ruthless and bloodthirsty evil-doers, of savage murders perpetrated upon defenseless members of the Jewish population regardless of age or sex, accompanied as at Hebron, by acts of unspeakable savagery, of the burning of farms and houses in town and country and of the looting and destruction of property. These crimes

have brought upon their authors the execration of all civilized peoples throughout the world."

All this happened long before Israel was established. When Israel was founded in 1948, the Jews of the Arab countries finally found a safe home. They therefore departed en masse to Israel. For example, 300,000 Jews lived in Morocco in 1948; only about 3,000 remained in the year 2014.

Tale: Jews always enjoyed a good life in the Islamic world.
Fact: There were regular anti-Jewish pogroms in the Islamic world.
Photo: A mass grave of victims of the Farhud, when 800 Jews were massacred in Baghdad in 1941.

61. Khazars

The Palestinian Tale: The Jews of the biblical past no longer exist. The current European Jews are descendants of the Khazars.

For those who have never heard of the Khazars before, they were a Turkish people that lived north of the Caucasus about 12 centuries ago. The Khazar nation dissolved about two centuries later, but a number of them supposedly converted to Judaism. The tale that all European Jews descended from the Khazars – and thus do not originate in the biblical-time Israel – is regularly mentioned in pro-Palestinian circles.

Unfortunately for them, Jewish genetic ancestry has been extensively researched. A 2013 genetics study by Wayne State University noted:
> *"Employing a variety of standard techniques for the analysis of population-genetic structure, we find that Ashkenazi Jews share the greatest genetic ancestry with other Jewish populations [so Sefardi, from the Middle East], and among non-Jewish populations, with groups from Europe and the Middle East. No particular similarity of Ashkenazi Jews with populations from the Caucasus is evident, particularly with the populations that most closely represent the Khazar region. There is no indication of a significant genetic contribution either from within or from north of the Caucasus region."*

Moreover, behind the Khazars Tale lies a dubious implication; namely, that the Jews could only be a nation if they were also a race – a genetically pure race at that. Such a requirement has never otherwise been raised in order to legitimize the existence of a people. Of course, after more than 3,000 years, the Jewish people are not "genetically pure." Nobody denies the influence of conversion to and from Judaism over the course of history.

However, the demand for Jewish purity is completely superfluous and conjures unpleasant associations with Nazism. There is no such thing as a "pure" people. That does not alter the fact that Jews constitute a people just like the Spaniards, Scots, Japanese, Americans, British and French. Jews have all the characteristics to be termed a people: they share a common language, culture, religion and history.

Tale: European Jews are descended from the Khazars.
Fact: Jews from all over the world show a strong genetic connection.
Photo: Jews of Yemen leaving for Israel.

62. Land development

The Palestinian Tale: The Jewish immigrants came to a populated, developed country.

Following centuries of neglect and deforestation, the land that is now Israel was unproductive and consisted mostly of desert, rocky soil or swampland without private owners (see Tale: Land theft). The neglect was due to many wars and brutal rulers who drove the population to flee violence and high taxes. A notorious example is Muhammad Djezzar, the pasha of Damascus and Jerusalem from 1783 to 1801. He was well known for his oppressive taxation and his violence. Many residents fled. The country therefore became the dwelling ground of traveling Bedouins and their goats. While cattle and sheep eat the green shoots, goats also eat the roots of plants. Without roots present in the ground, fertile topsoil is washed away by rain, and this had devastating consequences for the land.

Between 1831 and 1841, there were wars between Egypt and Turkey in the province of Syria, including present-day Israel. The city of Acre was destroyed in these wars. One in five men had to enlist in the Egyptian military and a rebellion against the military broke out, which was repressed violently by Egypt. Because of the wars in the area, many residents fled. Visitors in the nineteenth century spoke and wrote with astonishment of how empty the country was. In 1844, Jerusalem was just a big village, with 15,500 people. Jews constituted the largest group in the city, with 7,100 inhabitants. There were also 5,000 Muslims and 3,400 Christians. The next largest villages were Jaffa and Acre, with 9,000 and 5,000 residents respectively. Other villages counted at most a few hundred inhabitants. Bedouins mainly roamed throughout the country.

What was Mandatory Palestine (modern-day Israel, Jordan, West Bank and Gaza) is currently home to about twenty million people. In 1850, there were an estimated 500,000 inhabitants, which is 2.5 percent of the current population.

British Consul General James Finn reported in 1857: *"The country is in a considerable degree empty of inhabitants and therefore its greatest need is that of a body of population."*

The world famous writer Mark Twain wrote in 1867:

> *"Stirring scenes ... occur in the valley [Jezreel] no more. There is not a solitary village throughout its whole extent-not for thirty miles in either direction. There are two or three small clusters of Bedouin tents, but not a single permanent habitation. One may ride ten miles hereabouts and not see ten human beings.*
>
> *Nazareth is forlorn. ... Jericho the accursed lays a moldering ruin today. ... Bethlehem and Bethany, in their poverty and their humiliation, have nothing about them now to remind one that they once knew the high honor of the Savior's presence.*
>
> *A desolate country whose soil is rich enough, but is given over wholly to weeds... a silent mournful expanse... a desolation... we never saw a human being on the whole route... hardly a tree or shrub anywhere. Even the olive tree and the cactus, those fast friends of a worthless soil, had almost deserted the country."*

A clergyman, Samuel Manning, wrote in a travel book in 1874:

> *"But where were the inhabitants? This fertile plain, which might support an immense population, is almost solitude. Day by day we were to learn afresh the lesson now forced upon us, that the denunciations of ancient prophecy have been fulfilled to the very letter: 'the land is left void and desolate and without inhabitants.'"*

The development of the area that would comprise the British Mandate did not begin until the arrival of Jewish immigrants, from about 1860 onward. Rebuilding the damaged natural environment took tremendous effort. Soil erosion had to be countered by reforestation (Israel is therefore one of the few countries in the world that increased its amount of forest during the twentieth century) and the marshes had to be drained. These marshes were caused by the blockage of natural drains through erosion, and they were a source of mosquitoes and thus malaria, which claimed many lives. The US-educated Jewish bacteriologist Israel Kligler suggested various measures against malaria, which eradicated the disease from the area around 1925. Because of Jewish development efforts, the population density of the area west of the Jordan River is currently about ten times that of east of the Jordan River, although the soil possesses the same qualities.

This development of the British Mandate by the Jews, moreover, certainly did not happen at the expense of the Arabs, as noted by the British Peel Commission of Inquiry in 1937:

> *"The Arab claims that the Jews have obtained too large a proportion of good land cannot be maintained. Much of the land now carrying orange groves was sand dunes or swamp and uncultivated when it was purchased."*

Winston Churchill said the same on June 14, 1921, in a speech addressed to the British parliament:

> *"Anyone who has seen the work of the Jewish colonies which have been established during the last 20 or 30 years in Palestine will be struck by the enormous productive results which they have achieved. I had the opportunity of visiting the colony of Richon le Zion about 12 miles from Jaffa, and there, from the most inhospitable soil, surrounded on every side by barrenness and the most miserable form of cultivation, I was driven into a fertile and thriving country estate, where the scanty soil gave place to good crops and good cultivation, and then to vineyards and finally to the most beautiful, luxurious orange groves, all created in 20 or 30 years by the exertions of the Jewish community who live there.*
>
> *I am talking to the Committee of what I saw with my own eyes. All round the Jewish colony, the Arab houses were tiled instead of being built of mud, so that the culture from this centre has spread out into the surrounding district."*

The standard of living for Palestinian Arabs doubled between 1920 and 1937, resulting in much higher incomes than those in neighboring countries. These opportunities attracted many Arabs to the region (see Tale: Palestinian people). Moreover, the infant mortality rate was reduced by half in this time period.

The success of the Jewish efforts to redevelop the land was confirmed by the influential Muslim fundamentalist cleric, Sheikh Dr. Yousouf Al-Qaradawi, whose show on Al Jazeera has 60 million viewers worldwide. In one of his episodes preaching against laziness among the Arabs, he stated:

> *"We had the desert before our eyes but we didn't do anything with it.*
> *When they [the Jews] took over, they turned it into a green oasis."*

Tale: Arab farmers actively worked the land.
Fact: Israel was rendered fertile with great efforts by Jewish settlers, while the Arab regions remain barren.
Photo: In front the Israeli Yatir forest, in the background the barren West Bank.

63. Land for peace

The Palestinian Tale: The Arabs will grant peace in exchange for land.

In the 1990s, Israel gave land to the Palestinians to secure peace. Why has this not happened more recently?

First of all, currently 98 percent of Palestinians live under their own government, the Palestinian Authority.

Israelis yearn for the end of all violence and terror. However, they know that Palestinian promises of peace and ending violence and terror have not been kept (see Tale: Oslo Accords). In the first decade after the Oslo Accords, terror attacks increased enormously, contrary to the Palestinians' promise to dismantle terror infrastructure. As a result of the increased terror, Israel, for its security, set up many checkpoints at fences surrounding Gaza and the West Bank. Moreover, after Israeli withdrawals from southern Lebanon (2000) and Gaza (2005), the Palestinians showered Israel with 15,000 rockets as a "thank-you gift."

Palestinian President Abbas, in fact, has no mandate to speak on behalf of the Palestinians. In January 2005, he began his four-year term, which expired on January 9, 2009, yet as of 2016 he continues to be president. The parliament is in the hands of Hamas, which received 56 percent of the seats in parliamentary elections in 2006. Palestinian Prime Minister Haniyeh, Hamas political leader, refuses to implement the already signed peace agreements between the Palestinians and Israelis, and Hamas strongly opposes any new negotiations.

Hamas controls the Gaza Strip, where about half of the Palestinian population lives and where Abbas has close to zero authority. Therefore, Abbas really only negotiates on behalf of the PLO, the Palestinian "liberation organization." However, even within the PLO, most groups oppose negotiations with Israel or support it nominally simply to placate the outside world.

In 1937, mediators first proposed a two-state solution, which was agreed to by the Jews, but rejected by the Arabs. If the Palestinian leadership would now accept a two-state solution, it would become apparent to the Palestinian people that their suffering since 1937 has been in vain. The Palestinian leadership would have to explain why millions of descendants of Palestinian refugees have been kept in camps, oftentimes in appalling conditions, when they could have accepted a smaller state of their own. To have to explain this leadership failure to the Palestinian population would be very difficult for the current Palestinian leaders.

Ultimately, there is little support for a two-state solution among the Palestinian population (see Tale: Destruction of Israel). A whopping 80 percent of Palestinians agree with the Hamas Charter, which seeks the military defeat of Israel and its replacement by a Palestinian state. An appalling 73 percent agree with the Hamas Charter statement (which it attributes to Muhammad's sayings) that all Jews must be killed.

This belligerent attitude is encouraged by Palestinian leaders, who have much to gain from shifting focus to an external enemy (see Tale: Peace education). It diverts attention from all the corruption and abuses of power committed by the Palestinian leadership. In order for peace to take hold, the terrorist organizations must be disarmed and dissolved as stipulated in the peace agreements. The biggest terror groups affiliated with the main Palestinian parties are Fatah and Hamas. Disarmament and peace therefore remain virtually impossible.

In addition, all fundamentalist imams claim that "not an inch" of the area should be handed over to Jews. This extreme nationalism is the basic principle of Hamas, a radical Islamic terrorist movement. Is it even possible for any Arab leader to make peace without risking assassination by Muslim fundamentalists? Egyptian President Sadat was killed after he had made peace with Israel in 1981. The same thing happened to King Abdullah of Jordan and Prime Minister Riad al Solh of Lebanon in 1951, because they had held exploratory peace talks with Israel. Lebanese President Bachir Gemayel was assassinated in 1982, likely for the same reason.

Last but not least, money plays a role. Palestinians owe their relative prosperity to generous international aid funds. Palestinians have received more aid per capita than any other people. They may thus be fearful that if peace will come, the international donors will tell them to take care of themselves, after receiving 70 years of financial support.

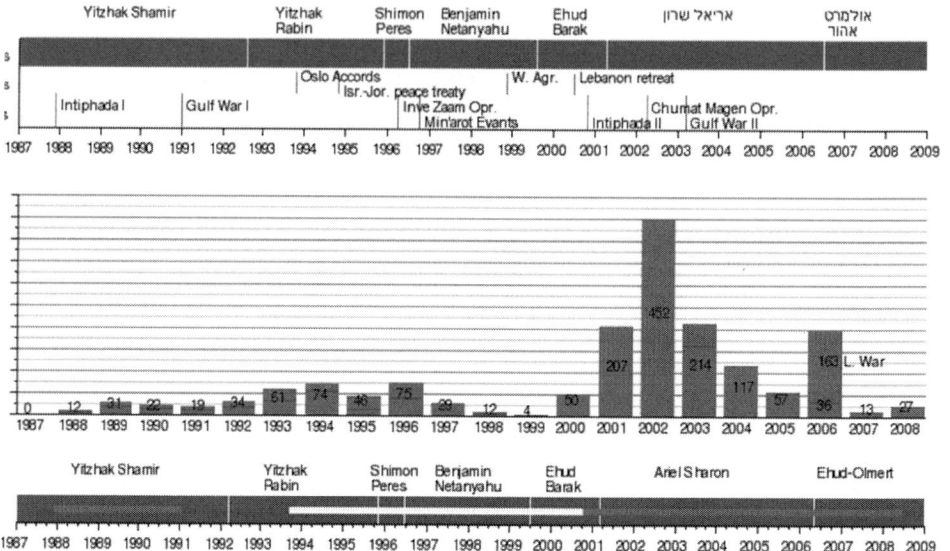

Tale: The Arabs grant peace in exchange for land.
Fact: Immediately after the Oslo peace treaties were signed, Palestinians took to terror, and the number of victims increased dramatically.
Photo: This graph shows the number of Israeli deaths from terrorism from 1987 to 2008.

64. Land, population

The Palestinian Tale: Exclusively Arabs lived in the area before the creation of Israel.

After the Jewish revolt in the year 135 CE, the Romans expelled many Jews from the country and renamed it Palestine. However, not all Jews left, and there remained a continuous Jewish presence in the region during the centuries that followed. For example, during excavations in Capernaum, archaeologists dug up the remains of a synagogue from the fourth century. In the year 351, there was another Jewish revolt in the north of Israel. In the year 438, the eastern Roman empress Eudocia abolished the prohibition against Jews praying on the Temple Mount in Jerusalem. The Mishna, the oral interpretation of the Bible, was compiled in written form in the first centuries of the Common Era in Yavne. The Jerusalem Talmud with commentary on the Mishna followed in subsequent years, and it was also written in the land that is now Israel.

Examples like these of Jewish settlement and accomplishment in the land that is now Israel exist for any period in history. For instance in 1696, the Dutch professor of geography Adriaan Reland noted that there were no cities of Arab origin. The existing cities, like Tiberias, Hebron and Gaza, originated from the Jewish or Roman period and were mainly inhabited by Jews and Christians.

The Muslims whom Reland encountered were mostly Bedouins. The Bedouins are a nation of nomads wandering throughout the Middle East, herding their livestock and working as seasonal help during harvests. Jerusalem was by far the largest city at that time. As Reland noted, Jerusalem had a majority of Jewish citizens, and Christians comprised the second largest population group.

For centuries there was an inflow of Jews, often supported with donations from foreign co-religionists. Due to the harsh living conditions, however, the population size remained static, similar to the experience of other groups.

Therefore, by 1844 Jerusalem was only a big village with 15,500 people. At that time, Jews constituted the largest group in the city, with 7,100 inhabitants. There were also 5,000 Muslims and 3,400 Christians. Bedouins mainly roamed around the country.

For centuries, people lived within the medieval city walls of Jerusalem, but in 1860 the Jews were the first to build and live in an area located outside these walls. Ironically, this area is nowadays known as part of "Arab East Jerusalem." It only became Arab East Jerusalem, however, after the ethnic cleansing of the Jews by the Jordanian army in 1948, when all Jews were driven out by force.

Tale: Exclusively Arabs lived in the land that is now Israel.
Fact: Cities such as Jerusalem, Tiberias, Safed and Hebron (photo) were inhabited by ancient Jewish communities.

65. Land promise

The Palestinian Tale: The world promised the same area to both the Jews and the Arabs.

Because of World War I, the massive Turkish Ottoman Empire imploded. The victors of the war – especially Britain and France – created new countries. In 1917 Britain – then the major world power – had promised Palestine to the Jews in the Balfour declaration, which was named after the then British foreign secretary. The declaration is clear:

> *"His Majesty's Government view with favour the establishment in Palestine of a national home for the Jewish people, and will use their best endeavors to facilitate the achievement of this object, it being clearly understood that nothing shall be done which may prejudice the civil and religious rights of existing non-Jewish communities in Palestine or the rights and political status enjoyed by Jews in any other country."*

According to the Arabs, the same land was two years earlier, in 1915, also promised to the Arabs because of their role in the war. The British government, however, stated in 1922:

> *"This representation mainly rests upon a letter dated the 24th October, 1915, from Sir Henry McMahon, then His Majesty's High Commissioner in Egypt, to the Sharif of Mecca, now King Hussein of the Kingdom of the Hejaz [Saudi-Arabia]. That letter is quoted as conveying the promise to the Sherif of Mecca to recognise and support the independence of the Arabs within the territories proposed by him. But this promise was given subject to a reservation made in the same letter, which excluded from its scope, among other territories, the portions of Syria lying to the west of the District of Damascus. This reservation has always been regarded by His Majesty's Government as covering the vilayet of Beirut and the independent Sanjak of Jerusalem. The whole of Palestine west of the Jordan was thus excluded from Sir Henry McMahon's pledge."*

Lebanon (for Christians) and the British mandate of Palestine as part of Syria are areas which were obviously not promised to King Hussein.

Tale: The mandate area was also promised to the Arabs.
Fact: The Balfour Declaration (photo) covered area that was not promised to the Arabs.

66. Land theft

The Palestinian Tale: The Jews stole their land from Arabs.

Through centuries of neglect, namely during the Turkish Ottoman Empire, a lot of land in the area had not been cultivated. Turkey had ruled over the region between 1512 and 1918, during which time most of the land remained barren (see Tale: Land development). Therefore, much Arab land was not privately owned but rather state property. In general, private land ownership was not common in the Turkish Ottoman Empire.

From the end of the 19th century onwards, Jews held fundraisers across the globe to buy land (first in the Turkish-Ottoman Empire, then the British Mandate), despite the many Muslim restrictions against selling land to Jews. Approximately 25 percent of the land purchased was swampland and another 30 percent had never been cultivated. The Arab landowners (almost half of them did not even live on these uncultivated properties) charged extortionate prices. The prices paid by Jewish buyers were ten times higher than the price of fertile land in the United States at the time.

In 1948, only 14 percent of the land in the British mandated territory was privately owned by Arabs. Jews had purchased more than a third of all private land and owned 9 percent of the mandated territory. The remaining 77 percent of the land was state property, which was mostly unused and undeveloped.

Contrary to the tale, it was the Jews from whom much land was stolen. Jewish landowners in Arab countries were forced to leave 100,000 square kilometers of land when they were expelled from these countries. This property was seized by the Arabs – a total landmass of more than four times the size of Israel.

Tale: The Jews stole Arab land.
Fact: Privately-owned land was purchased by Jewish immigrants.
Photo: Arabs and Jews celebrate a land sale.

67. Likud

The Palestinian Tale: Likud is an extremist party dominated by religious Jews.

In fact, Likud is a secular (non-religious), liberal and democratic party. Religious Israeli Jews can choose from a wide range of religious parties in the Knesset. If you support economic liberalism, you can join and get ahead in the party, no matter what your religion. Thus, Likud also has Muslims as prominent party members, such as the Arab-Israeli minister Ayoub Kara.

Tale: Likud is dominated by Orthodox Jews.
Fact: Likud is secular, and Arabs can participate without restrictions.
Photo: Member of Parliament and former Likud minister Ayoub Kara, a Muslim Arab-Israeli.

68. Media

The Palestinian Tale: The European mainstream media are pro-Israel.

It used to be that way, but pro-Israel bias is already ancient history, says Paul Brill, a Dutch foreign commentator in 2014: *"Where in the dim past there actually was a tendency to identify with Israeli positions, it is now rather the opposite the case."*

Much of the material in this book is rarely published. European media regularly report alleged Israeli racism or apartheid, but rarely mention the massive Arab hatred of Jews and the calls for a second Holocaust. The European media always report the alleged threats to Islamic holy places, but kept silent on the destruction of a Jewish holy place (the tomb of the biblical Joseph). They choose to report Israel's alleged unwillingness to achieve peace, but hide the fact that the Arabs rejected any proposed international compromise.

It is striking how often the standard principle of journalism, the right to reply, is omitted when it concerns Israel.
Nonsensical anti-Israel stories are repeated endlessly (see for example the Tale: Poisoning Arafat).

The difference in media focus is also striking (see Tale: Conflict). A Palestinian who was killed during an act of violence against Israelis virtually always makes the news, which hardly ever happens when it concerns one killed by fellow Arabs. Think of the dozens of Palestinians tortured to death because they oppose the Palestinian regime, or the thousands killed in the Syrian civil war.

What causes this bias?

First, there is a lack of knowledge and awareness of both the history and the causes of the conflict. This lack is compounded by the Arab culture of exaggeration with the possibility of manipulation of information by the (Arab) regimes. As a journalist, the only parts of the Gaza Strip you are allowed to visit are where you go with your Hamas guide.
There's even a term for the manipulated images distributed by (pro-) Palestinians: Pallywood. Best known are the dramatic images from 2000 of the boy Mohammed al-Dura caught in crossfire and cowering behind a wall. He was, allegedly, slain by

Israeli gunfire aimed at terrorists, although the Israeli shots were fired from the other side of the wall where al-Dura had taken cover.

Another force at work is the need for journalists to oversimplify. Journalists want to appear balanced, so if Arabs commit some wrong, Israel also needs to be blamed. Dutch political commentator Martin Sommer says: *"It is difficult to deny that report after report from Gaza has only one effect: what Israel wreaks there is shameful and the Palestinians are powerless victims."*

Repression of unpleasant facts also plays a role: it is not so pleasant to face and report the fact that there are persons who want to exterminate other people just because of their faith. Realize also that journalists are actually murdered when they report negatively on Islam, as happened after the Danish cartoons of Mohammed. Among journalists, this fear leads to self-censorship. The growth of the Arab population in Europe makes this fear ever stronger. In addition, there is a pro-Arab bias because of economic interests and energy dependence.

There is also a lot of guilt and fear around Europe's own past (see Tale: European Union). In some cases, this is outright anti-Semitism: one sometimes sees age-old anti-Semitic themes returning, such as *"Jews are cruel, manipulative, conspiratorial"* and so on. These days, this applies to "Israelis," "settlers" or "Zionists."

Finally, most importantly, most European mainstream media are left-wing, and therefore have more of a connection with the Palestinians because they are the "oppressed" people (oppression mainly caused by their own leaders). Even if you have a left-wing terror past (for instance, involvement in a planned bomb attack on an Israeli company in the Netherlands), you can become the chief editor for media such as the Dutch National Public Television. In recent years, this leftist political aspect has become even stronger because the multicultural society – the flagship accomplishment of the left – is under fire. Publicizing negative facts about Muslims is seen as supporting right-wing parties, especially those that are anti-immigration.

Hans Moll, former editor of Dutch newspaper *NRC Handelsblad*, compiled in his 2011 book *How the nuance disappeared from a quality newspaper* many examples of how that newspaper is biased in terms of the representation of the conflict.

Where does all the biased coverage lead to? To a totally distorted picture of Israel. For example, a study by the German University of Bielefeld in 2012 reports that 39 percent of the Dutch think that Israel is in a "war of extermination" against the Palestinians, which is totally absurd (see Tale: Genocide).

Among tourists to Israel, approximately two-thirds (65 percent) see Israel in a more positive light after their visit (see Tale: Tourism). This change happens simply because they see with their own eyes how the Israeli society functions.

"The huge lack of self-reflection, the lack of self-criticism. What I deemed impossible happened: after spending seven months in Muslim areas, I restored my sympathy for Israel. I haven't walked a day among the Arab population without hearing that Hitler was right, that Israel should disappear, that Jews were responsible for 9/11. I now understand how the Israelis feel threatened in that hateful sea of people."

– Rudi Rotthier about his prize-winning book *The Koran Route*, after he had gone to investigate the allegedly negative portrayal of Muslims in the media

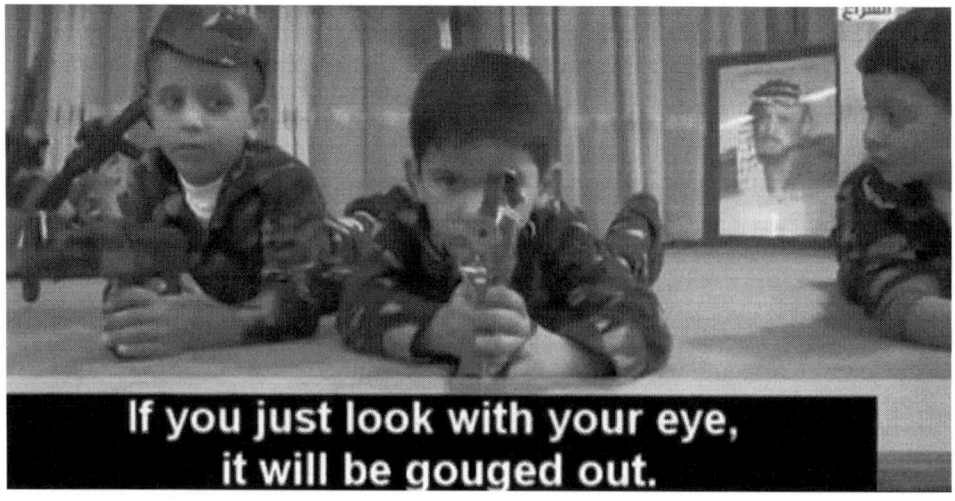

Tale: European mainstream media are pro-Israel.
Fact: Many Palestinian abuses are never reported.
Photo: Military parade and war slogans at a kindergarten graduation in Anabta in the West Bank.

69. Motherly love

The Palestinian Tale: Palestinian mothers of Jihadists are as much attached to the lives of their children as other mothers.

As a result of the Islamist death cult (see Tale: Death cult) Palestinian mothers often declare joy over the deaths of their children, if they have died in the struggle against the Jews.

As a wife of a Hamas parliamentarian argues on Hamas television on December 2, 2012:

> *"Women in Palestine play a great role in raising their children and in encouraging them to wage Jihad for the sake of Allah. This is absolutely the most glorious thing a woman can do.*
> *Women play their role and are not inferior to men. When a man goes to wage Jihad, his wife does not say, 'Don't go' or try to stop him. She encourages and supports him. She is the one who prepares his equipment, bids him farewell, and welcomes [his Jihad].*
> *She instills in her children the love of Jihad and martyrdom for the sake of Allah. Is not Allah's reward precious? Allah's reward is Paradise. Paradise requires from us our blood, our bodily remains, and our efforts for its sake.*
> *I am constantly praying: 'Allah, may the end of our days be in martyrdom.' I pray for this even for my husband and my children. None of us want to die in our beds. We pray that Allah will grant us Paradise."*

On the death of Maryam Farhat, the mother of three Palestinian suicide bombers, Palestinian President Mahmoud Abbas gave her a high posthumous Palestinian honor: the Order of Sacrifice. On Palestinian television she had previously explained her views on motherhood, including on the day of the death of one of her sons:

> *"By Allah, today is the best day of my life. I feel that our Lord is pleased with me, because I am offering something to His sake. I wish to offer more [sons] for Allah's forgiveness, and for the flag 'There is no god but Allah,' to fly over Palestine. That's what we want. We want the rule of Islam.*
> *I'm not parting from him [as he goes] to his death, but rather I'm parting from him as he goes to a better life, the Afterlife, which our Lord has promised us. By Allah, if I had a hundred children like [my son] Muhammad, I would offer them with*

sincerity and willingly. It's true that there's nothing more precious than children, but for the sake of Allah, what is precious becomes cheap."

Another mother explained in an interview on Arab News Network television how happy she was with the death of her son:

"I gave my son to Jihad for Allah. It's our religious obligation. If I wanted to have compassion for him, or to make him change his mind, it would be wrong, a mistake. I don't want to be guided by my feelings, a mother's feelings. I put them aside for a while for something greater, although a mother's feelings are involved.

Why? Because I love my son, and I want to choose the best for him, and the best is not life in this world. For us there is an Afterlife, the eternal bliss. So if I love my son, I'll choose eternal bliss for him. As much as my living children honor me, it will not be like the honor that the Martyr has given me. He will be our intercessor on the Day of Resurrection.

The greatest honor [my son] gave me was his Martyrdom."

The Israeli Prime Minister Golda Meir already noted in 1957: *"Peace will come to the Middle East when the Arabs love their children more than they hate us."*

Tale: All Palestinian mothers are as much attached to the lives of their children as other mothers.
Fact: Golda Meir (photo) concluded already 50 years ago that Arab hate often trumps love.

70. Muslim fundamentalism

The Palestinian Tale: Palestinian Muslim fundamentalist organizations are different than other Muslim fundamentalist groups, because Palestinian fighters are fighting an occupation.

In reality there is little or no distinction between the goals of al-Qaeda, Boko Haram, al-Shabaab, the Muslim Brotherhood, IS and Hamas.

The origin of all these organizations is in fact the same: that is, the spread of Wahhabism, the strict version of Islam, in Saudi Arabia. With wealth from the developing oil industry in the late 1970s, enormous financial flows spread from the Gulf across the Muslim world, funding Wahabi mosques, imam training and imam salaries.

That is why now around 80 percent of Muslims, for example in Egypt and Pakistan, believe that adulterous women should be stoned, that hands of thieves should be cut off and that apostate Muslims should be killed. The latter threat is the reason that Muslim fundamentalists face not much opposition from moderate Muslims. If anyone questions this interpretation of the Koran or of *Sharia* law, they run the risk of being regarded an apostate – and run the risk of getting killed.

Muslim fundamentalism is becoming more and more visible in the streets of many Muslim countries. Previously, headscarves in the street were an exception; now you will often find that the majority of women in Islamic countries wear headscarves.

Many members of all these Muslim fundamentalist organizations are willing to sacrifice their lives for Islam in the fight against "infidels" (the Jihad). According to their interpretation of Islamic faith, this will gain them admittance to paradise as Islamic martyrs. According to Islamic tradition, there they will be served by 72 virgins. Moreover, Muslim martyrs may designate 70 family members to also inherit the Islamic paradise.
It is the driving force for all Muslim fundamentalists.

Thus, the motto of the Muslim Brotherhood is:
"Allah is our objective; the Koran is the Constitution; the Prophet is our leader; Jihad is our way; death for the sake of Allah is our wish."

A *fatwa* (Islamic ruling) of al-Qaeda states:
"The ruling to kill the Americans and their allies – civilians and military – is an individual duty for every Muslim who can do it in any country in which it is possible to do it...
We call on every Muslim who believes in Allah and wishes to be rewarded to comply with Allah's order to kill the Americans and plunder their money wherever and whenever they find it."

The mission statement of Boko Haram in Nigeria declares:
"The Nigerian state and Christians are our enemies and we will be launching attacks on the Nigerian state and its security apparatus, as well as churches, until we achieve our goal of establishing an Islamic state."

The same with the Shiites, as the slogan of the Houthi's in Yemen is:
"Allah Akbar, Death to America, Death to Israel, Curse on the Jews, Victory to Islam."

Hamas is no different; its Charter says:
"The time [Day of Resurrection] will not come until Muslims will fight the Jews [and kill them]." (Article 7)
"Allah is its goal, the Prophet its model, the Koran its Constitution, Jihad its path and death for the case of Allah its most sublime belief." (Article 8)
"Jihad is the only solution." (Article 13)

"The coming century will be dominated by the struggle between modernity and fundamentalist Islam... There is no doubt that the secular state of Israel is the main barrier against the encroaching fundamentalism and the cradle of modernity in the region."

– Pim Fortuyn, a Dutch politician who was murdered in 2002 by an animal rights activist. He wrote these words in 1998

Tale: Palestinian Muslim fundamentalist organizations are different from others.
Fact: The goal of all Jihadi's is the same.
Photo: The slogan of the Houthi's in Yemen: *"Allah Akbar! [Allah is the greatest – bigger than the God of non-Muslims.] Death to America! Death to Israel! Cursed be the Jews! Victory is Islam!"*

71. Natural resources

The Palestinian Tale: Israel plunders the Palestinians' natural resources.

First of all, the Palestinian territories have few natural resources, so this Tale has few real-world examples. Best known is the so-called water theft allegation (see that Tale).

Another allegation is that the Israeli cosmetics company Ahava "steals" resources from the Dead Sea. However, the mud and minerals in Ahava's products are mined in Israel, within the Green Line. Only Ahava's factory is located just over the Green Line in the West Bank. The factory, however, predates the existence of a "West Bank." In 1929, the Jewish businessman Moshe Novomeysky received a 75-year concession to mine the minerals. He had already established his business in 1922. In 1939 there was a kibbutz built next to the factory. No one lived for miles around, given the totally barren, salty soil. The kibbutz and the factory were attacked during Israel's 1948 War of Independence, conquered and destroyed by the Iraqi army. In 1968 the factory was rebuilt.

Another Tale in this context is that Israel wants Gaza under its control because of the gas fields off its coast. However, insofar as these gas fields are situated in the sea area belonging to the Gaza Strip, Israel recognizes Palestinian ownership of these resources.

Tale: Israel plunders the Palestinians' natural resources
Fact: Only Ahava's factory is on the West Bank (photo).

72. Nazis

The Palestinian Tale: Israel behaves just like the Nazis.

This comparison is wrong, in all aspects.

In the Holocaust, 6 million Jews – a third of the Jewish people – were killed, all of them innocent civilians. The Palestinians suffer on average some 100 deaths a year, mostly combatants (see Tale: Genocide).

The Holocaust involved a planned industrial extermination. Palestinians are killed as a result of violence, which is initiated by Palestinian terrorists themselves.

In the Holocaust, extermination was the goal. The fight against the Palestinians is because of Jewish self-defense. Israel does not intentionally aim to kill Arab civilians (see Tale: War crimes). The reverse is indeed the case (see Tale: Violence).

Not only this comparison is nonsense, it is disgusting. It trivializes the enormous suffering of the Jews in the Second World War and the suffering of the survivors.

Yet this statement is popular in Europe, because if Jews can be viewed as behaving as badly as Nazis, Europeans can permit themselves to feel less guilt about the Holocaust, which was committed on European soil.

But the only similarity between this conflict and the Second World War is that Jews are again threatened based on an ideology – this time Islamic fundamentalism – that wants to exterminate them.

Tale: Israel behaves just like the Nazis.
Fact: Israel harbors no question of genocide, let alone a planned industrial extermination of the Palestinians, as happened to the Jews in the Holocaust.
Photo: Jews arrive in Auschwitz.

73. Nazism

The Palestinian Tale: Because the Jews were victims of Nazism, they were given their state, while we had nothing to do with either Nazism or the Holocaust.

The conflict between Arabs and Jews began in the 1920s by the first (self-proclaimed) leader of the Palestinian Arabs, the Grand Mufti (senior Islamic cleric) of Jerusalem, Amin Al-Husseini.

He was inspired to start the conflict by two then emerging ideologies; Nazism and Islamic fundamentalism. The latter was launched in the region by the establishment of the Muslim Brotherhood in Egypt in 1928.
These extremist movements emerged more or less simultaneously and also have major ideological similarities: the pursuit of world domination, the total subordination of the individual to the ideology, the rejection of democracy and human rights, militarism and a preference for conflict – and their enormous Jew-hatred.

Al-Husseini was an avid supporter of both movements. His Islamic youth movement was therefore called "Nazi Scouts." It distributed leaflets with Nazi slogans and swastikas.

For adults, his movement massively spread leaflets with texts like:
"O Arab! Remember that the Jew is your strongest enemy and the enemy of your ancestors since oldest Times. Do not be misled by his tricks for it is he who tortured Christ, peace be upon him, and poisoned Muhammad, peace and worship be with him. It is he who now endeavors to slaughter you as he did yesterday."

Al-Husseini began to incite the Muslims in Palestine to violence against the Jews. He established terrorist groups, like the emergent Islamic terror group led by Sheikh Izz al-Din al-Kassam in the Galilee and Haifa. This terror group still exists, now as a part of Hamas – the Palestinian branch of the Muslim Brotherhood. It has developed the Kassam rocket in Gaza, named after its first leader.

From the 1920s onward, these terrorist groups attacked the Jews in the British Mandate. They carried out large pogroms, including in Jerusalem, Safed, Tiberias and Hebron (see Tale: Hebron), following calls from Al-Husseini. He said in a sermon that a Muslim who kills a Jew earns his entrance to paradise. These pogroms were not directed against the Jewish immigrants but rather were all carried out against ancient Jewish communities. In Hebron in particular there was terrible bloodshed.

On April 19, 1936, Al-Husseini began a revolt against both the British Mandate rule and against the Jews, which lasted until 1939. Jews and Jewish villages were the targets of attacks.

Another important target was moderate Palestinian Arabs: those who were willing to cooperate with the Jews and the British. Among these victims were mayors, influential tribal leaders and Palestinian Christians. Arab terror groups used even more violence against fellow Arabs than against the Jews. Terrorists killed 239 Jews in 1938, but slaughtered more than 2,000 moderate Arabs, often in an extremely cruel manner.

The actions of the Arabs prompted the British to strictly limit Jewish immigration, in the hope to calm things down. Without immigration to Palestine, the last escape route for European Jews was closed off, and they remained trapped by the Nazis.

Of course, the Nazis were delighted with the rebellion of their ally against the British Empire, just before the start of the World War II. Nazi Germany supported the insurgency with money and weapons.
In turn, the Palestinian Arabs supported the Nazis. According to a 1941 poll, 88 percent of the Arabs in Palestine hoped that Nazi Germany would win the war. Only 9 percent backed the Allies.

Also in 1941, British pressure forced the grand mufti Al-Husseini to flee from his residence to Nazi Germany. Hitler promised Al-Husseini personally that his goal was the annihilation of the Jews in the Arab world. The German army in North Africa was specially equipped with an extermination unit tasked with hunting Jews in Arab countries.

> *"If Rommel had won the Battle of El Alamein and had arrived here, the remaining Jews here would have disappeared."*
> – Israeli Prime Minister Netanyahu on International Holocaust Remembrance Day 2012

Al-Husseini exerted himself intensively in Nazi Germany for the German war machine. For instance, he recruited tens of thousands of Muslims for an Islamic division of the Waffen-SS, the Handschar division. These soldiers committed the most heinous war crimes against Jews, partisans and the Serbian civilian population in the Balkans.

Furthermore, Al-Husseini personally blocked prisoner releases of innocent Jewish children to Palestine. A group of 500 children from Croatia ended up instead in the gas chambers.

Al-Husseini visited concentration camps and was very enthusiastic about the Nazi program. A Dutch Auschwitz survivor, Ernst Verduin, remembers the visit. He asked a guard about those people in strange clothes that were walking around. The answer was:

"Al-Husseini, the man in the robe, lives in Berlin, where he is under the personal protection of Hitler. He visits Monowitz [Auschwitz III] to see how the Jews have to work themselves to death in the factories. He is also in Auschwitz to see the gas chambers. When we will have won the war, he will return to Palestine to build gas chambers and then to murder the Jews there."

Al-Husseini's memoirs prove that he was fully aware of the existence of the gas chambers; he was proud that the Nazis entrusted him with this secret. Something like that had to be built in Palestine too, according to him. And this would have happened, had the Germans not been stopped in Egypt by the British at El Alamein.

Incidentally, it is said that Al-Husseini also suggested to Hitler the idea of the total extermination of the Jews, since in his younger years, he had been involved in the genocide of the Armenian Christians. The story goes that the Grand Mufti said to Hitler: *"No one is talking about it anymore, so you can do the same to the Jews."*
There is no hard evidence, but it is not improbable, as described in Barry Rubin and Wolfgang Schwanitz's 2014 book *Nazis, Islamists and the making of the modern Middle East*.
According to Bernard Lewis, arguably the world's most important Orientalist, Al-Husseini urged the Nazi regime to exterminate the Jews already in the 1930s.

Al-Husseini was put in charge of the Arabic broadcasts from Nazi Berlin Radio, the most important propaganda medium of the time, especially for the still often illiterate Arabs. Through these broadcasts he made appeals like:

"Arabs, rise as one man and fight for your sacred rights. Kill the Jews wherever you find them. This pleases Allah, history, and religion. This saves your honor. Allah is with you."

Historian Jeffrey Herf describes in his book *Nazi Propaganda for the Arab World* the enormous importance of the Nazis' thousands of Arabic radio broadcasts. The Nazis tried to coerce the Arabs to focus their anger on the British Mandate over Palestine, whereby they claimed that the attempts to establish a Jewish state were part of the Jewish plan to "rule the entire world." The Arabs were indoctrinated with all kinds of anti-Semitic conspiracy theories, which to this day are believed by many Muslims. Nazi propaganda also constantly pointed to the "fact" that the Islamic faith requires believers to eliminate all Jews.

Herf therefore called the broadcasts *"one of the most important cultural exchanges of the twentieth century"* and states that this Nazi propaganda has played an important role in the development of the Islamic Jew-hatred that continues until today; those anti-Semitic conspiracy theories are successfully (re)exported to large parts of the population of Europe in particular, but also the US and the rest of the world.

After World War II, Al-Husseini was held in French captivity as a war criminal. Unfortunately, France let him escape from house arrest, supposedly to maintain good relations with the Arab world, despite extradition requests from the United Kingdom and Yugoslavia – where his Muslim Waffen-SS divisions had caused enormous massacres – to bring him to trial for his war crimes.

Al-Husseini then once again led the fight against the Jews in the Mandate of Palestine (see Tale: War of Independence in 1948).

By the way, the legacy of Al-Husseini is still popular among Palestinians. In exile in Cairo, he was the mentor of the second leader of the Palestinians, Yasser Arafat. Arafat admired Al-Husseini and always affectionately called him "uncle."

The third leader of the Palestinians, Mahmoud Abbas, is also an admirer of Al-Husseini. He said in a speech on November 23, 2010:
"*We must recall the outstanding [early] leadership of the Palestinian people, the Grand Mufti of Palestine – Haj Mohammed Amin al-Husseini, who sponsored the struggle from the beginning.*"

The Arab-Israeli conflict can therefore ascribe a significant part of its origin to Nazism.

Incidentally, Nazism in the Middle East is still very popular. *Mein Kampf*, Hitler's autobiography, is a perennial bestseller across the Arab world and the Palestinians are no exception.

The Nazi salute is still regularly used, for example by student groups at the Palestinian Al-Quds University (November 5, 2013). And in *Zajzafuna*, a magazine funded by the Palestinian Authority for Palestinian youth, an article detailing "ten wisdoms of Hitler" was published in the August 2013 issue.

Hitler is also a childhood idol among Palestinians, as noted in a study by the University of Hamburg.

That the Palestinians had no connection with the Nazis is, in short, nonsense.

Tale: The Palestinians have no connection to the Holocaust.
Fact: The first Palestinian leader, Grand Mufti Amin Al-Husseini, advised Hitler during the Holocaust.

74. Normalization

Palestinian Tale: Palestinians seek normal relations with Israelis.

To live together peacefully, it is crucial that Palestinians and Israelis interact normally with each other and can meet. Unfortunately, this is prevented by Palestinian leaders.

Palestinians from Gaza can practically no longer come in contact with Israelis; this is prevented by Hamas. Employment in Israel or in the factories of the specially equipped industrial zone on the border with Gaza has stopped almost completely. An important reason is that those plants were at times also bombed from Gaza.

Again, in the West Bank under the Fatah regime, this is not much better than under Hamas. There are about 100,000 Arabs from the West Bank employed by Israeli companies. But Israelis who come to the West Bank are often treated aggressively. Month after month, at least 300 acts of violence are counted, mainly stabbings and throwing of stones and Molotov cocktails at Israeli vehicles. Israelis are killed or wounded regularly.

That this violence and this hatred certainly does not help the Palestinians apparently does not matter. For instance, two Arab businessmen in 2013 planned to open a big clothing store in Ramallah. Because those clothes came from an Israeli fashion chain, it resulted in a large protest; an "Israeli" clothing store in a Palestinian town would be a form of *"normalization of relations"* with Israel and was therefore unacceptable. The protests succeeded, the business did not open, and so the planned 150 jobs for Palestinians were not created.

In 2014, more than 80 Palestinian and Israeli children participated in a football tournament organized by the Peres Center for Peace. The aim was that the children would get to know and appreciate each other.
That objective was against everything Palestinian sportsmanship stands for, according to Jibril Rajoub, head of the Palestinian Football Association and prominent leader of the Fatah movement of Palestinian President Abbas. Rajoub termed the children's football a *"crime against humanity."* The daily *Al-Hayat Al-Jadida*, which is under control of the Palestinian Authority, published his statement on September 8, 2014:

"The game was an Israeli attempt to cover up their crimes against [Palestinian] athletes. It is a disgrace to use sports for this purpose.
For a while now the Palestinian sports leadership and community – the Supreme Council for Sport and Youth Affairs, the Palestinian Olympic Committee and the Palestinian Football Association – have opposed such activities.
I demand that all individuals and institutions distance themselves from such activities, especially because their recurrence would arouse disgust and aversion towards all members of the [Palestinian] sports community."

Tale: Palestinians seek normal relations with Israelis.
Fact: It's so unsafe in autonomous Palestinian territory that Israel cannot guarantee the security of its citizens and therefore prohibits entry (picture).
Translation of the text on the photo: *"This road leads to Area A, under control of the Palestinian Authority. Access to Area A is forbidden for Israeli citizens, mortally dangerous and a punishable crime."*

75. Occupation Gaza Strip

The Palestinian Tale: The Gaza Strip is occupied.

The Gaza Strip is not occupied; there are zero Israeli soldiers in the territory. Despite the fact that for almost 3,000 years Jews had lived continuously in Gaza, today there are zero Jews living there.

However, there is an arms blockade around Gaza, and there is a strict border control. The blockade and control are executed by Gaza's two neighboring countries, Egypt and Israel. There are very good reasons for this. Hamas, which controls the Gaza Strip, regularly commits terrorist attacks in Egypt and Israel (see Tale: Gaza blockade) and has fired more than 15,000 rockets at Israeli villages and cities. Incidentally, Gaza's border traffic with Egypt is even more restricted than its border with Israel.

Obviously, strict border control does not mean occupation. By comparison, no one says that North Korea is occupied by South Korea because South Korea does not allow weapons to enter across their border.

Since Israel withdrew completely from Gaza in 2005, the administration has been in the hands of the Palestinians. Hamas was elected to rule the government in 2007, and that organization continues to employ its own civil servants, levy taxes, determine foreign policy, govern the police and judiciary system, and control the media.

There is also no question of an occupation as defined by international law. Article 6 of the 1949 Fourth Geneva Convention describes occupation as *"to the extent that such Power exercises the functions of government in such territory."*

Moreover, Article 42 of the Hague Convention on the law of war says: *"Territory is considered occupied when it is actually placed under the authority of the hostile army. The occupation extends only to the territory where such authority has been established and can be exercised."*

Neither Israel nor Egypt exercises the functions of government in the Gaza Strip. The Gaza Strip is controlled by the radical Islamic terrorist organization Hamas, not by Israel.

Tale: Gaza is occupied.
Fact: Israel is bombarded with rockets from Gaza.
Photo: In this apartment in 2012, three Israelis were killed by a rocket.

76. Occupation Golan

The Palestinian Tale: The Golan is occupied.

Originally part of the Golan Heights belonged to the British mandate of Palestine that the League of Nations – the forerunner of the United Nations – in part assigned to the Jewish people. In 1923, however, a new boundary was defined by Britain and France. These two countries as mandate holders claimed the reign of the countries of Palestine and Syria. The Golan Heights were a late addition to the French Mandate of Syria.

In 1944, Syria became independent and thus governed the Golan Heights. The land transfer later had serious consequences for Israel. Because Syria now controlled the mountainous Golan, it could put the entire adjacent Israeli lowlands under fire. And that Syria did very regularly in the years 1948-1967. In April 1967, there were sizable Syrian artillery bombardments on Israeli villages, one of the causes of the Six-Day War, which started two months later.

Israel captured the Golan Heights in the Six-Day War after two decades of Syrian aggression. Under international law a state can lose an area as a result of aggression. For example, think of Nazi Germany after World War II. Because Syria was the aggressor against Israel it is legal and logical that Syria lost the Golan Heights. Especially since the League of Nations had previously assigned part of the area to Israel. (Quite apart from the fact that Syria now hardly exists as a state.)

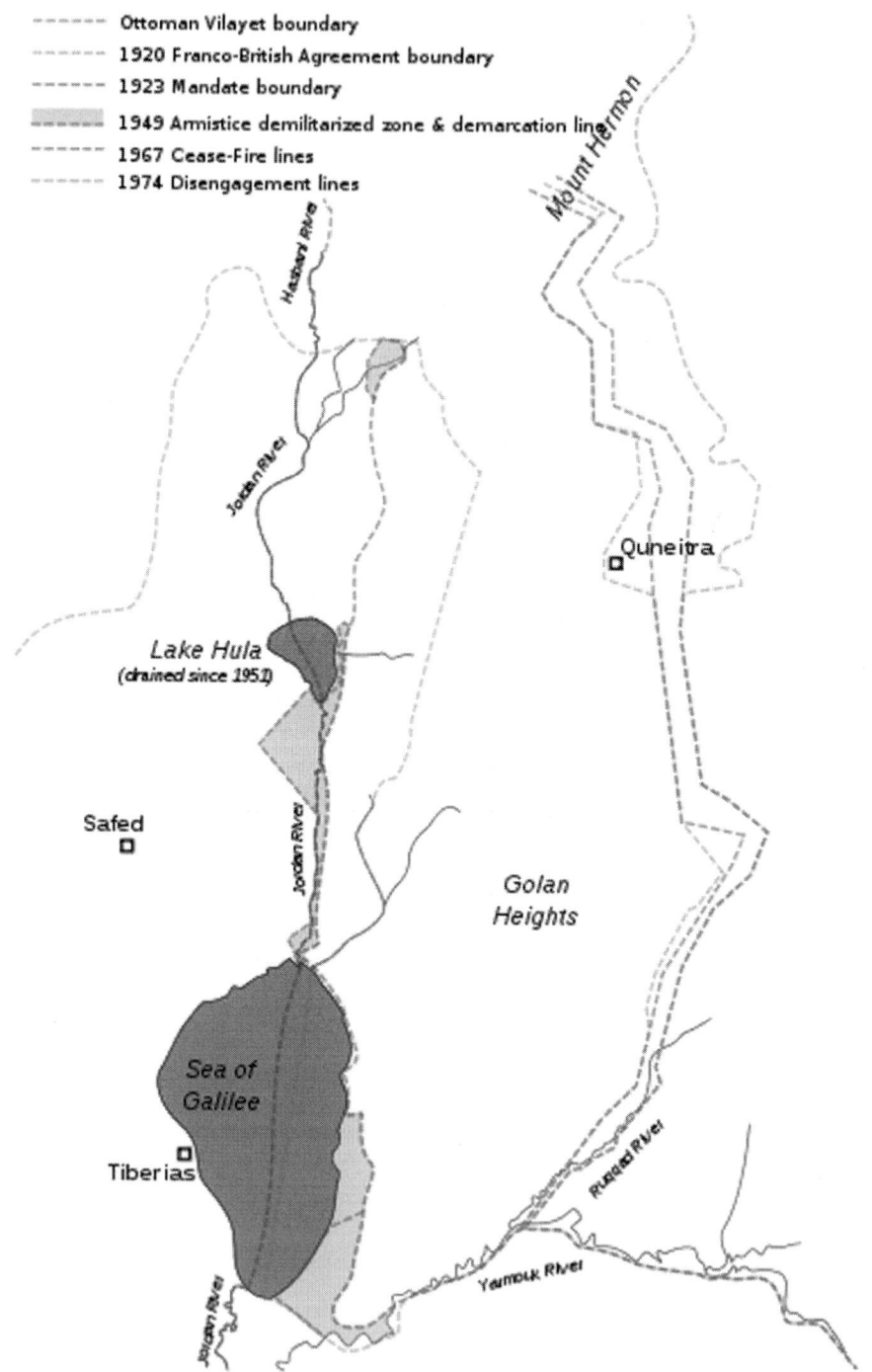

Tale: The Golan is occupied.
Fact: The Golan partially belonged, according to the international decision in 1922 by the League of Nations to the Jewish National Home.

77. Occupation Lebanon

The Palestinian Tale: Lebanon is occupied.

According to the Arab League and the Lebanese terrorist organization Hezbollah, Israel occupies Lebanese territory. Hezbollah gives this as a reason why it fights against Israel and has committed during the past 30 years many attacks against Israeli and Jewish targets, like blowing up a building of a Jewish association in Argentina in 1994. More than 80 people were killed in the blast.

The area that Hezbollah claims is the "Shebaa Farms," a small strip of land of seven by one miles.

The United Nations (certainly not pro-Israel, see Tale: United Nations) has investigated the claim and instead came to the conclusion in Resolution 425 (2000) that the Shebaa Farms is not historically Lebanese territory – and that Israel therefore indeed has fully withdrawn from Lebanon.

Of course, this "occupation" is not the real reason for the violence and terror of Hezbollah. For that one need only read the Hezbollah's charter:

> "Therefore our struggle will end only when this entity [Israel] is obliterated. We recognize no treaty with it, no cease fire, and no peace agreements, whether separate or consolidated."

The attacks perpetrated by Hezbollah on Jews worldwide – not Israelis, but Jews – also show otherwise. They are about hatred of Jews. Hezbollah leader Nasrallah let there be no misunderstanding:

> "If the Jews all gather in Israel, it will save us the trouble of going after them worldwide."

Tale: Lebanon is occupied.
Fact: The Israeli army has completely withdrawn from Lebanon.

78. Occupation West Bank

The Palestinian Tale: The Palestinians in the West Bank live under occupation.

This has been a tale for about 20 years. Since the mid-1990s, following the Oslo Accord, 96 percent of the Palestinians in the West Bank live under self-rule in an autonomous region with its own government. The Palestinian Authority controls Palestinian foreign policy, issues passports, employs Palestinian civil servants, levies taxes, directs the police, judiciary system and prisons, controls the media, and so on.

This autonomy is unprecedented and is matched in Europe only in Basque Country. Palestinians in the Gaza Strip even have the ability to wage war against Israel – talk about autonomy!

Under international law, a territory is occupied if another state forms its government and has military power within it (see more in Tale: Occupation Gaza Strip). For the large Palestinian population centers this is not the case.

Furthermore, according to case law, there can be no question of occupation in the West Bank according to international law, as the affected area did not previously belong to any country. Before Israel conquered the West Bank in 1967, the area had been annexed by Jordan, but this annexation was virtually unrecognized by the rest of the world.

The West Bank therefore was considered disputed territory prior to the Oslo Accords, and since the mid-1990s the official name of (the Arab populated part of) this region has been the (autonomous) Palestinian Territories.
The West Bank as a whole is still disputed territory (see Tale: West Bank claims).

The Palestinian citizens are indeed oppressed, that's true, but that is by their own Palestinian administration and not by Israel. In the Palestinian autonomous area there are no elections; there are executions of dissidents; honor killings are common; Palestinian children in Palestinian schools are taught that Jews are bad people; torture is widespread in Palestinian prisons; gays and Christians are persecuted; women are discriminated against and there is a huge amount of cronyism and corruption.

Tale: The Palestinians in the West Bank live under occupation.
Fact: There is Palestinian self-government.
Photo: Palestinian passport.

79. Olive trees

The Palestinian Tale: Jewish settlers constantly destroy Palestinian olive trees.

Olive trees should be pruned annually, like willows; otherwise they stop bearing fruit. Palestinian farmers do this themselves. To the layman, the trees look maimed afterward. Palestinians show these pruned trees to gullible visitors, to prove that "settlers" have damaged their trees. How can these settlers be so mean?!
From Wikipedia: *"Olive trees can live for several centuries and can remain productive for as long if they are pruned correctly and regularly."*

It even happens that Arabs themselves cut down their olive trees, to blame Israelis. For example, this occurred on October 13, 2014, irrefutably, because the Arabs were filmed without knowing it.

This is a case of Arab projection, in which Jews are accused of something while the atrocities are on the contrary committed by Arabs. The aggression against Jews in the West Bank is in fact gigantic, see the Tale: Normalization.

Tale: Jewish settlers constantly destroy Palestinian olive trees.
Fact: The branches of an olive tree must be pruned regularly for optimum growth of the olives.

80. Organ theft

The Palestinian Tale: Israel kills Palestinians for their organs.

The Iranian ministry of Education invented this tale. In 2004, the ministry produced a television series based on this lie. In the show, the Israeli president is kept alive by organs stolen from Palestinians. The series revolves around a Palestinian girl with very beautiful eyes. Those eyes are taken from her, so she becomes blind. The series was translated into Arabic and broadcast in Arab countries.

It is reminiscent of the medieval anti-Semitic blood libel which claims that Jews need blood of non-Jews to bake their matzos (unleavened bread) for their Passover celebration (see Tale: Blood libel).

In 2009, this tale reached the West, when it was published by the small Swedish newspaper *Aftonbladet*, using Palestinian "witnesses" as its primary evidentiary basis.
The story seemed to have come into the world by the confession of an Israeli pathologist who, about 20 years earlier, removed organs in his institute without the consent of family members. This happened to both Palestinian and Israeli victims, but only at this single institute.
This was done only at a single institute, years before, and it did apply not only to Palestinians. However, the Swedish newspaper enlarged this story, claiming that it had happened with many deceased Palestinians. The publication even suggested that this might have been the reason of the deaths of the people whose organs were extracted. After protests, the writer admitted that he *"had no idea whether it's true."*

As with all anti-Israeli tales, this tale regularly returns. Even *Time* magazine published it in 2014 (and retracted it after protests). Egypt broadcasted a television series about it during Ramadan in 2015.

The Palestinian Authority also spreads this Tale. For instance, on November 3, 2015, the Palestinian ambassador to the United Nations (UN) Riyad Mansour stated in a letter to UN Secretary General Ban Ki-moon that bodies of Palestinians killed by Israeli forces are *"returned with missing corneas and other organs, further confirming past reports about organ harvesting by the occupying power. A medical examination conducted on bodies of Palestinians returned after they were killed by the occupying power found that they were missing organs."*

And on January 29, 2016 the official Palestinian Authority daily newspaper *Al-Hayat Al-Jadida* reported:

"The minister of justice clarified to the Martyrs' families that he has given instructions, based on the directives of President Abbas and Prime Minister Rami Hamdallah, to all medical and legal staff to work around the clock, every day of the week, especially in cases of the handing over of Martyrs' [deceased terrorists] bodies ... to make sure that no body parts or organs were stolen from the bodies of the released Martyrs."

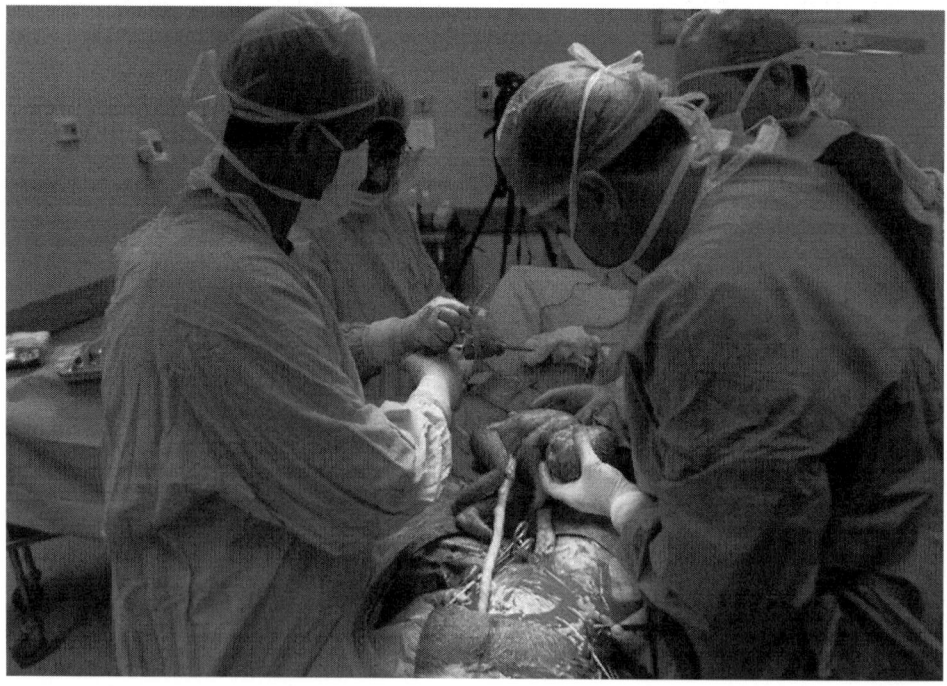

Tale: Israel kills Palestinians for their organs.
Fact: Israel provides medical treatment to a hundred thousand Palestinians yearly and saves many lives that way.
Photo: A Palestinian woman gives birth to quadruplets in an Israeli hospital.

81. Origin

The Palestinian Tale: The Jews in Israel are not from the region but come from America and Russia.

In the early days of the State of Israel, 56 percent of Jewish immigration was from Arab countries. They fled in a mass exodus because of discrimination and pogroms. In 1948 there were nearly 1,000,000 Jews in the Arab countries and Iran; more than 850,000 Jews from Arab countries went to Israel (see Tale: Jewish refugees). Interesting in this is that the number of Jewish-Arab refugees since 1948 is greater than the number of Palestinian refugees. Nevertheless, you never hear anything about this high number of Jewish refugees or the possessions they had to leave behind and for which they received no compensation. According to their interest group these Arab Jews lost 100,000 square kilometers of land in Arab countries – more than four times the size of all of Israel.

Due to the massive emigration of Jews from countries such as Morocco, Yemen, Egypt and Iraq, Arab Jews are the largest population group in Israel. Of the Jewish population in Israel, the majority was born in an Arab country or has at least one ancestor from an Arab country.

Tale: The Jews in Israel are not from the region but from America and Russia.
Fact: As early as the 19th century, Jews were the largest population group in Jerusalem.
Photo: Women praying at the Wailing Wall.

82. Orthodox Jewish power

The Palestinian Tale: Israel is a Jewish theocracy (a state based on religion, where clerics exert authority) – Orthodox Jews make the rules.

Israel is a democratic state in which independent, non-affiliated judges who are not bound to any religion administer justice. In Israel, fewer people vote for religious political parties than, for instance, in the Netherlands.

Further, there is complete freedom of religion. The only exception is for Jews who are prohibited from practicing their religion on the Temple Mount in Jerusalem. This is done to not offend Muslims.

There are only a few points where the Jewish character of Israel appears in public life. The food is mostly kosher. Pigs may only be reared in some Christian areas. Saturdays and Jewish holidays are days off.

At the time of the signing of Israel's Declaration of Independence, there was much debate about whether to include the word God. A compromise was reached, and the Declaration ends:

> "Placing our trust in the rock of Israel, we affix our signatures to this proclamation."

Marriage is an area that is still subject to religious rules. This is because this law to a large extent is based on the Turkish legislation from before 1917. As in many Arab countries, civil marriages are not possible. Weddings must be done religiously. This is not discriminatory because it applies to Jews, Muslims and Christians alike.

In short, contrary to the implications of this tale, Judaism is not the mandated religion of the only Jewish state, even though many states have Christianity or Islam as their state religion (see Tale: Jewish state). There are five European countries where the head of state must adhere to the state religion. That does not apply to Israel, where a Muslim can legally be head of state.

This is a case of projection in which Israel is blamed for something that the Islamic nations themselves are guilty of. In many Islamic countries, the legislation is based on *Sharia* (Islamic rule of law), which discriminates against non-Muslims.

The power of the Orthodox Jews in politics is also highly exaggerated. About 12 percent of the Israeli population is made up of religious Jews – moderately religious 4 percent and strictly orthodox 8 percent. Their political influence is greater because they are often required in the government coalitions. In Israel, like in many other countries, these religious parties not indispensable: in the Israeli government of 2013-2015 no Orthodox parties participated.

According to a global poll conducted by Gallup in 2015, Israel is even one of the least religious countries in the world: only 30 percent of the population consider themselves religious. Thus Israel scores equally with the United Kingdom, but much lower than for example the United States (56 percent), Germany (59 percent) or the average of the Middle East and North Africa (82 percent).

Tale: Orthodox Jews make the rules in Israel.
Fact: The Gay Pride Parade in Tel Aviv (photo) is the largest – and almost only one – in the Middle East and North Africa, with around 150,000 visitors annually.

83. Orthodox Jews

The Palestinian Tale: Many Orthodox Jews are anti-Zionist.

This tale is frequently spread on social media, often accompanied with a photo of Orthodox Jews protesting against Zionism or Israel.

It always concerns members of the Jewish sects *Neturei Karta* or the even more radical small splinter group, the *Sicari*. These are small groups; their total membership is estimated at five thousand. They are strange sects that oppose all authority, including the Israeli government. They are the same sects whose members spit on women and want women to travel separately from men on busses. They are just two small groups, and the majority of the Jews – Orthodox and non-Orthodox – are not affiliated and do not interact with them. Both chief rabbis of Israel condemned separated travel and have declared it not in accordance with Jewish law. Anti-Israel sites, however, proudly produce these small radical groups of Jews as proof that even *"Orthodox Jews are against Israel."*
Incidentally, sect members are paid for their anti-Israel activism. Documents intercepted by Israel state that one of the leaders of *Neturei Karta* received $ 55,000 from Palestinian leader Arafat.

The larger and more moderate group of Satmer Hasidim is also against Israel as a Jewish state. They believe that a Jewish state can only be founded after the arrival of the Messiah.

Out of around one million Orthodox Jews (out of a total population of 8 million) who live in Israel, about 20,000 fall into these categorized beliefs. These 20,000 that are against Israel are less than 2 percent of the Orthodox population and 0.25 percent of the total population. A percentage so small makes it clear that the claim that Orthodox Jews are anti-Zionist is indeed a big Tale.

Tale: Orthodox Jews are anti-Zionist.
Fact: The Chief Rabbinate of Israel (photo) consists of Orthodox Jews.

84. Oslo Accords

The Palestinian Tale: The Palestinians adhere to the Oslo Accords, and Israel does not.

The Oslo Accords were signed in 1992 in the Norwegian capital Oslo. The agreement is based on the principle of "land for peace," as defined in the binding resolution 242 in 1967 by the United Nations Security Council. Israel would give land to Arabs and in return Israel would get peace.

The land was undeniably given. As a result, 98 percent of the Palestinians (100 percent in the Gaza Strip and 96 percent in the West Bank) live under Palestinian self-rule. Also, Israel is fully compliant with its other obligations under these agreements, such as tax collection and distribution of water. Often, Israel is reproached for building in East Jerusalem and the West Bank, but these actions do not violate its obligations as set forth in the Oslo Accords (just as the promise of a Palestinian state is not in those accords, although this is also often claimed).

The real problem with the Oslo Accords is the fact that the Palestinians have not fulfilled their seven key obligations under these peace agreements.

These obligations include the Palestinian recognition of Israel's right to exist, including the redaction of passages from the charter of the PLO that deny this right and that advocate the destruction of Israel. This has not happened.

These obligations include stopping terror attacks. This has also not happened. On the contrary, Palestinian leaders still promote and organize terror (see Tales: Hamas and Fatah). Palestinians who advocate peace and oppose terror are often executed as "collaborators" (see Tale: Collaborators).

These obligations include dismantling terrorist organizations. That has also not happened, as not even one is gone. Hamas, the Al Aqsa Martyrs Brigades, the Islamic Jihad and so on, all of them still exist more than twenty years after the signing of the Oslo Accords.

These obligations state that only parties recognizing Israel should participate in Palestinian elections. Nevertheless, Hamas participated in all elections that have been held.

The population was to be taught that a peaceful solution to the Palestinian-Israeli conflict would be pursued from then on. This has not happened. On the contrary, acts of terrorism are celebrated on Palestinian TV, and terrorists are made role models of in Palestinian society (see also Tales: Fatah, Terrorists and Peace education).

A final peace treaty was to be signed with Israel. However, President Abbas of the Palestinian Authority consistently refuses to negotiate if pre-conditions are not first fulfilled. If that happens, as happened in 2013–2014 with the release of 76 Palestinian murderers from Israeli prisons, Abbas wants new concessions or raises new barriers (see Tale: Two-state solution).

Finally, the Palestinian Authority is required by the Oslo Accords to achieve peace in mutual negotiations, and therefore may not take unilateral steps. Everyone knows that this promise has also been broken, with the request for recognition of 'Palestine' made to all countries and the United Nations, without first achieving peace.

In 1993 it seemed that the Oslo Accords would finally result in a lasting peace between Israel and the Palestinians. Unfortunately, they have turned into a farce.

Tale: The Palestinians adhere to the Oslo Accords and Israel does not.
Fact: After twenty years, no Palestinian terror organization has been disarmed.

85. Palestinian leaders

The Palestinian Tale: Palestinian leaders want only what is best for their people.

In reality, a combination of abuses of power and corruption by Palestinian leaders motivate their decision making and policy. Foreign money (see Tale: Development aid) fuels the corruption.

Palestinian leaders are amassing fortunes by skimming foreign aid money. The foreign aid skim adds to local corruption. In Palestinian business deals a percentage must always be paid to a Palestinian official.

Yasser Arafat was at the forefront of this corruption. US government officials estimate the personal wealth of Arafat to be between one and three billion dollars. The wealth of his successor, Mahmud Abbas, is estimated at one hundred million dollars. However, that estimate is separate from the wealth of his two sons, who are able to enrich themselves because their companies get preferential treatment – and even possess monopolies (such as a monopoly on cigarettes).

Other Palestinian leaders also take part in this corruption. According to the former Palestinian minister, Mohammed Dahlan, 1.3 billion dollars have "disappeared" during Abbas's presidency. An example of the blatant corruption enacted under his presidency is the disappearance of money said to be going to pay the salaries of workers. These salaries were paid to nonexistent officials or non-existing projects, such as six million dollars for an Italian-Palestinian pipe factory – which existed only on paper.

It is ironic that Hamas members relied on anti-corruption rhetoric to win the last Palestinian legislative elections held in 2006: The leaders of Hamas got rich after the election, mainly by collecting "tax" on goods smuggled through the tunnels to Egypt.

Egyptian Professor Ahmed Karima of the Al-Azhar University in Egypt concluded in 2014 that Hamas, in recent years, has become a movement of millionaires. According to Karima, Hamas has no fewer than 1,200 millionaires among its leaders and middle managers. The absolute winner is the supreme leader of Hamas, Khaled Mashal, who claims to be "living in exile." In reality, he lives in great luxury in Qatar. According to Jordanian media, he owns $2.6 billion in personal assets.

According to a poll in 2014, 25 percent of Palestinians named corruption as the biggest problem of Palestinian society. This was second to the issue of the settlements (29 percent).

Tale: The Palestinian leaders want only what is best for their people.
Fact: Hamas leader Khaled Mashal (pictured) has personally misappropriated $2.6 billion.

86. Palestinian people

The Palestinian Tale: There is a distinct Palestinian people.

Until the middle of the nineteenth century, the area that is now Israel and Jordan was very sparsely populated (see Tale: Land development). That is why in the same nineteenth century the Turkish Ottoman government allowed refugees from other parts of the Ottoman Empire to settle there.

There were indeed streams of refugees, for example caused by the Austrian occupation of Bosnia and Herzegovina and the Crimean War. In 1878 land was therefore distributed by the Turkish Ottoman government to Muslim settlers from the Balkans and the Crimea.

The Encyclopaedia Britannica in its edition of 1911 therefore describes a territory where *"no less than fifty languages"* are spoken:

> *"There are very large contingents from the Mediterranean countries, especially Armenia, Greece and Italy, a number of Persians and a fairly large Afghan colony, tribes of Kurds, German 'Templar' colonies, a Bosnian colony and the Circassian settlements placed in certain centers by the Turkish government, in order to keep a restraint on the Bedouin and a large Algerian element in the population still maintain(s)."*

In a handbook in 1920 of the British Foreign Office it is also noted:

> *"The people west of the Jordan are not Arabs, but only Arabic-speaking.*
> *In the Gaza district they are mostly of Egyptian origin; elsewhere they are of the most mixed race."*

In addition to fleeing from wars elsewhere, Arabs were also attracted by the Jewish immigration, which increased steadily after 1880. Jewish immigration created a lot of jobs, higher salaries and unprecedented medical facilities. The British Peel Commission concluded in 1937 that the Jews had increased the absorption capacity of the country by their economic development.

Thus the establishment of 40 Jewish families in the newly founded village Rishon le-Zion in 1882 drew also more than 400 Arab families to it.

Already in 1913 a report of a British Royal Commission notes:
> "The area was under-populated and remained economically stagnant until the arrival of the first Zionist pioneers in the 1880's, who came to rebuild the Jewish land. Jewish development of the country also attracted large numbers of other immigrants – both Jewish and Arab.
> The road leading from Gaza to the north was only a summer track suitable for transport by camels and carts.
> Houses were all of mud. No windows were anywhere to be seen.
> Schools did not exist.
> The rate of infant mortality was very high.
> The western part, toward the sea, was almost a desert. Many ruins were scattered over the area, as owing to the prevalence of malaria, many villages were deserted by their inhabitants."

In the 1920s and 1930s, the Arab population growth had accelerated, by (illegal) immigration. As noted US President Roosevelt in 1939:
> "Arab immigration into Palestine since 1921 has vastly exceeded the total Jewish immigration during this whole period."

Governor El-Hurani of the Syrian Hauran province declared in 1934:
> "In the last few months from 30,000 to 36,000 Hauranese [Syrian] had entered Palestine and settled there."

Churchill refuted in 1939 the tales – already then – that Arabs were made to suffer:
> "So far from being persecuted, the Arabs have crowded into the country and multiplied till their population has increased more than even all world Jewry could lift up the Jewish population."

The British governor of Sinai Claude Jarvis reported even more cynically:
> "This illegal immigration was not only going on from the Sinai, but also from Transjordan and Syria, and it is very difficult to make a case out for the misery of the Arabs if at the same time their compatriots from adjoining states could not be kept from going in to share that misery."

The figures confirm this. Cities with a mixed Jewish and Arab population flourished and grew during that period, at a much higher rate than is possible with natural growth. In just nine years between the (British) censuses of 1922 and 1931, the Arab population of Jerusalem grew by 37 percent, that of Tel Aviv by 62 percent and Haifa even 86 percent. For a large part, this must have been the result of Arab immigration.

Nevertheless, as indicated in the Tale "Palestinian state, history," the Russian Soviet Union in 1964 invented the term "Palestinian people." So this concept is only fifty years old.

The Palestinians therefore do not meet the criteria of most other nations: they have no unique language, culture, religion or ancient history that is different from other Arabs in the area.

For instance, in Dutch parliament, the word "Palestinians" was only first used for in 1968 by a socialist MP. It is striking that in the beginning of his text he speaks still traditionally about "Palestinian Arabs" or "Arab Palestinians." The single word "Palestinians" he uses only once, later in his text.

And sometimes, the Palestinians make "a slip of the tongue." Thus, Palestinian leader Zuhayr Mohsen explains in an interview with the Dutch daily *Trouw* in 1977:

"In fact, there exists no Palestinian people. Between Jordanian, Palestinian, Syrian and Lebanese there are no differences. We are part of one nation, the Arab nation. Only for political reasons we endorse our Palestinian identity carefully. Yes, the existence of a separate Palestinian identity exists only for tactical reasons. The foundation of a Palestinian state is a new tool in the fight against Israel."

Similarly spoke the Hamas Minister of the Interior and National Security Fathi Hammad, in a televised address on March 23, 2012. He was indignant about the lack of Arab solidarity with the Palestinians, because:

"We all have Arab roots, and every Palestinian, in Gaza and throughout Palestine, can prove his Arab roots – whether from Saudi Arabia, from Yemen, or anywhere. We have blood ties.
Personally, half my family is Egyptian. We are all like that. More than 30 families in the Gaza Strip are called Al-Masri ["Egyptian"].
Brothers, half of the Palestinians are Egyptians and the other half are Saudis.
Who are the Palestinians? We have many families called Al-Masri, whose roots are Egyptian. Egyptian! They may be from Alexandria, from Cairo, from Dumietta, from the North, from Aswan, from Upper Egypt. We are Egyptians. We are Arabs. We are Muslims. We are a part of you."

This does not mean that there are no persons that consider themselves Palestinian. Also, it does not mean that these people have no rights. But as a nation, it is conceived (by Moscow).

"One day during the 1960s I went to bed a Jordanian Muslim, and when I woke up the next morning [after the Six Day War], I was informed that I was now a Palestinian Muslim, and that I was no longer a Jordanian Muslim."
– Former PLO terrorist Walid Shoebat

"The Palestinian people have no national identity. I, Yasser Arafat, man of destiny, will give them that identity through conflict with Israel."
– Yasser Arafat in his biography, by Alan Hart

Tale: There exists a Palestinian people.
Fact: At the time of the British Mandate, stamps said in Hebrew: Palestine – Eretz [land] Israel.

87. Palestinian state is missing

The Palestinian Tale: There is no Palestinian state.

In 1922, the state of Jordan was split off from Mandatory Palestine by Britain and designated to be a state for Arabs. In this way, 78 percent of the territory which was unanimously endorsed by the League of Nations (the forerunner of the United Nations) to be the Jewish national home was taken away. So, there is already a Palestinian Arab state: Jordan.

> *"The truth is that Jordan is Palestine and Palestine is Jordan."*
> – King Hussein of Jordan in 1981

> *"The relationship between Jordan and Palestine is the relationship of one people living in two states."*
> – Palestinian President Mahmoud Abbas on June 2, 2015

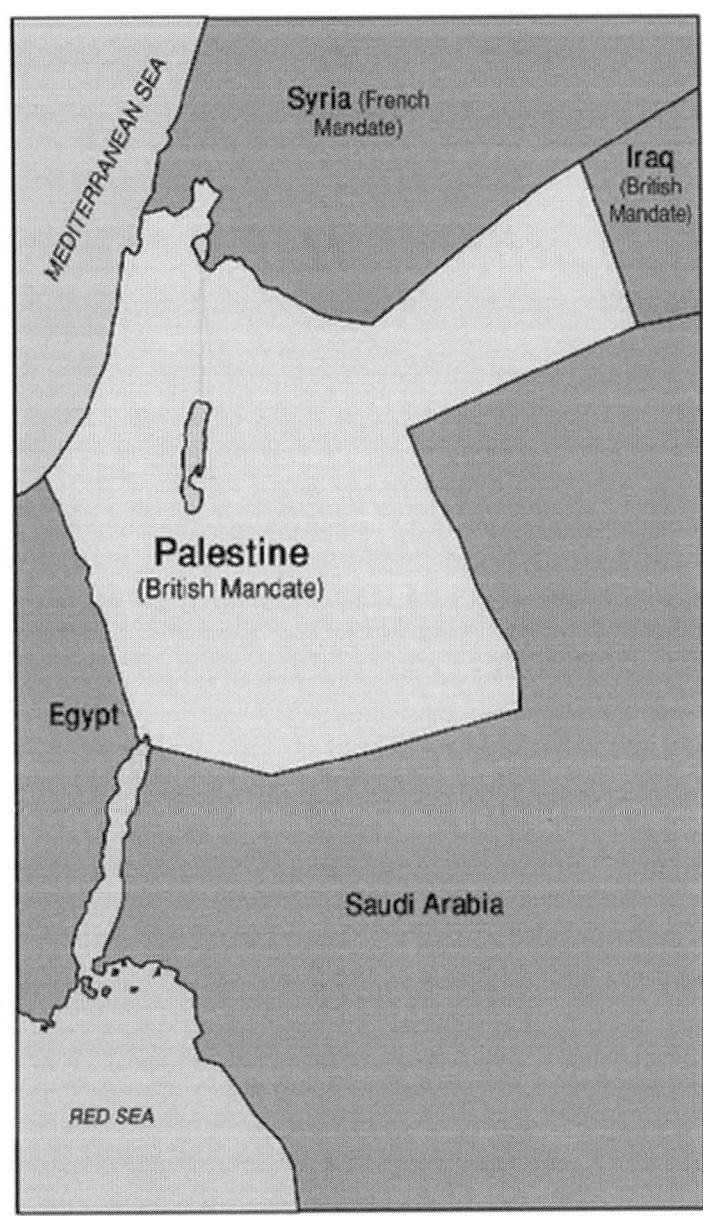

Area Allocated for Jewish National Home
San Remo Conference, 1920

Tale: There is no Palestinian state.
Fact: Jordan is the Arab state in Mandatory Palestine.

88. Palestinian state, future

The Palestinian Tale: All conditions for a Palestinian state are met.

According to the international convention of Montevideo, a state should meet four conditions to be recognized: it needs to have a clear population, a clear area, a functioning government and international relations.
The current Palestinian Authority does not fulfill any of these criteria of international law. There has never been a Palestinian state. There are no clear boundaries, for in the Oslo Accords it was agreed that they will in future be determined by mutual agreement. So far any proposed international compromise, however, has been rejected by the Arabs (see Tale: Two-state solution). There is not a single government with international relations. This is because there are two governments: one of Fatah in the West Bank and one of Hamas in Gaza. Moreover, no elections have been held since 2006. Palestinian President Abbas was elected in 2005 for a four-year term, but reigns endlessly. According to his own Palestinian law he is in fact no longer a legitimate head of state.

Also, the Palestinians committed themselves to making peace with Israel in a final peace treaty, and not to appeal directly to the UN for recognition. This is agreed to in the Oslo Accords, which are guaranteed by the UN and the EU. However, the Palestinian Authority has asked the UN to recognize a Palestinian state, while at the same time refusing to conclude a final peace treaty with Israel. With this behavior, the Palestinians have not complied with international agreements. It is particularly remarkable that the UN and EU do not point this out to the Palestinians, as everyone should, after all, obey the law.

Moreover, a Palestinian state would be in violation of some of the United Nations's fundamental values about freedom and equality. President Abbas and other Palestinian leaders have repeatedly stated that Jews would not be allowed to live in a Palestinian state. How can an openly racist state receive recognition if it plans to ethnically cleanse a part of its population?

Last but not least: a state must be peaceful. Article 4 of the UN charter provides:
> *"Membership in the United Nations is open to all other peace-loving states which accept the obligations contained in the present Charter and, in the judgment of the Organization, are able and willing to carry out these obligations."*

That description is at odds with Palestinian incitement to hatred and terrorism – as promoted by both Hamas and Fatah – and the desire of both organizations to destroy Israel (see Tale: Destruction of Israel). The Hamas regime in Gaza is even regarded worldwide as a terrorist organization.

> *"Germany supports a two-state solution. We see how difficult that is, so we also believe that unilateral recognition of the Palestinian state won't move us forward toward that goal."*
> – German Chancellor Angela Merkel, 2014

Tale: All conditions for a Palestinian state are met.
Fact: States must be peaceful.
Photo: Hamas fired missiles at a preschool.

89. Palestinian state, history

The Palestinian Tale: A Palestinian state is a historic necessity.

A Palestinian state never officially existed. In the nearly 2,000 years from the year 70 until the recreation of Israel in 1948, there was no independent political entity in the area. In the Koran, Palestine is not even mentioned once, while Israel is mentioned 44 times.

In the West, over the past centuries, the area was commonly referred to as "Palestine" or "the Holy Land." Palestine was the name the Romans gave to the country, replacing historic Judea (where the word Jew comes from). This renaming was meant to wipe out the memory of the Jewish state after the Romans had beaten down several Jewish revolts. In the Islamic world, the area was normally referred to as "southern Syria."

In 1922, the League of Nations – the forerunner of the United Nations – assigned the area to the Jewish people in the Mandate for Palestine due to the defeat of the Ottoman Turks and the breaking up of that empire. The name itself was a point of resentment for Arab nationalists. The name Palestine was judged an idiotic Jewish invention. There existed no Palestinians, as the area's Arab residents were considered South Syrians.

In 1919, at a conference in Paris where the British mandate of Palestine was proposed, Arab delegates, both Muslim and Christian, were also opposed to the name Palestine:

> "We consider Palestine as part of Arab Syria, as it has never been separated from it at any time. We are connected with it by national, religious, linguistic, natural, economic and geographical bonds."

The name Palestine was therefore used only by Jews at the time. Thus, the largest Jewish newspaper was named *The Palestine Post* (now the *Jerusalem Post*). Jewish associations and foundations were created to support the Jewish presence in Palestine. Take for example, the still existing The Netherlands Foundation for Training and Deployment of Palestinian Pioneers. Money was raised by the Jewish United Palestine Appeal (now United Israel Appeal).

Frank Sinatra performed in 1947 at the charity Action for Palestine because he wanted to support its Jewish residents.

When for the first time the two-state solution was proposed in 1937, the leaders of the Palestinian Arabs gave the same response: *"There is no country with the name Palestine. Palestine is a Zionist invention. There is no Palestine in the Bible; our country was for centuries part of Syria."*

They rejected the partition plan for a Jewish and an Arab state in Palestine on that basis. The Arabs' solution was to add the territory to Syria, as it had been for centuries.
This was the message of Arabic leaders for a long time. Even in 1956, Ahmed Al-Shukairy, deputy secretary general of the Arab League, spoke these words before the UN Security Council:
"It is common knowledge that Palestine is nothing but southern Syria."

Incidentally, this would not prevent this same Ahmed Al-Shukairy from establishing the PLO as a "Palestinian" liberation organization eight years later.

> *"Palestine is nothing but a drop in an enormous ocean. Our nation is the Arabic nation that stretches from the Atlantic Ocean to the Red Sea and beyond it.*
> *The PLO is fighting Israel in the name of Pan-Arabism. What you call 'Jordan' is nothing more than Palestine."*
> – Palestinian leader Yasser Arafat in 1993

Even as recently as June 20, 2012, Palestinian writer Hassan Yousouf stated on Palestinian television:
> *"Let's speak openly. I think that the Palestinian cause is fundamentally and essentially a Syrian matter, whether we like it or not.*
> *Obviously, it is an existential, Arabic, regional matter. Essentially and fundamentally it is a Syrian matter, since it [Palestine] is part of the Levant, Greater Syria."*

However, in a huge twist, the Palestinian Arabs in the 1960s suddenly called themselves "Palestinians." This was an invention of the KGB, the Russian secret service. The KGB started many "liberation organizations" that wanted to win "self-determination" – from Western-oriented countries, of course. Until then, Arab terrorists claimed their aim was the destruction of Israel. The KGB made it clear to them that, as this would not make them popular in the West, they should claim to strive for "liberation," which would be especially appealing to the political left.

Thus, the PLO as the "Palestinian Liberation Organization" was founded in Moscow in 1964. The 422 members of the "Palestinian National Council" were all handpicked by the KGB. A Palestinian flag was created by removing a star from the flag of Jordan. Weapons were supplied by the KGB and the Stasi (the East German secret service) and everything else by the Romanian secret service, from uniforms to stationery. The "Palestinians" had been launched.

It was thus no surprise when in 2016 it was revealed that Palestinian President Abbas had been an agent for the Russian KGB. Of course, it was already known that Mahmoud Abbas received a doctorate from the Patrice Lumumba University in Moscow (see Tale: Holocaust denial). According to KGB defectors, 90 percent of the university's faculty and staff received their paychecks from the KGB. Its purpose was to train KGB agents from the developing world, including terrorists. Abbas's fellow students included master terrorist Carlos the Jackal and future Iranian dictator Ayatollah Ali Khamenei.

The "liberation" movement thus pursued the conquest of Palestine. That emphatically did not mean the West Bank and Gaza, because those two areas were at that time still occupied by Arab countries, respectively Jordan and Egypt. No, the PLO only wanted to conquer – and destroy – Israel.

Currently, however, the concept of Palestinian statehood is starting to wear down in Arab circles. After all, the goal of all Muslim fundamentalist organizations is gaining ground: one great Islamic empire in the Middle East and North Africa – the caliphate.
Thus, the goal of the Egyptian president Morsi of the Muslim Brotherhood, stated in his election campaign and after his election victory was:
"The capital of the Caliphate – the capital of the United States of the Arabs – will be Jerusalem."

The same applies to Palestinian Muslim fundamentalists. In an interview on October 17, 2014, on official Palestinian Authority television, Sheikh Kamal Khatib, deputy leader of the Islamic Movement in Israel said:
"Jerusalem will not be only the capital of the Palestinian state, but also the capital of the coming righteous Islamic caliphate."

Tale: An Arab Palestinian state previously existed.
Fact: The Mandate of Palestine was not a state, and its territory was intended for the Jews.
Photo: Palestine flag according to the Larousse Encyclopedia of 1924.

90. Palestinian state, viability

The Palestinian Tale: Israeli construction makes a viable Palestinian state an impossibility.

This Palestinian Tale was launched after the Israeli announcement of the construction of the so-called E1 area east of Jerusalem. This would make West Bank too narrow and "split in two."
However, after implementation of the plan, the West Bank would not be narrower than Israel itself is near the city of Netanya (9 miles).
So, this tale is a case of projection, in which Arabs condemn Israel for something they are promoting themselves.

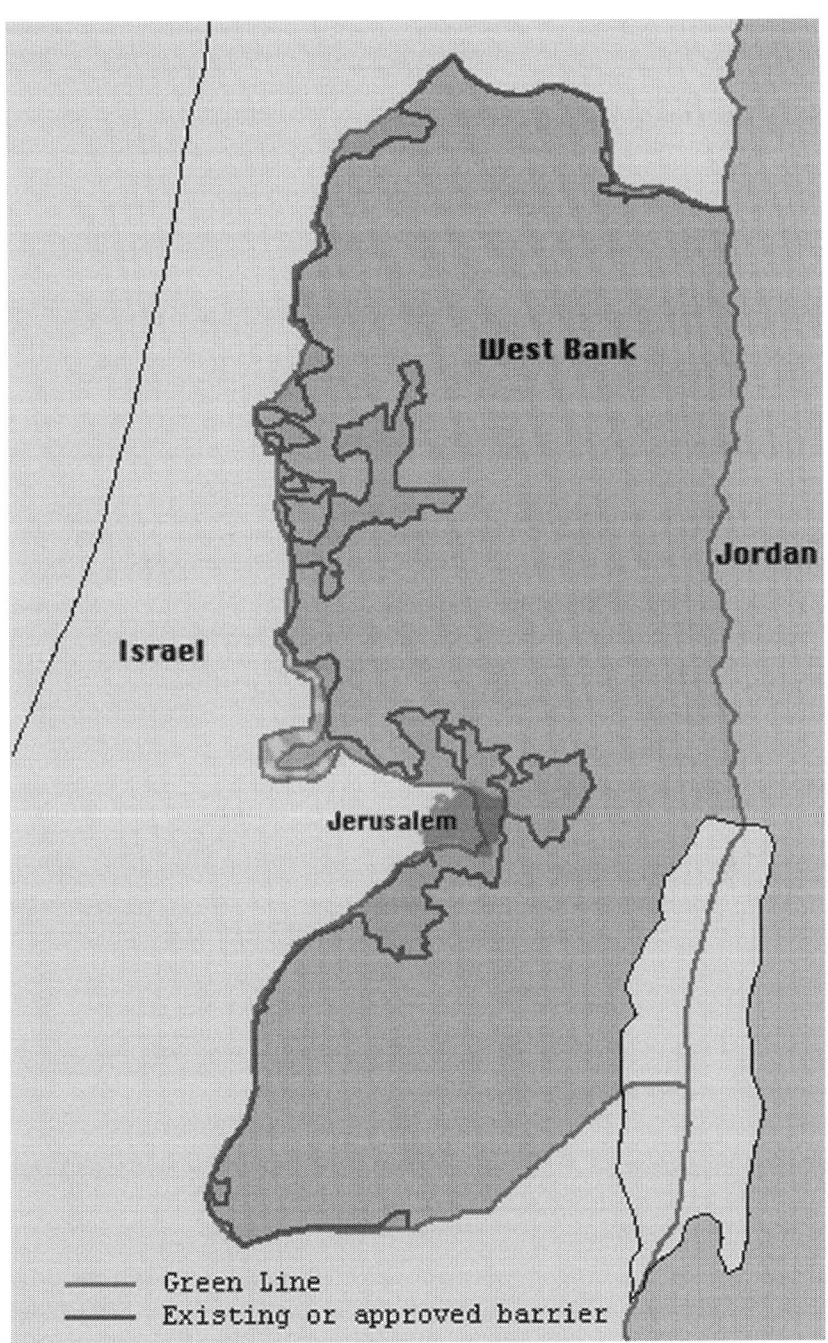

West Bank barrier – May 2005

Tale: Israeli construction preempts a viable Palestinian state.
Fact: Only 5 percent of the West Bank is on the Israeli side of the security fence, the possible future border.

91. Palestinian state, wish

The Palestinian Tale: The Palestinians have always wanted their own state.

Like the Arab countries, the leadership of the Palestinian Arabs in 1947 refused the UN Partition Plan (see that tale), which proposed an Arab state in the West Bank and Gaza. In 1947 there could already have been a Palestinian state!
After Arab countries attacked Israel in 1948, Jordan captured the West Bank, and Egypt conquered Gaza. But neither country planned to create a Palestinian state there. No one asked for it on the Arab side. The king of Jordan hosted a conference in Jericho in 1948, in which thousands of Palestinian Arabs – including many prominent ones, such as the mayors of Hebron, Bethlehem and Ramallah – asked for the annexation of the West Bank by Jordan.

The only country that still called for a Palestinian Arab state was Israel! That can be read in an article in the Israeli newspaper *The Palestine Post* of May 15, 1949, which tells about the head of the Israeli delegation to the peace negotiations, Walter Eytan:

"An independent sovereign Jewish State had come into existence despite the Arab War and the only result of that war had been to prevent the creation of an independent Arab state, he said. Dr. Eytan was also understood to have insisted that the future of Arab Palestine must be decided by the Arab inhabitants themselves. The General Assembly gave the neighboring States no title to any part of the country, he said.
Dr. Eytan suggested that the Commission hold a plebiscite in the Arab area to ascertain the wishes of the inhabitants, and assist in the establishment of a genuine representative body for Arab Palestine."

It was not to be. Jordan annexed the West Bank (illegally, according to the Arab League and the UN), and Egypt did not give up Gaza.

From 1948 to 1967, there appeared no national aspirations whatsoever on the part of the Palestinian Arabs. Instead, they frequently made terrorist attacks on Israel from the Gaza Strip, the West Bank and neighboring countries. In 1964 these terrorist groups formed the PLO, the "Palestine Liberation Organization." This "liberation," however, focused not on the West Bank and Gaza, where most Palestinians lived, but on Israel. As is apparent from the first charter of the PLO, it's about *"getting back the homeland"* – a euphemism for the destruction of Israel. It was not so much in the interests of the Palestinians, but in Arab interests generally. So the title of the charter is: "The Palestinian Pan-Arab Charter." Article 24 even says explicitly that they would not exercise any territorial rights in the West Bank and Gaza: *"This Organization does not exercise any regional sovereignty over the West Bank in the Hashemite Kingdom of Jordan or on the Gaza Strip."*

That changed after Israel conquered the West Bank and Gaza in the Six Day War of 1967, when Israel was attacked by Jordan, Syria and Egypt. The charter of the PLO was rewritten and given a new title: "The Palestinian National Charter."

So for the first time, in this charter in 1968, the emphasis is on a "Palestinian state." But still, both the PLO and Hamas highlight that a Palestinian state would be subordinate to the "Arab nation" and the "Islamic nation."

> *"The State of Palestine is an Arab state, an integral part of the Arab nation and that nation's heritage and its civilization."*
> – "Declaration of Independence" of the Palestinian National Council in 1988

> **"Islamic and traditional views reject the notion of establishing an independent Palestinian state.**
> **In the past, there was no independent Palestinian state.**
> **Hence our main goal is to establish a great Islamic state, be it pan-Arabic or pan-Islamic.**
> **Our position stems from our religious convictions. This is a holy land. It is not the property of the Palestinians or the Arabs. This land is the property of all Muslims in all parts of the world."**
> – Hamas leader Mahmoud Zahar in 2005

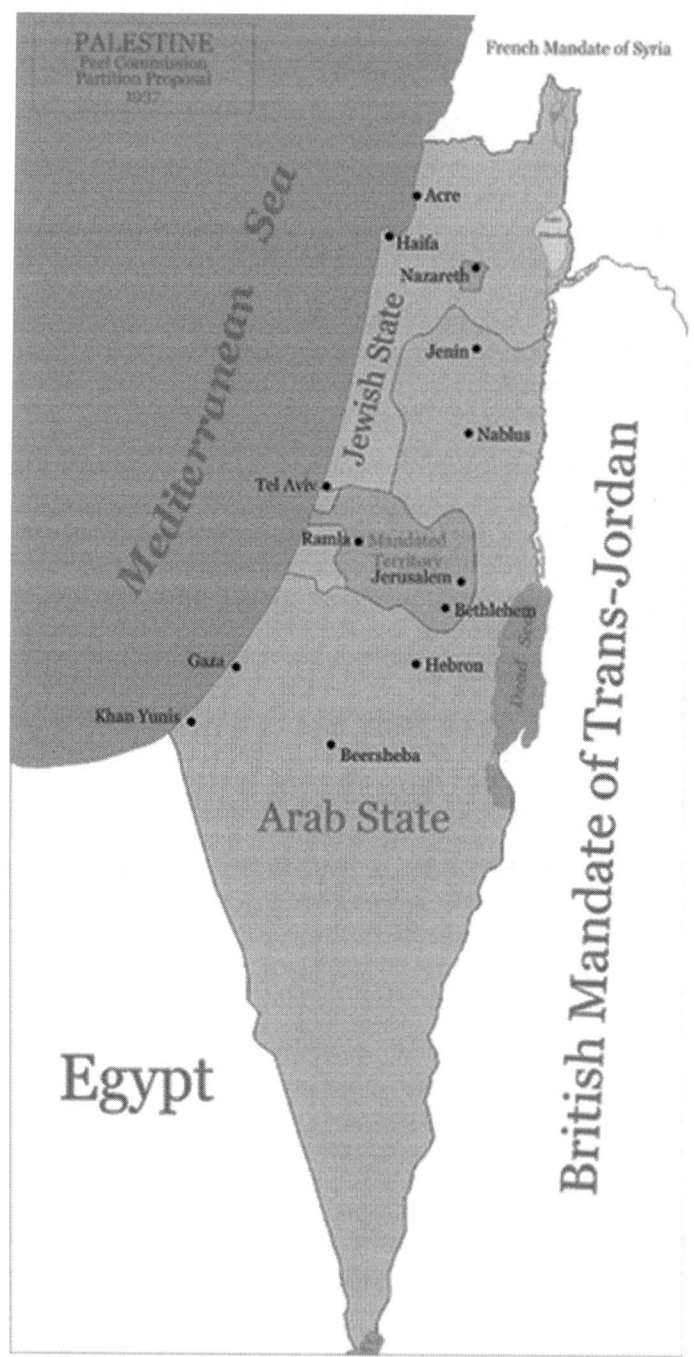

Tale: The Palestinians always wanted their own state.
Fact: When independence was internationally proposed, it was always rejected by the Arabs – even when it was first proposed in 1937 and the Jews would have received only a mini-state (map).

92. Partition Plan

The Palestinian Tale: The proposed partition plan by the United Nations in 1947 was unfair to the Arabs – and was therefore rightly rejected.

Palestinians call the partition plan of 1947 a colonial plot. But the number of countries that voted for it was almost three times as large as the number of countries that voted against it. Among the pro voters there were many former colonies that had become independent states in Asia, Latin America and Africa, including Thailand, Bolivia, Liberia, Brazil and Costa Rica. Only Muslim countries voted against (with only three others proving the exceptions).

The partition plan proposed by the United Nations was based on the population situation on the ground in 1947. Cities and regions with a Jewish majority would become part of the proposed Jewish state and those with an Arab majority of the Arab state. The Jewish state would cover 55 percent of the Palestine Mandate area west of the Jordan with almost the same percentage of (mostly Jewish) inhabitants, 53 percent.

Nevertheless, it was indeed a very unfavorable distribution, for the Jews:
1. Jordan was already separated as an Arab part of Mandate Palestine, despite the fact that this land was promised to the Jews in 1922 by the League of Nations, the UN's predecessor. Without Jordan a whopping 78 percent of the area promised to the Jews was lost!
2. Jerusalem was excluded from the Jewish state – it would become an international city – although in 1947 Jews already formed a large majority of its population.
3. The large anticipated immigration of Jews from Europe and the Arab countries was ignored.
4. Approximately 60 percent of the territory allotted to the Jews consisted of the barren Negev desert.
5. The emphasis on the local demographic situation made the proposed borders very long and therefore difficult to defend (while Arab aggression was already declared. See Tale: War of Independence in 1948).

Nevertheless, the Jews agreed with the proposed distribution and the Arabs essentially rejected it.

Had the Arabs also accepted, the Palestinians would already have had an independent state in 1948.

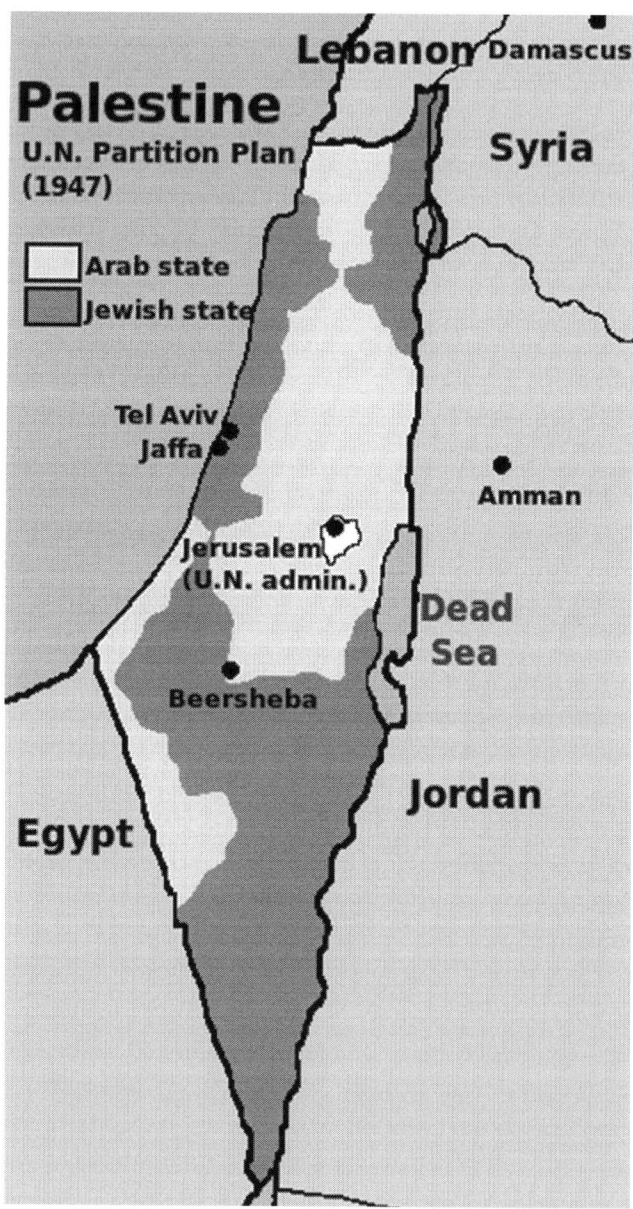

Tale: The Partition Plan was unfair, and the Arabs were right to reject it.

Fact: The Partition Plan was unfair – to the Jews.

93. Peace

The Palestinian Tale: That there is no peace is Israel's doing.

The Arab-Israeli conflict began in the 1920s under the first Palestinian leader, the Grand Mufti of Jerusalem Al-Husseini. Ideologically, he started the war against the Jews, inspired by Nazism, Arab nationalism and, in particular, Islamic fundamentalism (see Tale: Nazism).
In the sixties and 1970s, the conflict became less religious and more nationalistic, because the Soviet Union made use of it in the Cold War against the West (see Tale: Palestinian state, history).

However, since about 1980, Muslim fundamentalism increased sharply in the Muslim world, because since then organizations supporting it are financed with huge sums of petrodollars. The Arab-Israeli conflict has become almost entirely religiously motivated, again. This is shown by the fact that even Fatah (by origin, secular) now also makes use of Islamic principles. Today, Fatah also refers to the Koran, uses Islamic religious symbolism and speaks of their killed terrorists as "Islamic martyrs" (see Tale: Death cult).

Hamas, obviously, has always been Muslim fundamentalist. It has the support of the majority of the Palestinians. According to an opinion poll held among Palestinians in 2011, 73 percent agree with article 7 of the Hamas charter, which says that it is an Islamic duty to exterminate the Jews. It indicates that the conflict stems from religiously motivated hatred of Jews for about three-quarters of the Palestinians.

Jew hatred is very much alive across the whole of the Islamic world. The former Malaysian Prime Minister Mahathir accused the Jews of all that is evil in the world, Turkish Prime Minister Erdogan is openly anti-Semitic, King Salman of Saudi Arabia called the attacks of September 11 an Israeli conspiracy and the then Egyptian president Morsi prayed openly for the destruction of the Jews on Egyptian state television.

> *"The core of the conflict in the Middle East is that the Arab states have never accepted the existence of the State of Israel. Their anti-Semitism does not focus so much on what Israel does, but on its existence as such."*
> – Former European commissioner Frits Bolkestein, 2003

But is it true that all (Palestinian) Muslims are Muslim fundamentalists?
No, but there is a second motivation playing a role, which is strongly associated with the Muslim beliefs. For centuries Jews (and Christians) were second-class citizens in Arab countries. They led a second class life among the Muslims; they had to act in a submissive way towards Muslims and had to put up with all kind of humiliations.
For Muslims this was an indirect proof that Allah was favoring Muslims and that Islam was the superior religion.

And then those despised Jews founded their own state. A state with initially only one million inhabitants, which became much more successful than the entire Arab world in the economic, cultural, military and scientific areas. This is not easy to digest for nationalistic Muslims:

"The Palestinian cause is central for Arab thinking. It's because we always lose to Israel. It gnaws at the people in the Middle East that such a small country as Israel, with only about 7 million inhabitants, can defeat the Arab nation with its 350 million. That hurts our collective ego. The Palestinian problem is in the genes of every Arab.
The West's problem is that it does not understand this."
– *Al-Jazeera* chief editor Ahmed Sheik

So it is in essence not a conflict over land or borders. If that was the case, the conflict would have been resolved already eighty years ago, when the two-state solution was presented for the first time – with a very tiny Jewish state.
A two-state solution means that there will be a Jewish state living in peace. That is still unacceptable for many Arabs. That is why all proposals for peace or a two-state solution have already failed sixteen times in the past eighty years (see Tale: Two-state solution).

The two-state solution was the idea behind the UN Partition Plan of 1947. Quite literally, Resolution 181 of the General Assembly of the United Nations proposes the creation of "an Arab state" and "a Jewish state." But to this day the Palestinians refuse to recognize a Jewish state. Palestinian President Abbas stated clearly, on March 4, 2015, in a speech to the PLO's Central Council, broadcasted on Palestinian television:
"We do not accept a Jewish state; we will never accept a Jewish state."

That is quite a travesty; at the same time Abbas demands a Palestinian state with a constitution based on Islamic *Sharia*, which discriminates against non-Muslims.

But does Israel not risk international isolation by holding on to security demands, in exchange for peace? Or is this a frightful tale that has simply been told for a long time?

> *"Without a fundamental change, Israel could wind up in an international diplomatic ghetto, with the United States as her only friend. Even in the United States, Israel's position will not be secure unless it changes her policy.*
> *This may be Israel's last chance to make a peace that won't be imposed upon her."*
> – The then American secretary of state Henry Kissinger in December 1973

So when will there be peace? The then Prime Minister of Israel, Golda Meir, already in 1957 gave the answer:

> ***"Peace will come when the Arabs will love their children more than they hate us."***

It seems that we have not moved closer to this, more than half a century after these words.

> *"The truth is that if Israel were to put down its arms, there would be no more Israel. If the Arabs were to put down their arms, there would be no more war."*
> – Israeli Prime Minister Benjamin Netanyahu in 2006

Tale: That there is no peace is Israel's doing.
Fact: Jews and Israel are blamed for everything that goes wrong in the Arab world.
Photo: Demonstration in Tahrir Square in Cairo, Egypt.

94. Peace education

The Palestinian Tale: The Palestinians abide by their commitment to peace education.

The most important obligation that the Palestinians have accepted in the Oslo peace agreements is that of peace education. After all, what is the sense of peace agreements if new generations are not brought up with a desire for peace? Only then, with the next generation, can indeed true peace and an end to violence come about.

To the contrary, unfortunately, there is education for war. Palestinian youth are told that war, strife and violence against Israelis are good. This indoctrination comes from mosques, schools, newspapers and television. Children learn from Hamas children's television programming that they must exterminate the Jews (see Tale: Hamas). Children in Gaza receive, from the age of eight, military training; they are deployed by Hamas as child soldiers.

The Fatah movement of Palestinian Authority President Mahmoud Abbas in the West Bank is not much better.

For starters, many schools are named after Palestinian terrorists because they are the role models for Palestinian society (see Tale: Terrorists). An official Palestinian Authority television broadcast on March 27, 2014, focused on the Dalal Mughrabi School. The Palestinian girl for whom the school is named hijacked an Israeli bus with others and killed 38 passengers, including 13 children. A teacher of the school tells:

"Dalal Mughrabi is a fighter who carried out Jihad and struggle from the beginning of her life. She was one of the brave female fighters who carried out Martyrdom-seeking operations [i.e., terror attacks]. We in the Ministry of Education had the honor of naming our school after the Martyr Dalal Mughrabi, so that her eternal memory will stay for a long time."

A pupil agrees:

"Dalal Mughrabi is a great leader who put the Palestinian cause more and more on the forefront and worked on it to protect the pure land of the homeland, by defending Jerusalem and to liberate it. This fighter may have died and her soul may have ascended to Heaven, but still our mothers give birth to thousands like Dalal, and

she still walks among us. Dalal Mughrabi has given us a lot, and I personally am proud to attend the Dalal Mughrabi School, which bears this pioneering name."

In Palestinian schoolbooks, children are "educated" that: the struggle against Israel is a religious war, a Palestinian state means the disappearance of Israel, Israel has no right to exist, the Holocaust was exaggerated or did not happen, Palestinians are the victims of *"racist Zionists"* and that the creation of Israel was *"the greatest catastrophe in the history of mankind."*

As a result, children in Palestinian schools are raised with the idea that Israel must disappear, as the head of the Palestinian Teachers Association in Jerusalem confirmed on official Palestinian Authority television on November 15, 2014:

"In our schools, we teach what our religion and conscience dictate: That Jerusalem is Arab and that Palestine – from north to south, from the [Jordan] River to the [Mediterranean] Sea – is Islamic Palestinian Arab, and will remain so in spite of the damned occupier."

Children learn that according to Islam, Jews are criminals and unclean creatures. Thus spoke an approximately eight-year-old girl in the children's program *The best home* on official Palestinian Authority television on March 22, 2013:

"Allah's enemies, the sons of pigs [i.e., Jews, in Islamic tradition] destroyed and uprooted the olive and fig trees. They murdered children with guns; they are snakes. They cut off their limbs with stones and knives. They raped the women in the city squares. They defiled Allah's book [the Koran] in front of millions.
Where is the nation of Islam? Where are the nation of Islam and the Jihad fighters? Where is the fear of Allah in Jerusalem, which has been defiled by the Zionists?"

This is reflected in the Palestinian textbooks. After an investigation of 250 Palestinian textbooks, the Center for Near East Policy Research noted in January 2016 that they contain:

"delegitimization of both Israel and of the Jews' very presence in the country, demonization of Israel and the Jews, non-advocacy of a peaceful solution to the conflict and, instead, emphasis on a violent struggle for the liberation of Palestine without limiting it to the areas of the West Bank and Gaza. Jihad and martyrdom are part and parcel of that violent struggle."

Some examples from the study:

"Lesson four: Palestine is Arab and Muslim."
Above a map where Israel is called "Palestine."
– *National education*, Grade 2, Part 1, 2015, p. 16.

"Hearing [weapons'] clash is pleasant to my ear.
And the flow of blood gladdens my soul,
as well as a body thrown upon the ground,
skirmished over by the desert predators
By your life! This is the death of men
and whoever asks for a noble death – this is it!"
– *Our beautiful language*, Grade 7, 2014, p. 75.

"Fighting the Jews and the victory over them: The Messenger [Muhammad] already announced the end of the Jews' oppression upon this Holy Land and the removal of their corruption and of their occupation thereof. [It is told] by Abu Hurayrah that the Prophet said: 'The End of Days will not take place until the Muslims fight the Jews, and the Muslims will kill them.'"
– *Faith*, Grade 11, 2013, p. 94.

What is the result of this brainwashing? That 80 percent of Palestinians support the murder of Israeli babies (see Tale: Violence) and that Palestinian teenagers take to the streets to stab Jewish civilians to death.

Tale: The Palestinians abide by their commitment to peace education.
Fact: Even in Palestinian schools, posters which venerate terrorists as martyrs are hung (photo).

95. Peace from the right

The Palestinian Tale: Peace can only be made by the Israeli left.

It is precisely the political right in Israel that has often recognized the real opportunities for peace – peace for which land was ceded. The first peace treaty between an Arab country and Israel was made by Likud Prime Minister Menachem Begin, the peace with Egypt, signed in 1979. Under Likud Prime Minister Yitzhak Shamir the first peace conference with Arab countries and the Palestinians was held. And in 1997 Likud Prime Minister Netanyahu signed the agreement of Hebron. Also, it was a Likud Prime Minister, Ariel Sharon, that in 2005 evacuated the entire Jewish population from the Gaza Strip, so that only Palestinian Muslims and Christians remained.

Nowadays also, only the Israeli political right seems to be able to really negotiate for peace and get popular support for it. But the Palestinians have to be willing too.

> *"I negotiate with every enemy who wants to stop being my enemy. That is the way to make peace. An enemy who wants to destroy you and stays committed to your extermination is not someone you can negotiate with. You don't negotiate with al-Qaeda. You don't negotiate with the khalif Baghdadi, because these people only want to destroy you.*
> *As long as Hamas remains committed to our destruction, what's there to negotiate? As a method of suicide or what?"*
> – Israeli Likud Prime Minister Benjamin Netanyahu

Tale: Peace can only be made by the Israeli left.
Fact: Likud leader Menachem Begin (photo) made peace with Egypt.

96. Peace negotiations

The Palestinian Tale: Peace negotiations fail because of Israel's demands.

In the Tale "Two-state solution" it is described how the Arabs have rejected all sixteen peace proposals since 1937, both the Israeli proposals and the internationally proposed compromises. The only peace treaty that the Palestinians have signed with Israel was intended as a temporary one and has been sabotaged by them (see Tale: Oslo Accords).

The compromise proposal by the then US president Clinton in 2000 is a poignant example. The proposal conceded that the Palestinians would have a Palestinian state in Gaza and almost all of the West Bank, with East Jerusalem as the Palestinian capital. In addition, the Palestinian refugees would be financially compensated with $30 billion for their damages. All of the Palestinians' requests, which they continue to demand, were addressed in the proposed agreement.

However, to the astonishment of President Clinton and the world, the Palestinian leader Yasser Arafat refused. Prince Bandar attended the negotiations on behalf of Saudi Arabia. He was convinced that this proposal was a great offer, the best the Palestinians could ever expect. He warned Arafat: *"If you don't accept what is available now, it won't be a tragedy, it will be a crime."*
Arafat chose the crime.

> *"President Barack Obama started negotiations between the parties, exactly what the Muslim world asked from him. And exactly on the day these started, one of the parties involved – Hamas – bombards innocent Israeli civilians, in order to thwart the peace process. That makes you wonder how sincere they are about that peace process."*
> – British former Prime Minister and negotiator for the Middle East Tony Blair, in 2010

Tale: Peace negotiations fail because of Israel's demands.
Fact: When Prime Minister Netanyahu (photo) offered the Palestinians a state in 2009, they did not even want to negotiate with him.

97. Philistines

The Palestinian Tale: Palestinians are descendants of the Philistines.

To "prove" their historical presence in the region, the Palestinians assert that they are descendants of the Philistines of the Bible. In the Bible, the Philistines were defeated by Israel's King David. The last mention of the Philistines in history dates back to 7 BCE. After two thousand years of obscurity, no one can definitively claim that they are descended from the Philistines; just as a Dutch person can't say that he or she is descended from the Batavians. Ironically, the word Philistines means "invaders," referring to non-Semitic people of Greek origin. Moreover, the Arabs invaded the area fifteen centuries after the Philistines and conquered Jerusalem in the year 637 CE – about two thousand years after the Jewish state had been established.

After realizing that the Philistines did not arrive in Israel before the Jews, Palestinian propaganda began to claim that they are descended from the Canaanites. However, the absurdity of this claim remains the same, as history has not mentioned the Canaanites for almost 3,000 years.

Nonetheless, Saeb Erekat, the Palestinian representative in peace negotiations with Israel, continues to claim that he is a descendant of the Canaanites. This is an asinine assertion from a man in such a position. However, at a conference in Munich on February 1, 2014 he stated flatly (with the cameras rolling):
 "I am the proud son of the Canaanites, who were there 5,500 years before [the Jewish] Joshua Ben Nun burned down the town of Jericho."

According to the Bible, Joshua Ben Nun lived some 3,300 years ago. Saeb Erekat now claims his family lived there 5,500 years earlier than Ben Nun, which would mean that his family would have lived there 9,000 years ago. To claim to know precisely where one's ancestors lived 9,000 years ago is absurd.

However, the lie continues further. On their Facebook page, his family stated that the Erekats originated in Medina, Saudi Arabia. Afterwards, they settled in Jordan until about 1860, closer to the vicinity of Jerusalem. His ancestors are said to have settled rather recently in the area as economic immigrants, like many Palestinians have (see Tale: Palestinian people).

Ultimately, Saeb Erekat exaggerated his family's presence in Jerusalem by about 8,800 years.

Palestinian Basic Law associates Palestinians with Arab nations, unrelated to Philistines and Canaanites. This is clear in Article 2:

"Palestine is part of the Arab homeland. The state of Palestine abides by the Charter of the League of Arab States. The Palestinian people are part of the Arab and Islamic nations."

The words say it all: Jews originated in Judea (the area around Jerusalem), and Arabs in Arabia.

Tale: The Palestinians are descendants of the Philistines.
Fact: Nothing has been heard from the Philistines for two thousand years, while history of the Jewish people has been chronicled during this whole time period.
Photo: The oldest known mention of the land of Israel on the more than 3,200 year old Merneptah column in Egypt.

98. Pigs

The Palestinian Tale: Israel breeds pigs to pester Palestinians.

This Tale emerges regularly in the Palestinian media, and it is perpetuated through this media exposure like other conspiracy theories (see the Tale). Even the serious English-language Arab newspaper *Gulf News* devoted attention to it in 2013:

"*A Palestinian youth was accidentally shot and killed by his cousin on Saturday night as a group of young Palestinians attempted to defend their village against a herd of wild pigs released by Israeli colonists during the snowstorm that has hit Palestine since last Tuesday.*
Local sources in Kafr Al Deek told Gulf News *that Israeli colonists have used the bad weather to set free a group of the wild pigs to attack the Palestinian farms and properties in the village.*"

Pigs are, for Jews – as for Muslims – considered to be unclean animals. Therefore, breeding pigs is only allowed in a designated number of residential areas inhabited by Christians in northern Israel. Moreover, of course, unleashed pigs would eat the harvest of Israeli farmers as readily as that of Arabs – a pig sees no difference between potatoes planted by Arabs or Israelis. In reality, the pigs that were referred to in this tale were wild pigs.

Tale: Israel breeds pigs to pester Palestinians.
Fact: These are wild pigs that damage crops.

99. Poisoning Arafat

The Palestinian Tale: Arafat was poisoned by Israel.

The tale that Yasser Arafat was murdered with polonium was very popular in Europe and the Netherlands. The main major news agency *ANP* devoted as many as 20 news reports to it in 18 months.
These reports were often published by the main Dutch media. The story, however, was mainly a show put on by Arafat's widow to damage Israel.

Of the many international research teams that investigated Arafat's death, a Swiss team was the only one that found indications that might imply that Arafat had indeed been poisoned with polonium. Other teams from different countries did not find anything. The Russian research team found the measured values of the poison polonium in Arafat's mausoleum to be no higher than expected from natural causes. The British professor Nicholas Priest, an expert in the field of polonium poisoning, even stated that *"any scientific credibility for polonium poisoning is lacking in the Swiss report."* Coincidence or not, the Swiss team was paid by Arafat's widow.

That same widow had refused to allow an autopsy shortly after Arafat's death in 2004; probably she feared that another cause of death would be discovered.

The only indication of poisoning was that the detection of a high amount of polonium (a radioactive, toxic substance) on Arafat's underpants. But even then it was dubiously high – as concluded by different research teams – given the time elapsed and the rapid disintegration of the radioactive poison. The dose was so huge that it could have killed a herd of elephants, so to speak. These levels make it plausible that the polonium was applied much later.

This suspicion was confirmed in 2012 by Professor Roland Masse, a radiation expert from the Percy Hospital in Paris, the hospital where Arafat spent his last days. He claimed that Arafat could not have been contaminated in any way with polonium, because Arafat was tested back then also: *"A lethal level of polonium simply cannot go unnoticed."*

Also, Arafat did not show some typical characteristics of polonium poisoning, like hair loss. Anyone can see from the pictures that Arafat during his hospitalization had grown a beard. The accusation therefore makes no sense, as was also concluded by the official French investigation.

But Arafat's widow had a big personal interest in pushing this story and so promoting herself in the Palestinian cause. She is very much at loggerheads with the Palestinian Authority over the ownership of the hundreds of millions of dollars – if not billions – which Arafat kept for himself. She likely thought that it would not hurt to show her "Palestinian nationalism" by blaming Israel for her husband's death. And the mainstream media had no problem accommodating her.

Tale: Arafat was poisoned by Israel.
Fact: Arafat (photo) was 75, had already been sick for a long time, after an unhealthy life and Parkinson's disease.

100. Poisoning wells

The Palestinian Tale: Israel poisons Palestinian water sources.

That Jews poison the water sources of non-Jews, is an old anti-Semitic Tale, already found during the Middle Ages. Thousands of Jews were killed because of the false accusation, as at the time of the Black Death plague. In Strasbourg on February 14, 1349, nine hundred Jews were burned alive on the grounds of this accusation. Like other nonsensical classic anti-Semitic allegations, such as the Blood libel and quest for World domination (see those Tales), this one is also happily recycled by the Palestinians, without any basis of truth.

As was reported in a news broadcast of the official television of the Palestinian Authority on September 24, 2014:

"Water experts have warned of the consequences of the attack by the occupation [Israel] on water wells, as a result of its use of poisonous bombs that threaten public health."

A reporter added:

"The policy of attacking water wells is a war strategy used by the occupation in its aggression against Gaza. Not only were the people deprived of water, but poison was also injected into main [water] sources, destroying agriculture."

The Palestinian president Abbas himself has spread this ridiculous Tale, and even in the European parliament.

In his speech to the parliament on June 23, 2016, he said:

"Only a week ago, a number of rabbis in Israel announced, and made a clear announcement, demanding that their government poisons the water to kill the Palestinians.

Isn't that a clear incitement, to commit mass killings against the Palestinian people?"

Tale: Israel poisons Palestinian water sources.
Fact: This absurd anti-Semitic accusation led to the death of many Jews during the Middle Ages.
Photo: Jews at the stake during the "Black Death" plague, in 1349.

101. Population growth

The Palestinian Tale: If there is no Palestinian state, the Jews will become a minority in Israel, because the Arab population grows faster.

This can be heard regularly, that Israel will be overwhelmed by an Arab population that will destroy the Jewish character of the state. It comes from all sides, not only from Palestinians but also by US Secretary of State Kerry, left-wing Israeli politicians and the ayatollahs of Iran.

The numbers predicting this Arab population explosion are not too reliable. The population figures from the West Bank are inflated for political reasons by the Palestinian authorities, for instance by counting Palestinians that have emigrated to countries abroad. Unlike the Palestinians, Israel does have an immigration surplus (see Tale: Emigration).

The hundreds of thousands of Arabs living in Jerusalem are counted twice, by both Israel and the Palestinian Authority. A study in 2007 suggested that the Palestinian statistics thus counted approximately 30 percent more Arabs in the West Bank and the Gaza Strip than actually lived there (2.4 million instead of 3.8 million).

Furthermore, this tale is an absurd representation, because there is virtually no Israeli that wants to regain control of the Gaza Strip or the part of the West Bank that has Palestinian self-rule.

The number of Arab residents in the West Bank will not grow so quickly in any case, says the Israeli expert Dr. Guy Bachor:
> *"Obama, Kerry, Clinton and all those who talk about the demographics are wrong. The data shows, and it's true throughout the Middle East, a collapse in the Arab birth rate... including [among] the Palestinians and Israeli Arabs.*
> *At the same time, there is an astounding rise among the Jewish population in Israel."*

The key number is 2.1 children per woman. Less than that number represents a negative population growth. Many nations around Israel remain below that threshold, while in Europe the figures are much lower.

This tale turns out to be based on outdated figures. In 2003, the average number of children per Israeli Arab woman was more than five. But in 2013 it was already reduced to 2.7 and this number continues to decline. This is caused, like everywhere else in the world, by a higher standard of living, better education and the stronger position of many women, who do not want to spend their days caring for children. In Israel, the birth rate increased in this period, to more than three children per woman.

Remarkably, if birth rates remain as they are now, there will be more Jews living in Israel by the end of this century than native Germans living in Germany.

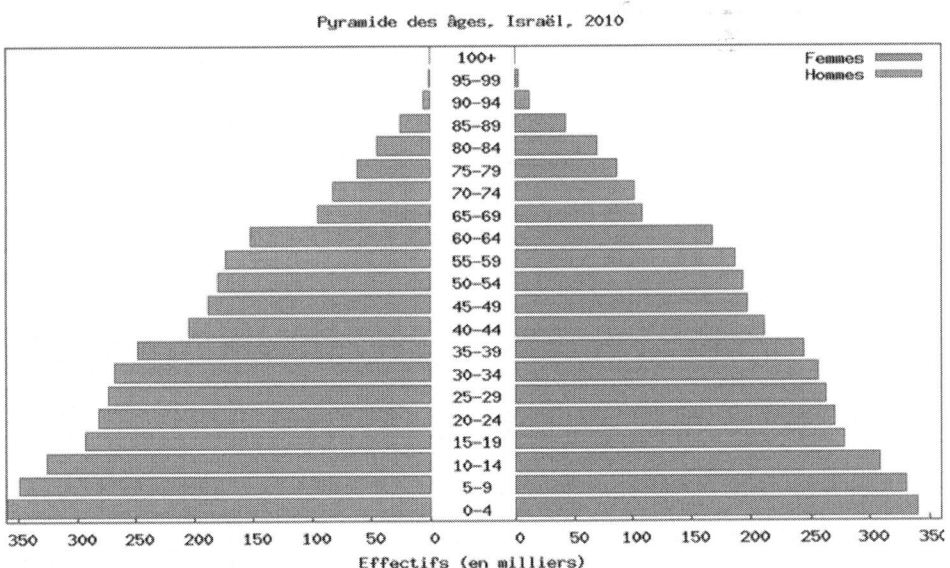

Tale: The Jewish population in Israel will be overtaken by the Arabs.
Fact: Israel has a young, rapidly growing population.
Photo: The population pyramid of Israel.

102. Prisoners

The Palestinian Tale: The Palestinians in Israeli jails are political prisoners.

In Israel, there are about 4,000 Palestinians in prison. The vast majority of these prisoners were convicted after a fair trial. Often, they are convicted of murder or other very serious and violent crimes. More than half have been convicted of terrorism and have blood on their hands. Often, this blood is the blood of children.
Palestinians are not detained for their political opinions and are not "political prisoners."
These prisoners have been found guilty of deliberate violence against civilians, which is, by definition, a war crime (see Tale: Terror).

At the end of 2011, 1,027 of the prisoners who committed lighter crimes were released in the prisoner swap in exchange for the safe return of Israeli Gilad Shalit. Thus, all of Israel's current Palestinian prisoners are all being held due to severe crimes.
This begs the question, what is "light" in the case of Palestinian terrorists? One prisoner, Ahlam Tamimi, was set free in this exchange after organizing the suicide attack on an Israeli pizzeria in 2001. This attack killed 16 civilians, including eight children.

About three hundred prisoners have not been convicted. These Palestinians are in preventive detention, which involves only 7 percent of Palestinian prisoners. Preventive detention – also known as administrative detention – exists in many countries, including other Western democracies such as Australia, England and the United States.
The objective of administrative detention is to prevent attacks by persons with known violent and terroristic intent. Therefore, administrative detention is a preventive measure and not a punitive measure. This is permitted under the Fourth Geneva Convention, Article 78. The Dutch government agreed:
"Based on international law, detention for security imperative reasons without this associated with a criminal trial, is permitted as an exceptional measure."

Information that serves to indicate the intent of individuals to commit terrorist acts is reviewed by a court while remaining confidential in order to protect police informants. This process exists to ensure that innocent people do not become prisoners and that all prisoners are convicted based on their actions.

Additionally, some prisoners (less than 0.5 percent) are subject to solitary confinement. These prisoners are considered to be extremely dangerous terrorists; to the extent that there is reason to believe that they will continue to organize terrorist attacks if not placed in solitary confinement. One such prisoner is Abdullah Barghouti; a Hamas ringleader who organized suicide attacks in which 66 Israeli civilians were killed. And what does he have to say about his actions today? *"I am sad because there were only 66."*

Tale: The Palestinians in Israeli prisons are political prisoners.
Fact: All prisoners are in jail because of their own violent actions.
Photo: The pizzeria in which 16 civilians were slain in 2001, including five members of the Dutch family Schijveschuurder.

103. Rabin murder

The Palestinian Tale: If Israeli Prime Minister Rabin had not been assassinated, there would now be peace.

This is a Tale because the socialist Yitzhak Rabin held exactly the same positions on security issues as have recent Israeli governments. Rabin explained those views in his last speech to the Knesset, the Israeli parliament, on October 5, 1995, a month before his murder. Rabin said that there was no question of a withdrawal to the 1967 lines.

He, like the other Israeli signatories to the Accords, saw Palestinian autonomy as an experiment that could possibly bring peace. But if the autonomy failed, it would have to be reversed. He furthermore was in favor of Palestinian autonomy, but not a Palestinian state. In his book *The New Middle East*, which was published in 1993, the year of the first Oslo Accord, Rabin wrote:
> *"Even if the Palestinians agree that their state may have no army or weapons, who can guarantee that a Palestinian army would not be mustered later to encamp at the gates of Jerusalem and the approaches to the lowlands?"*

In 1995, terrorist attacks had already started. The ink on the Oslo Agreement was barely dry before the radical Islamic group Hamas began an unprecedented series of suicide bombings in Israel. At times, innocent Israeli civilians were blown up almost daily in supermarkets, pizza parlors and street markets; some of the attacks were massive, causing dozens of deaths.

Israel pressured the Palestinian leadership to stop terror, but that did not help to curb the attacks, although the leadership had so obligated itself under the peace agreements. It became increasingly clear that Yasser Arafat himself – who had signed the Oslo Accords on behalf of the Palestinians – still had a hand in the terror wave (see Tale: Arafat).

The Israeli people elected Benjamin Netanyahu of the Likud party as Prime Minister six months after Rabin's assassination. Rabin's socialist party suffered losses despite the wave of sympathy following his murder. The terror attacks convinced the Israeli voter that the experiment of the Oslo Accords had failed.

Rabin himself understood so too, shortly before his death. His daughter Dalia Rabin, former Israeli defense secretary, said in a newspaper interview in 2010:

"Many people who were close to Father told me that on the eve of the murder he considered stopping the Oslo process because of the terror that was running rampant in the streets, and that Arafat wasn't delivering the goods. Father, after all, wasn't a blind man running forward without thought.

At the end of the day he was someone for whom the security of the state was sacrosanct."

Tale: If Israeli Prime Minister Rabin had not been assassinated, there would now be peace.
Fact: Rabin (photo) was a military man for most of his career and never lost sight of Israel's security.

104. Racism

The Palestinian Tale: Israel is racist.

As shown in the tale "Democracy, Israel," Arabs in Israel have the same civil rights as Jews. The principle of equal citizenship for all peoples is explicit in Israeli law and is therefore strictly enforced by Israel, including by the Israeli Supreme Court. Any citizen can hold any function. Thus Arab-Israeli Majalli Wahabi was acting president of Israel in 2007, when the incumbent president was indicted.

Yet this tale is very actively publicized, apparently under the motto: if a lie is repeated often enough, it will be believed at some point. It is often even claimed that over 50 Israeli laws are discriminatory. It is not true: half of the laws on this list have to do with the religion of the majority of the people, as is common in Muslim and Christian countries too (see Tale: Jewish state). As for the rest, they are utter nonsense; for instance the *Trading with the Enemy Act* is on this list. It is claimed to be discriminatory because *"thus far, all enemy states are Arab and/or Muslim states."*

On the contrary, there is no country in the Middle East where Arabs have more civil rights than in Israel. They have more civil rights in Israel than in all of their own Arab countries!

Equality for men and women, freedom of religion, democracy, women's suffrage, gay rights, freedom of the press, freedom of expression – even for atheists, property protection, protection of the rights of minorities such as Christians and Druze, protection of women against child marriage, female genital mutilation and honor killings and so on. Arabs in Arab countries can only dream of these kinds of freedoms and civil rights.

Also, even compared to other Western countries, there are examples where Israel takes greater care of minorities. Unlike Switzerland, Israel has no ban on minarets. France may not recognize the Celtic language of Brittany minority; Arabic is in Israel a normal, officially recognized language. In the summer of 2016, there was a discussion in many European countries if burqas and burkinis should be forbidden. Burqas are already forbidden in certain European countries, like France. In Israel they are allowed.

So this is a case of Arab projection, whereby Israel is falsely accused of something that is common in Arab countries. In almost all Arab countries, minorities don't enjoy most of these civil rights.

Some wry examples: In Saudi Arabia and Iran, gay are men publicly hanged. In Lebanon, Palestinians cannot own property and cannot have certain professions, like being a doctor. In Egypt under the Morsi government Bahai children were not allowed to attend school (because Bahai was an "illegal" religion). Until 2012 lessons in the Kurdish language were banned in Turkish schools. In Bahrain, the Shiite majority has no voice. Mecca is off-limits to all non-Muslims.

Jews may not live in Saudi Arabia, Jordan or in the Palestinian territories. Racism against Jews is propagated by the Palestinian leadership, even by the president. See the Tales Fatah and Hamas, which also show that both these parties – which the vast majority of Palestinians has voted for – are overtly racist. Compare that to Israelis, of which only 1 percent voted for the racist Kach party – before it was banned.

In Israel, gays are properly protected, even Arab gay men. Gay men from Gaza and the West Bank have therefore in recent years fled to Israel, which gives them safety.

This does not mean, unfortunately, that discrimination does not exist in Israel. But no society is totally free from discrimination. However, research shows that discrimination against Arabs in Israel is not greater than – for example – against Moroccans in the Netherlands. That is surprising, given the fact that Israelis suffer daily from Arab violence, such as throwing stones at cars.

Arabs in Israel are therefore not dissatisfied. See more in the Tale: Arabs in Israel.

Tale: Israel has racist laws.
Fact: The rights of minorities are protected, for example in the Declaration of Independence (photo).

105. Refugee problem

The Palestinian Tale: Israel is solely responsible for the refugee problem.

This is a tale for many reasons.
Firstly, the Arabs started the war of 1947-1948 (see Tale: War of Independence in 1948).
Secondly, only 10 percent of the Palestinian Arab refugees were actually expelled by Israel (which was as a result of continued aggression on the part of that population (see Tale: Expulsion of 1948).
Thirdly, it was the Arab countries and their leaders themselves that banned the return of the refugees. The Arab High Command stated: *"It is inconceivable for the refugees to return to their homes. It will serve as a first step to Arab recognition of the state of Israel and the idea of partition."*

In the fourth place, there was a kind of unintended population exchange. At that time there were even more Jews fleeing from Arab countries (about one million) than Palestinian refugees coming into these Arab countries (see Tale: Jewish refugees). Would it not have been very logical to resettle the Palestinian Arabs in the abandoned houses of the Jews in the Arab countries?

The main reason that there are still people considered to be Palestinian Arab refugees is because it is an artificially maintained problem. According to the UN refugee agency, anyone who cannot return to their country of origin should integrate in the places where they live. In the case of the Palestinian Arab refugees this was not allowed, on purpose.
In the 1940s there were tens of millions of other refugees, such as Germans, Cossacks, Tatars, Silesians, Pakistanis and others. All those other refugee problems no longer exist, because those refugees integrated into their new surroundings.
The comparison with the founding of Pakistan is striking, because it also took place in 1948. That created approximately ten times more refugees on both sides: seven million Hindus and seven million Muslims. Nobody speaks about it anymore, because these refugees have all for a long time been integrated, in India and Pakistan.

This was not to be with the Palestinian Arab refugees; they were seen as a political weapon against Israel and used accordingly. Because of that, the Palestinian refugees were not allowed to integrate into any of the 22 Arab countries (see Tale: Arab treatment of Palestinians). The head of the UN agency for Palestinian refugees (UNRWA), Ralph Galloway, said in August 1958:

"The Arab states do not want to solve the refugee problem. They want to keep it as an open sore, as an affront to the UN and as a weapon against Israel. Arab leaders don't give a damn whether the refugees live or die."

Indeed, even Palestinian "refugees" living in Palestinian autonomous areas this very day, are discriminated against by their own government. For instance, they must remain in their camps and have fewer rights than other Palestinians. A notorious example is the Balata refugee camp in the West Bank. The growing population there – now 30,000 – lives locked in only one square kilometer. It is therefore one of the most densely populated places in the world. However, the residents are not allowed to live outside the camp or build homes there. They cannot vote in local elections. The children are not allowed outside the camp schools. Their life is horrible, thanks to their own Palestinian leaders.

Even if there was a two-state solution in the future and thus a Palestinian state, the situation in Balata would likely remain unchanged. The Palestinian ambassador to Lebanon explained this clearly, in an interview in 2011 with the Lebanese newspaper *The Daily Star*:

"Even Palestinian refugees living in refugee camps inside the Palestinian state are still refugees. They will not be considered citizens."

It is ironic that the Palestinians claim their own state because of their right to self-determination but deny their own citizens to become citizens therein!
The Palestinian President Abbas in 2013 even said about Palestinians who were likely to be killed in the Syrian Civil War: *"It is better they die in Syria than give up their right of return."*

The conclusion cannot be any other than that the Palestinian refugee problem is totally artificial.
It has been, to begin with, very much exaggerated (see Tale: Refugees, numbers) and – under pressure from the Arab world – nobody has ever seriously tried to solve it, like all other refugee problems from that time have been. Many of the descendants of the refugees still live in camps, some 70 years later, and are fully taken care of by the United Nations. The cost of this, over all those years, has not been paid by the Arab world – which caused it – but mainly paid by us, in the West.

The problem, as a matter of fact, could be solved tomorrow: Arab governments need only stop their discrimination of Palestinians, by declaring that all Arabs will automatically be considered citizens of the country in which they were born.

This would also be beneficial for the approximately 18 million new, genuine refugees and displaced people, coming from seven countries, all Muslim (Afghanistan, Iraq, Libya, Pakistan, Somalia, Syria and Yemen), as there would be a better use of the money otherwise spent by the West on Palestinian "refugees" for decades to come.

And don't forget: the main victims are the Palestinians themselves. They are forced by the Arab world to a sad existence: discriminated against and imprisoned in camps. As Syrian former Prime Minister Khalid al-'Azm wrote in his memoirs:
"It is we who made them leave. We brought disaster upon Arab refugees, by inviting them and pressured them to leave. We have rendered them dispossessed. We have accustomed them to begging. We have participated in lowering their moral and social level."

Tale: Israel is responsible for the refugee problem.
Fact: The problem is artificially maintained – everywhere refugees are resettled and integrated, for example by the division of India and Pakistan.
Photo: Train of refugees, Punjab (India), 1947.

106. Refugees, numbers

The Palestinian Tale: There are more than five million Palestinian refugees.

According to the UN High Commissioner for Refugees of the United Nations (abbreviation: UNHCR) a refugee is someone that *"because of a well-founded fear of persecution remains outside his country of nationality."*
Under Arab pressure the UN has a different set of rules for the Palestinians than it has for any other group of refugees.

In the first place, most of them can hardly be called refugees; they are rather the descendant of refugees. It is sufficient for someone to have one parent or a grandparent or a great-grandparent who was a Palestinian refugee to be considered a refugee. In all other cases of refugees anywhere in the world, whether it is a Christian from Iraq or a family from Afghanistan, this curious rule does not apply. So that while other refugee problems tend to shrink over time, the number of Palestinian "refugees" has multiplied almost tenfold and will – inevitably – continue to grow. Meanwhile already one-third (!) of the total number of refugees worldwide are Palestinians. This is expected to result in 2040 in no less than 13 million Palestinian "refugees" – of which none will actually have fled.

This rule seems even more ridiculous when you consider that at the moment as many as two million of these "refugees" already are living in the autonomous Palestinian areas. In fact, they comprise 41.6 percent of the population there, according to the Palestinian Central Bureau of Statistics in 2016. So why are they considered 'refugees'? It is puzzling that they are living in their own territory, under their own Palestinian administration and legislation, they still be considered "refugees." Even more remarkable is that they have fewer rights in those Palestinian autonomous areas than the Palestinians who are not registered as refugees. Another 40 percent of all "refugees" live in Jordan, where the vast majority of them are full Jordanian citizens, so not real refugees either.

In the second place, many of such "refugees" were not even Palestinians, or are no longer so. The above mentioned regular international definition – a refugee must have the nationality of the country where he fled from – as we saw is not applied to Palestinian refugees. For them it was enough to have lived in Mandatory Palestine for at least two years. It means that many Egyptians, Bosnians, Syrians, Jordanians etc. that had come as guest workers to Palestine because of the favorable economic development and good medical facilities because of the Jewish contributions, transformed into "Palestinian" refugees.

Other "refugees" have since long acquired other nationalities. Such is the case in Lebanon where the reported number of Palestinians is almost double that of the actual number, the other half has already acquired a different nationality (see Tale: UN UNRWA). The fact that former Palestinian refugees then still retain their rights as "refugees" is a gross violation of the 1951 Convention on the Status of Refugees, which states that a person will no longer considered a refugee if he *"has acquired a new nationality."*

Then there are 'refugees' who did not live in the Mandate of Palestine, and therefore never have fled! Based on the population figures of 1948, it is possible to accurately reconstruct that about 600,000 Palestinian Arabs fled. Of those, tens of thousands if not hundreds of thousands of refugees could easily integrate in other countries and did so, like the Bedouins and wealthy Palestinians. Nevertheless, the organization of the United Nations for Palestine Refugees in 1950 registered 957,000 "refugees" in its care. So the number had almost doubled! This can only explained by the fact that poor, non-Palestinian Arabs also registered as "refugees," in order to benefit from the care provided by the United Nations – especially in Lebanon, Syria and Jordan. That this was indeed so, was noted in a report made by the UN itself in 1951 – without doing anything to change this travesty.

Thirdly, no one had to flee out of fear of persecution, as is required under the above mentioned UN definition. It was not necessary: to those who stayed peacefully, no harm happened and they became Israeli citizens. The reason to leave was mainly to avoid the fighting, as advised by the Arab leadership (see Tale: Expulsion of 1948). Thus said Iraqi Prime Minister Nuri Said, while the Iraqi army attacked Israel:
"We will smash the country with our guns and obliterate every place the Jews seek shelter in. The Arabs should conduct their wives and children to safe areas until the fighting has subsided."

In addition, in order to be considered as refugee, one should have had to flee to another country, according to the above criteria *"outside the country of nationality."* This is not the case by most of the Palestinians. Three-quarters of them went to another part of the territory of the Mandate of Palestine – namely the West Bank, Gaza or Jordan. Only a quarter left the Mandate of Palestine (mainly to Lebanon and Syria).

With this watered-down definition of a refugee, someone who was born in Gaza, worked in Haifa and who, because of the war, went back to his hometown in Gaza is counted as a refugee. This is not a far-fetched example. The economic boom started by the Jews attracted many Arabs, both from inside and outside the Mandate of Palestine.

Conclusion: If the normal, internationally recognized definition of a refugee – not yet helped and because of persecution having to flee outside the country of their own nationality – is used, there exist today only a very small number of Palestinian refugees.

Tale: There are more than five million Palestinian refugees.
Fact: Many so-called refugees are living in Palestinian autonomous areas.
Photo: Jalazone "refugee" camp in the West Bank.

107. Resistance

The Palestinian Tale: The Palestinian terrorists are like the European resistance fighters against the Nazi's of World War II.

The planned murder and intentional targeting of civilians is in no way a legitimate resistance and should never be regarded as such.

In May 1940, Nazi Germany invaded the Netherlands. After the devastating bombing of the city of Rotterdam the Dutch surrendered, after that the Nazis abolished the Dutch democracy and laws. From 1943 on, violent resistance against the Nazis increased: railways were blown up, population registries were attacked or destroyed, collaborators and high-ranking German military were liquidated.

The Germans often responded in a beastly manner to these acts of resistance. For example, almost the entire male population of the Dutch village of Putten was deported to concentration camps in 1944, after an attack on German officers by resistance fighters. Almost none of the villagers came back alive. Despite occasional operational accidents by European resistance fighters, their actions were for a rightful cause; they fought for the restoration of freedom and democracy. Moreover, their attacks targeted military objects: German soldiers, commanders, tanks and weapons depots.

German children, who of course could not help that someone like Adolf Hitler had come to power, were never a target of the European resistance. How different from our European resistance fighters, operates the radical Islamic terrorist movement. On October 4, 2003 the 28-year-old recently graduated lawyer Hanadi Jaradat walked inside the Maxim restaurant in the Israeli city of Haifa. There she blew herself up. As many as 21 people, Jews and Arabs, were killed. Among the dead were three children aged 4, 9 and 11 years old and a baby of just two months.

It's just one example in an endless series in which Palestinian terrorists almost exclusively focus their attacks on civilians, preferably children.

For example, 22 Israeli schoolchildren were killed by an attack on their school in Ma'alot in 1974, the baby Shalhevet Pass was slain by a Palestinian in 2001, 21 young people were slain in 2001 by a bomb attack on a disco in Tel Aviv, the 2-year-old Dutch Hemda Schijveschuurder was murdered with her parents, brother and sister in 2001 in a pizzeria in Jerusalem, the 5-year-old Danielle Shefi was murdered under her bed in 2002 where she had tried to hide from the Palestinian terrorists, the three-month old baby Hadas Fogel was, after her parents and two brothers had been killed, beheaded in 2011, the student Daniel Viflic was killed by an anti-tank grenade fired at his school bus in 2011, 13 year old Hillel Yafa Ariel in 2016 was killed while sleeping in her bedroom.

Nothing what the "fighters" of Hamas and other Palestinian terror organizations are doing, was done by the European resistance fighters. Despite how brutal and how violent the Germans often were – think of the above-mentioned example of Putten – there never was a Dutch resistance fighter that walked with five kilograms of explosives on his body into a German school to blow himself up together with innocent children.
To contrast that, between the years 2000 and 2005 blew 134 Palestinian "fighters" themselves up amongst Israeli women and children, resulting in 603 innocent victims.

There is another big difference between the European and Palestinian "resistance fighters." The European resistance fought against the Nazi ideology, for freedom and democracy. How different are Hamas and the other organizations. In fact, Hamas has an ideology that is eerily similar to that of Nazism, as any honest reader of the Hamas Charter would surely admit (see Tale: Hamas). Organizations like Hamas, Islamic State and al-Qaeda are fighting to end freedom and bring oppression to their own people, with the establishment of an undemocratic Islamic state where freedom of speech does not exist, women and infidels are second-class citizens and homosexuals are thrown to their deaths from high buildings.

The planned murder and intentional targeting of civilians is terror, nothing else and therefore is not in accordance with the international laws of war under any circumstances (see Tale: Terror, right to).
This applies even more in this conflict, as the Palestinians have signed peace treaties with Israel, in which they have agreed to stop the terror and dismantle terrorist organizations in exchange for land and autonomy.

Therefore, it is awful to compare Palestinian terrorists to European resistance fighters.

European resistance fighters had respect for human life, that is why they were willing to put their own lives at risk in order to save innocent Jewish men, women and children. A more stark contrast, one between them and the Palestinian "fighters," is hard to fathom.

Tale: Palestinian terrorists are resistance fighters
Fact: Palestinian terrorists almost always target civilians.
Photo: The graves of the children killed in the Palestinian attack on their school in Ma'alot.

108. Right of return

The Palestinian Tale: There exists a right of return for refugees.

Such a right does not exist. As the UN agency for refugees (UNHCR) writes on its website, there are not one but three solutions to resolve refugee problems: repatriation, integration in the host country or integration into a third country.

Palestinians refer to UN Resolution 194 of the United Nations (1948), which states that refugees *"wishing to live in peace with their neighbors"* should be able to return. Refugees that do not want to return should be compensated for their lost possessions. However, this does not guarantee a "right of return," not even remotely.

Firstly, it is a resolution of the United Nations General Assembly. By definition, that assembly can only give recommendations; these are not binding and therefore there are no penalties for failure to fulfill them – they have no legal force and effect.
Secondly, so far there is very little evidence of Palestinian refugees who wish to live in peace with their Jewish neighbors (see Tale: Violence).
In the third place, the resolution also refers to the Jewish refugees from Arab countries (which were higher in number). It would be nice if all the refugees (or their descendants) would be compensated for their lost possessions, but that also holds true for the Jewish refugees, which were more numerous and have lost assets about twice the value of those of the Arab refugees.
Fourth, the UN resolution relates to the refugees from the war in 1948. Seventy years later, few of them are still alive.
Finally, the return of Arab refugees was immediately banned by the Arab leaders themselves, and was therefore impossible. Facilitating their return would include an implied recognition of the State of Israel. The Arab High Command, as the then leadership of the Palestinians called itself, said:
> *"It is inconceivable for the refugees to return to their homes. The very suggestion to do so is an attempt for those culpable for the problem to shun responsibility, and will serve as a first step to Arab recognition of the state of Israel and the idea of partition."*

For the same reason – it would mean recognition of Israel – all Arab countries at the time voted against UN Resolution 194 – which they now invoke to claim right of return! This is nothing more than irony and hypocrisy.

In their eyes, there was only one possible solution to the refugee problem: the destruction of Israel.

Tale: There exists a right of return for refugees.
Fact: This "right" does not exist, not even equally so for the Jewish refugees of 1948.
Photo: Israeli refugee camp for Jewish refugees from Arab countries.

109. Right to exist

The Palestinian Tale: Israel has no right to exist.

Israel was founded on the basis of:

- The recognition that the Jewish people – like other peoples – has the right to self-determination in the land where it is the majority.
- The recognition that elements of the Jewish people have continuously resided in the land for 3,000 years.
- International decisions by the League of Nations in 1922 and the United Nations in 1947.

Items 2 and 3 are quite unique. Few countries can boast of these origins, other than Israel. *In view of this, countries like Suriname and Australia have a lot less right to exist.*

Yet Israel is the only country in the world whose destruction is continuously called for, for instance by the ayatollahs in Iran.

> *"I first saw Palestine in 1939. There the neglect and ruin left by centuries of Ottoman misrule were slowly being transformed by miracles of labor and sacrifice...*
> *Israel was not created in order to disappear – Israel will endure and flourish. It is the child of hope and the home of the brave. It can neither be broken by adversity nor demoralized by success. It carries the shield of democracy and it honors the sword of freedom; and no area of the world has ever had an overabundance of democracy and freedom."*
> – John F. Kennedy, then President of the United States

Tale: Israel has no right to exist.
Fact: The land of Israel has for 3,000 years continuously been inhabited by Jews.
Photo: The mosaic floor of the synagogue at Ein Gedi, from the third century.

110. Roadblocks

The Palestinian Tale: Israeli roadblocks cause hours of delay in travel.

It is regularly claimed that Israel complicates the lives of the Palestinians in the West Bank by a multitude of checkpoints and roadblocks. Of course Israel had to set up roadblocks, not with the purpose to make the lives of the Palestinians difficult, but to stop terrorist attacks. Between 2000 and 2005, during the second intifada (Palestinian uprising), over a thousand innocent Israeli men, women and children were killed in more than a hundred (suicide) attacks.

However, the construction of the security fence has created a kind of border. There the checks are now made, like other countries do at the border. Since the fence stops most terrorists, the roadblocks and controls are less and less necessary, and so they have decreased steadily. The number was reduced from hundreds during the second intifada to 48 in 2008. Since 2012, under normal circumstances there are no more roadblocks, and Palestinians throughout the West Bank can travel without obstacles in the autonomous Palestinian territories.

Tale: Israeli roadblocks cause hours of delay in travel.
Fact: Normally, the checkpoints are no longer in operation (photo).

111. Sabra and Shatila

The Palestinian Tale: Israel killed Palestinians in the massacre of Sabra and Shatila.

This tale is a total distortion of the facts. It was Christian Arab militias who massacred hundreds of civilians in Sabra and Shatila in 1982. No Israeli soldier slew even one Palestinian. Christians behaved as cruelly as they did in these camps because a few weeks earlier the Palestinians had killed hundreds of Christians with axes and knives, in the Christian town of Damour.

The Israeli army was nearby at the time, but it is doubtful whether it could have prevented the events in Sabra and Shatila. Moreover, there was a war situation where many very difficult decisions about life and death were made under great pressure.
An Israeli investigation a few months after the incident found that the then Israeli defense minister Sharon nevertheless bore indirect responsibility because of negligence; he had not immediately responded to the signals that a massacre might have been taking place.

In that respect, the situation is similar to the massacre of Bosnian Muslims in Srebrenica (Yugoslavia), an area that was then under the protection of Dutch UN forces. There also was negligence on the part of the Dutch in responding to signals of an impending massacre. The Dutch responsibility is actually much larger: in Srebrenica many more Muslims were killed (at least 6,000), the massacre should have been easier to anticipate because the Dutch were already on the spot, the Dutch mission was precisely to protect the civilian population there, and it took seven years for the Netherlands to start an investigation by a parliamentary committee of inquiry (Israel investigated itself within 10 days. Likewise, the allegations that Moluccan train hijackers, who had already laid down their arms, were executed on orders of the Dutch minister for the interior in 1977 have not been seriously investigated for over 40 years.

Incidentally, you never hear anything about the real perpetrators – nor of the other 150,000 deaths from the Lebanese civil war between Palestinians and Lebanese Christians, Shiites and Sunnis. Only those deaths where a connection can be made to Israel are repeatedly brought up – while it was Arabs that massacred other Arabs in Sabra and Shatila.

Tale: Israel killed Palestinians in the massacre of Sabra and Shatila.
Fact: They were killed by Christian Phalangists.
Photo: Phalangists during a Mass in a training camp.

112. Safety fence, construction

Palestinian Tale: Israel is unique in that it needs a fence to keep people out.

Worldwide, there are many border and security fences. Some examples: the United States's fence against illegal Mexican immigrants, the fences of Spain, Greece, Norway and Hungary against illegal immigrants, the Great Wall of China, India's fence against Pakistan's terrorists, Saudi Arabia's fence against Yemeni terrorists, the fence that divides Cyprus into a northern and a southern section, and so on. Why does only the Israeli fence outrage?

Tale: Only Israel has fences.
Fact: Dozens of countries have border fences.
Photo: The border fence between Spain and Morocco.

113. Safety fence, necessity

The Palestinian Tale: The purpose of the security fence is to make life miserable for Palestinians.

Countries have the right to build security fence against terrorists, and many do so (see Tale: Safety fence, construction).

The need for the security fence cannot be reasonably disputed. In the 34 months prior to the construction of the fence – from September 2000 to July 2003 – 73 terrorist assaults were perpetrated by terrorists from the West Bank, in which 293 Israelis were murdered and 1,950 were injured.

After the construction of the fence, the number of terrorist assaults decreased enormously, by more than 90 percent.

Therefore the fence has probably already saved the lives of thousands of Israelis and prevented many more injuries. Also, there is now much less need for Israeli anti-terror operations, so many Palestinians lives were spared too.

Opponents point to a negative, although non-binding, advisement of the International Court of Justice. That response, however, was made to a highly partisan question of the United Nations General Assembly – where virtually any motion directed against Israel can count on an automatic majority (see Tale: United Nations). So the Israeli argument of self-defense was disregarded, and the Palestinian terrorism that necessitated the fence was not condemned.

The Court even contradicted itself in the ruling. On the one hand, it declared that Article 51, on the right to self-defense, was not applicable because it was not a conflict between two UN member states. Nevertheless, the Court ultimately gave an opinion, while it usually only handles disputes between two sovereign states.

The Israeli Supreme Court, having considered the international law, came to the conclusion:
> *"It is permitted, by the international law applicable to an area under belligerent occupation, to take possession of an individual's land in order to erect the separation fence upon it, on the condition that this is necessitated by military needs. To the extent that construction of the fence is a military necessity, it is permitted, therefore, by international law. Indeed, the obstacle is intended to take the place of combat*

military operations, by physically blocking terrorist infiltration into Israeli population centers."

The route of the fence was determined carefully, partly because Palestinians can appeal the Israeli Supreme Court if they disagree with the planned course of the fence. Because of this, about 99 percent of the Arabs in the West Bank live on the Palestinian side of the fence. And now – because violence has quieted down a lot – most Israeli roadblocks in the West Bank are no longer in use (see Tale: Roadblocks), which benefits the Arabs in the West Bank by shortening travel times.

Further, opponents call it a wall. That is incorrect. Only 5 percent consists of a wall, and that is only at locations where gunmen could take Israeli housing under fire from across an open fence.

Opponents even nonsensically call it an "apartheid wall." Before the massive Palestinian terror, there was no fence. And when the terror will stop, Israel would be very happy to demolish the fence. It costs a fortune to guard the fence and checkpoints. And, of course, Palestinians can still go into in Israel. As the Tale "Economy, Palestinian" shows, about 100,000 Arabs from the West Bank go to work for Israeli employers daily.

Tale: The safety barrier consists of a solid wall.
Fact: Where there are no houses to protect against sniper fire, it is not a wall but a fence (photo).

114. Saudi peace initiative

The Palestinian Tale: It is incomprehensible that Israel rejected the Saudi peace initiative.

The Saudi peace initiative was made shortly after the attacks of September 11, 2001, when Saudi Arabia was on the defensive because of the news that 15 of the 19 hijackers proved to be Saudis. Therefore, Saudi Arabia wanted to make a positive-looking gesture. So, it is questionable how serious the Saudi peace initiative really was.

The proposal contains two elements which, everyone knows, are unacceptable to Israel, but which according to Saudi Arabia cannot be negotiated.

The first is the return to the armistice lines of 1949. Apart from the safety aspect, Israel will not give up the old Jewish quarter of Jerusalem. By doing so it would agree to the ethnic cleansing, for the second time, of the centuries-old Jewish Quarter of Jerusalem. This was done before by the Jordanian army, in 1948, so that from then on the Jews could not pray anymore at their holiest place of worship, the Wailing Wall.

The second element relates to the "return" of the descendants of the six hundred thousand Palestinian refugees of 1948, a total of 5 million people. The inclusion of all these Palestinian offspring is contrary to the idea of the two-state solution – each people its own state. Most of these "refugees" are already living in the West Bank and the Gaza Strip – and it would mean the demographic destruction of Israel.

The biggest problem with the peace initiative of the Arab League was the way it was delivered: non-negotiable and Israel had to act first and then wait and see what would become of the Arab promises. The Arab League did not even react when Israeli Prime Minister Ariel Sharon offered in response to attend the Arab League 2002 summit. An offer of Prime Minister Netanyahu to negotiate was likewise rejected in 2016 by the Arab League.
And in general, there has been not much proof of an Arabic desire for peace. The economic boycott of Israel by Arab countries still exists, as do the political and cultural boycotts.

For instance, this was demonstrated in October 2014 by Saudi MBC television. During a broadcast of the Arab version of *Idols* the program showed a map of the Middle East that included Israel because two participants were Israeli Arabs. After furious reactions, however, the network made apologies to its hundreds of millions of Arab viewers and from then on the two participants were called "Palestinians." And Israel was taken from the map of the Middle East and replaced by "Palestine." Likewise, in 2015 Saudi Arabia broke its contract with a Portuguese air carrier because it had ordered an overhaul of an aircraft in Israel.

Tale: It is incomprehensible that Israel rejected the Saudi peace initiative.
Fact: It is questionable whether a real desire for peace is behind it.
Photo: Hitler's *Mein Kampf* in a bookstore in Indonesia, it is a bestseller in the Islamic world.

115. Second Intifada

The Palestinian Tale: The Second Intifada (uprising) was caused by Ariel Sharon's visit to the Temple Mount.

This is completely untrue, as the international Commission headed by US Senator Mitchell concluded in its official report.
How could Sharon's half-hour-long walk cause this much violence? These attacks were planned far in advance, and the plans of attack were already verifiably publicized. Months before the visit, international media reported that then Palestinian leader Yasser Arafat was planning violent attacks. These articles are still on the Internet, for instance: *Arafat talks of battles in a few weeks* and *Palestinians prepare for September war.*

These messages date from about three months before the start of the second intifada. By then, it was already generally known that Arafat was preparing violence. As these articles show, Arafat's aim was to begin a second intifada, after torpedoing the American peace proposals of the year 2000. He intended to divert attention from that failure.
Incidentally, many Palestinian leaders admitted this in public, from Hamas leaders to Arafat's widow – see the interview with her on Dubai TV on December 16, 2012.

And so it happened. Those 4,000 Palestinians and Israelis who were killed during the second intifada were not a result of Sharon's visit – this violence was planned in advance and led by Arafat.
In 2015, the PLO and the Palestinian Authority were sentenced to pay $218 million compensation to victims with the US nationality for specified Palestinian terrorist attacks. The US court found convincing evidence for the responsibility of the Palestinian leadership in those assaults during the Second Intifada.

This is another case of Arab projection, in which Israel is blamed of something where the Arabs are guilty themselves. It was Arafat who knowingly started the violence of the Second Intifada.

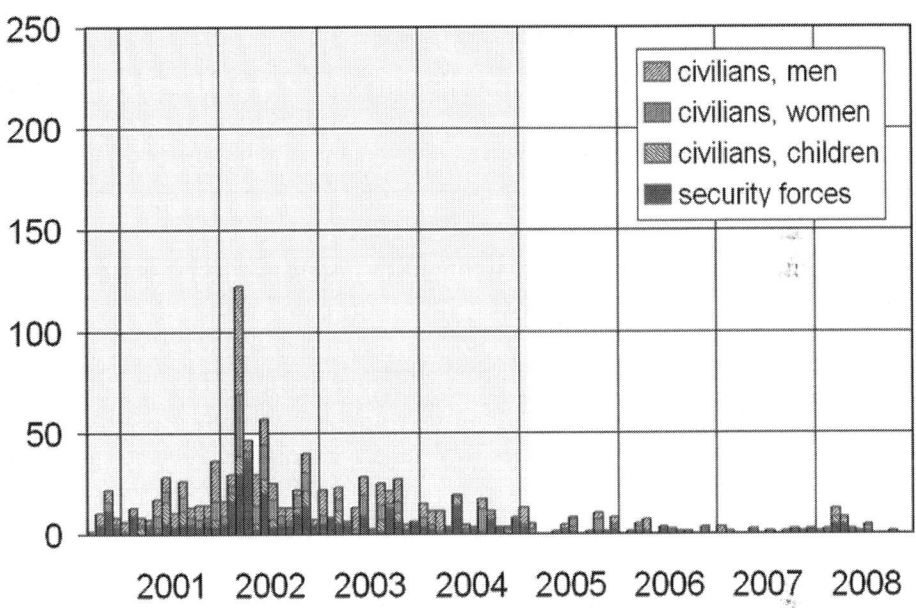

Tale: The Second Intifada was triggered by anger about Ariel Sharon's visit to the Temple Mount. Fact: The terrorist attacks went on for years and only subsided after the construction of the security fence (graph).

116. Settlement construction

The Palestinian Tale: Israel massively builds new settlements and houses in the West Bank, leaving no room for the Palestinians.

This Tale you can read regularly: Israel builds and builds still more, and has done so for 50 years now. The impression thus created is that all the space in the West Bank is occupied by Israel. But in reality, according to a brief look at Google Maps, Israeli housing – even after 50 years of construction – covers not even 2 percent of the area of the West Bank. The largest "settlement" is Pisgat Ze'ev – in reality a suburb of Jerusalem – with a population of 50,000. By the way, it was built on land that was purchased by Jews in the 1930s.

And new settlements are almost no longer being built. Even the Israeli Peace Now movement – which opposes the settlements – had to acknowledge this in a report of April 19, 2012; since 1990, only three settlements have been newly built.

In the negotiations for a final peace treaty, there is a considerable degree of consensus on the partition of the West Bank. This is clear from leaked documents. Israel will keep a small percentage of the West Bank – the areas where almost only Jews live – in exchange for territory elsewhere (see also the Tale: West Bank claims).

Israel's urban planners are not stupid and therefore do not build houses (anymore) in places which they know Israel will possibly have to leave. Building therefore takes place almost exclusively in areas which everyone involved acknowledges will remain part of Israel. So building homes in existing settlements is not a *"threat to the peace process,"* another Palestinian Tale that often can be heard.

And how about the impression that huge numbers of new houses are being built?

To begin, one must know that in Israel – as in other democratic countries – there exist comprehensive, long-term bureaucratic procedures for new construction. In total, as many as eight phases must be completed, from the approval of the zoning to the publication of the plan in several newspapers:

1. The approval of the zoning (or modification thereof) through an assessment by the relevant municipality.

2. The approval of the zoning through an assessment by the relevant province.
3. The submission of the building plan and its publication in several newspapers.
4. Consideration of any objections submitted.
5. The approval of the (modified) building plan through an assessment by the relevant province.
6. The publication of the final plan in various newspapers. Fifteen days after publication, the construction plan is valid.
7. The launching of the tender among contractors of the construction plan.
8. The application for planning permission by the contractor who has been awarded the project tender and the construction permit itself.

By no means will all plans be realized. In any phase, construction plans may be partially abandoned, and this happens regularly. This sometimes results in a new building plan for the same location, and that also will be repeatedly reported in the media.

This is the explanation of how it was possible for anti-Israeli circles to circulate – by adding up all these construction phases for the same houses – a figure of 14,000 new homes that were planned during the nine months of the last peace negotiations in 2014. In this way, the impression is created that Israeli construction efforts increase exponentially.

In reality fewer houses are being built in these territories than before because, as described above, houses are only built in areas in the West Bank where there already are existing Jewish neighborhoods and villages. Compared to 15 years ago, about half the number of houses are being built. It involves about a 1,000 homes a year, at most.

If such a small number of houses would be built anywhere else, this would get – understandably – no coverage in the media. But when it comes to Israel, you will read about these plans in newspapers, and sometimes even eight times about the same construction project.

Tale: Because of the settlements there is no room left for the Palestinians.
Fact: The construction of Israeli settlements covers less than 2 percent of the West Bank. Including the surrounding area, it is 3 percent.

117. Settlements

The Palestinian Tale: The settlements are illegal.

Israel suffers from the Arabs because of violence, incitement to genocide, rockets, terrorism and murder. The Palestinians say they mostly suffer from Jewish house construction. This is symbolic for this conflict: the Jews want to build, the Arabs want to destroy.

As described in the Tale "West Bank claims," there is no question of occupied territory there, but rather of disputed territory.

Also, Israel builds exclusively in areas that it governs lawfully under the Oslo peace accords of the 1990s. There is no ban on building there, although that is a Tale often heard. Demands that only non-Jews build in these areas testify to Arab racism.

The Palestinians base this Tale on the Fourth Geneva Convention, which prohibits the deportation of population to territory of another country. The West Bank, however, does not belong to another country; the British Mandate does not exist anymore and Jordan has surrendered its claim to it. The final partition of the area has yet to be agreed, as set forth in the internationally guaranteed Oslo accords (see Tale: West Bank claims). Moreover, there is no question of Israel's government forcibly deporting Jewish residents to the West Bank; those who live there volunteer to so do.

The allegations that the Israeli settlements are contrary to international law therefore are disputed. Many internationally renowned lawyers do not agree with this position, on the grounds above.

Important is this regard is also Resolution 242 of the United Nations from 1967. It states that Israel *"has the right to live in peace within secure and recognized borders."*

On this basis, Israelis settled primarily in military-strategic places on the west side of the West Bank. At its center, Israel before 1967 was only 15 kilometers wide, and because of this it was very easy for an enemy army to split it in two.

Therefore Israel was militarily very vulnerable to the many hostile actions from the Arab countries.

"I would like to see which international law has declared them illegal."
– Julie Bishop, Australian foreign minister and lawyer, 2014

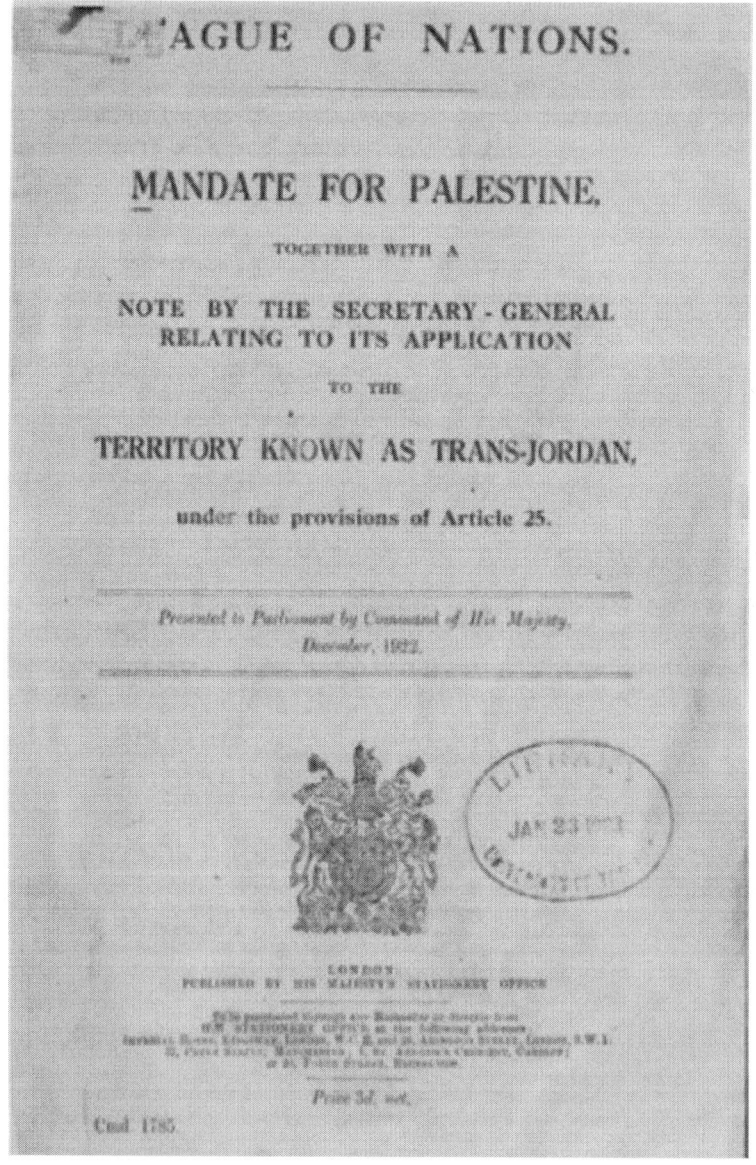

Tale: The settlements are illegal.
Fact: In the Mandate for Palestine (photo) this area was also assigned to the Jewish people.

118. Sexual harassment

The Palestinian Tale: Israeli women sexually harass Palestinian men.

The leading English-language Arab newspaper *Gulf News* published an investigation that concluded that Palestinian workers are sexually harassed by Israeli women on a massive scale:

"Palestinian laborers working in Israel are at a high risk of sexual harassment by Israeli women, according to a recent field study conducted by the Palestinian Central Bureau of Statistics. The study found that 77 percent of the Palestinian laborers in Israel had been subject to sexual harassment by Israeli women.

In an interview with Gulf News, *Shaher Saad, the President of the Union of the Palestinian Laborer Federations, said the Palestinians face a real problem with the laborers who work in Israel:*

'There are about 55,000 Palestinian laborers who enter Israel for work through illegal and unacceptable methods. The real focus needs to go to those illegal labourers who get sexually harassed.'

Saad said his union has come up with extensive programs to raise the awareness of the Palestinian laborers, mainly targeting illegal workers. 'AIDs is a key enemy fought by the union. The [female] Israelis only care for their joy and interests and pay no attention or consider judicial consequences when they handle Palestinian laborers.'"

A massive pandemic of Jewish women who seduce Palestinian men and transmit all kinds of venereal diseases; it sounds not very plausible. And it is not true. The story is based on completely distorted facts from the report *Risky behavior by workers* written by the United Nations in 2010.

The United Nations study intended to learn how much Palestinian Arab workers knew about safe sex. Indeed, according to the study 77 percent of Palestinian men who work in Israel said that they had been *"sexually harassed"*. However, these "sexual harassments" were interpreted very broadly in the study. Aside from actual sexual assault, it could also mean that a male Palestinian had seen an Israeli woman in shorts on the bus. Not being used to that, at home in the Palestinian territories, their imaginations could have run wild.

Harassment also appeared to apply more the other way, in another case of projection, in which Israelis are criticized of something that on the contrary is done by Arabs. In the study, many male Palestinians pointed out that they had gone to work in Israel in order to have sex, something that for unmarried men is almost impossible "at home." These men, for example, hung around in clubs or discos to take advantage of Jewish women, mostly of Russian origin because they are considered "easy." Apart from the sex itself, some wanted to gain experience with a Jewish Israeli woman. In this way they would learn how to perform after their wedding. The study finds that the sexual deprivation experienced by Palestinians in youth is an important factor in their risky behavior in Israel.

But there is yet another, very different factor, according to the above study. Some Arabs view sex with Jewish girls as a form of Jihad, as a way to punish and humiliate Jews.

It is distressing that this study of the United Nations has elicited not a word of criticism of the therein apparent Arab misogyny and anti-Semitism. Imagine that the investigation would have found the opposite, that Israeli men seek sex with Arab women to humiliate them. Would newspapers not for weeks been full of Israeli "feelings of superiority, misogyny and racism"?

Tale: Israeli women sexually harass Palestinian men.
Fact: Palestinian men are not accustomed to female exposure.

119. Six Day War

The Palestinian Tale: Israel started the Six Day War.

The Six Day War began on June 10, 1967. As anyone who followed the news at that time knows, it was the Arabs who consciously sought the confrontation with Israel. Almost daily, war language sounded from the Arab world.

Egyptian President Gamel Abdel Nasser said on May 26 and 28, 1967:
"Taking over Sharm el Sheikh meant confrontation with Israel (and) also meant that we were ready to enter a general war with Israel. The battle will be a general one and our basic objective will be to destroy Israel. Our basic objective will be the destruction of Israel. The Arab people want to fight.
We will not accept any coexistence with Israel. The war with Israel is in effect since 1948."

The president of Syria, Nureddin al-Attasi, proclaimed on May 22, 1967:
"We want a full-scale, popular war of liberation... to destroy the Zionist enemy."

Syrian Defense Minister Hafez Assad, father of the current president Bashar Assad, stated on May 20, 1967:
"The Syrian army, with its finger on the trigger, is united. I believe that the time has come to begin a battle of annihilation."

The president of Iraq, Abdel-Rahman Aref, confirmed on May 31 and June 1, 1967:
"The existence of Israel is an error which must be rectified. This is our opportunity to wipe out the ignominy which has been with us since 1948. Our goal is clear – to wipe Israel off the map. We shall, God willing, meet in Tel Aviv and Haifa."

The president of the Palestinian Liberation Organization, Ahmed Shukairy, spoke openly on June 1, 1967:
"This is a fight for the homeland – it is either us or the Israelis. There is no middle road. My impression is that none of them will survive."

Beginning years earlier, several Arab leaders had expressed themselves in similar words. Thus said the Egyptian president Nasser on March 8, 1965:

"We shall not enter Palestine with its soil covered in sand; we shall enter it with its soil saturated in blood."

So the threat existed already for years, and was widely supported in the Arab world. The final declaration of the Arab summit in September 1964 was:
"The Council was unanimous in defining national objectives for the liberation of Palestine from Zionist colonialism.
The Council welcomed the establishment of the Palestine Liberation Organization to consolidate the Palestine Entity, and as a vanguard for the collective Arab struggle for the liberation of Palestine. It approved the Organization's decision to establish a Palestinian Liberation Army."

Even long before the 1967 war, Israel was constantly attacked from Egypt and Syria. In 1965 there were 35 attacks from Egypt by Arab terrorists. In 1966 there were even more attacks: 41. And in the first four months of 1967 alone there were 37.

Syria was regularly shelling northern Israel. In April 1967, the Soviet Union gave (false) information to Syria that Israel was preparing for an attack on them. Syria then appealed to Egypt for military support, based on a treaty that bonded these countries.

On May 15, 1967, Egyptian President Nasser requested the United Nations to withdraw its peacekeeping force, which had acted as a buffer in the Sinai since 1956. His troops should in this way have clear passage to Israel: an evident proof that the Egyptian army planned attack. Without waiting for a resolution of the General Assembly – which his predecessor had promised if this request would be made – UN Secretary-General U Thant immediately granted this request. More than 50,000 Egyptian troops then marched in the direction of the southern Israeli city of Eilat.

The radio broadcaster of *Voice of the Arabs* noted, satisfied on May 18, 1967:
"As of today, there no longer exists an international emergency force to protect Israel. The sole method we shall apply against Israel is a total war which will result in the extermination of Zionist existence."

On May 22, 1967 Egypt set up a full military naval blockade of the port of Eilat, which was essential for Israel's fuel imports. According to the laws of war this has to be regarded as an act of war. The Egyptian state broadcast left no doubt about the intent:

"With the closing of the Straits [of Tiran], Israel faces two possibilities, both of which are blood-soaked: either it will die by strangulation in the wake of the Arab military and economic blockade, or it will die by shooting from the Arab forces surrounding it in the south, north and east."

Both the intention to attack and the first act of war came by the Arab countries. Because of this, Israel attacked the Egyptian and Syrian air force.

At the same time Israel made an urgent appeal to Jordan to stay out of the war. Israeli Prime Minister Levi Eshkol even made a personal appeal to the Jordanian King Hussein not to engage in combat operations. Nevertheless, Jordanian artillery shelled West Jerusalem from the West Bank, which had been in Jordanian hands since 1948. Israel fought back and then captured the West Bank. The Sinai desert and the Golan Heights were conquered from Egypt and Syria, respectively.

A further tale-within-a-tale: during the war, Israel shelled a US spy ship, the *Liberty*. It had sailed, in violation of American instructions (whereof Israel had been notified), within a 100-mile zone of the coast. It even came as close as 14 miles of the shore and was therefore mistaken for an Egyptian warship that was carrying out shelling in the area. Nevertheless the accusation that Israel had consciously strafed the ship keeps popping up, although 10 US and three Israeli investigations did not find any indication or proof of that.

Even after their massive defeat in the war the Arabs still refused to make peace with Israel, so Israeli Foreign Minister Abba Eban noted:
"I think that this is the first war in history that on the morrow the victors sued for peace and the vanquished called for unconditional surrender."

Tale: Israel started the Six Day War.
Fact: Egyptian President Nasser prepared this war for years.
Photo: Nasser with pilots of the Egyptian Air Force.

120. Suffering of Palestinians

The Palestinian Tale: Palestinians suffer terribly and that is Israel's fault.

The suffering of the Palestinians is quite relative. Contrary to propaganda stories about "appalling" living conditions, the quality of life of the average Palestinian is one of the highest in the Arab world, higher than in Turkey and higher even than in some European countries.

Economic prosperity is relatively high when compared to the rest of the Arab world (except the oil states, of course) thanks to Israeli employment (see Tale: Economy, Palestinian). There is no hunger (as is the case in neighboring Egypt) and there is hardly any illiteracy (in Egypt, 40 percent of the population is illiterate), 80 percent of Palestinians own a mobile phone and all schoolchildren receive a laptop from the United Nations.

The Israeli government's improvement of the standard of living and quality of life in the West Bank and the Gaza Strip between 1967 and 1993 is telling. Before that, in the period between 1948 and 1967, these territories were ruled by Jordan and Egypt, and practically without progress.

In the period of Israeli control after 1967, income per capita rose extraordinarily, far above that of the Arabs in surrounding countries: from approximately $450 in 1967 to about $2,250 in 1993, and these numbers are adjusted for inflation. That is an average growth of 5.5 percent per year, which is higher than the Israeli economy's expansion during that period.

Water pipes and connections to the electricity grid were built by Israelis. In the years between 1972 and 1992, the percentage of houses with running water rose from 24 percent to 79 percent in the West Bank and from 14 percent to 93 percent in the Gaza Strip. In the same period, the number of homes with access to electricity rose from 8 percent to 98 percent in the West Bank and from 35 percent to 98 percent in the Gaza Strip. Health care also improved greatly: the number of health centers increased from 113 to 378. Malaria was vanquished. The infant mortality rate fell by three-quarters: the number of Palestinian children who died prematurely decreased from 86 to 20 children per thousand births.

The percentage of children receiving education past primary school increased from 15 percent to 49 percent from 1967 onward. In the same period, the Israelis founded seven universities and colleges in the West Bank. Previously, there had been no institutes for higher education. After gaining autonomy in the region, the Palestinian government has built no new universities or hospitals.

The Palestinian people have a relatively high level of education; they have the highest percentage of university graduates among the Arab world.

After the Palestinians were granted autonomy in 1993, these developments came to a halt in the Palestinian territories which, in turn, resulted in an economic decline.

This decline was mainly due to the following four reasons: First, the number of terror attacks grew enormously, with many suicide attacks on buses, schools and shops. Israel was forced to limit free access of Palestinian guest workers for safety reasons: only married Palestinian men over a certain age were allowed into Israel. It was not a measure that Israel took eagerly: Israel has no interest in poverty among Palestinians. Moreover, this change of policy required to attract more expensive Eastern European workers.

The Hamas government obstructs Palestinians working for Israeli companies. The Erez industrial zone in Gaza, where 187 companies provided more than 5,000 well-paying jobs for Palestinians, was attacked from Gaza beginning in 2001. In the three years after 2001, five-hundred grenades launched by terror groups had rained down on the area, and companies abandoned their factories in 2004. The terror also greatly affected the Palestinian tourist industry.

Secondly, for political reasons, the building of new facilities for the Palestinian people was slowed down by the Palestinian leadership, in order to blame Israel. This occurs even if there is money available from development assistance. Examples include the construction of water treatment and water desalination plants (see Tale: Water theft).

Thirdly, there was a massive power divide, lack of legal security, and corruption in the Palestinian autonomous area (see Tale: Palestinian leaders). So every Palestinian entrepreneur must contribute a set amount of its sales to members of the regime. A true private sector is therefore almost nonexistent. A study of the Washington Institute for Near East Policy describes corruption as one of the biggest problems of Palestinian society.

Fourth, much money from the regime went to the oppressive security forces, which exercise a reign of terror. You would expect that in the Gaza Strip under Hamas, where everyone must behave according to the Muslim fundamentalist rules. But the same happens in the West Bank, where people are regularly tortured and oppressed. For instance, a person who put a picture of a soccer-playing President Abbas on his Facebook page was sentenced to a year in prison. In the West Bank there is also still a lot of money going to terrorist organizations to buy weapons and missiles.

In the Gaza Strip, most of the budget goes to military goals and oppressing the local population. Little money remains for institutions that benefit the population, such as schools or hospitals. All metal is used in the manufacturing of rockets, and building materials are used for war tunnels (the digging of these cost at least 160 Palestinian children their lives). Rather than being involved in violence and the waste of money for war purposes, Palestinian rulers could have greatly improved living standards in Gaza.

Again, this accusation is Arab projection, in which Israel is blamed for something which the Arabs cause themselves.

The bill for mismanagement is mostly paid by Western taxpayers (see Tale: Development aid). Incentives are perverse, because Palestinian mismanagement continues to be financially compensated by the West. Thus the Palestinian leadership can proceed unhindered on their path to self-destruction.

Tale: The Palestinians are suffering terribly.
Fact: In Gaza there is a lot of luxury.
Photo: BMWs cross the Israeli border at Kerem Shalom into Gaza.

121. Suicide bombers

The Palestinian Tale: Suicide bombers act out of despair.

It has repeatedly been scientifically proven that this is not true, neither for Palestinian terrorists nor other Islamic terrorists. Terrorists often come from middle or upper social classes and are better educated than average.

A study by Queen Mary University in 2014 found that Muslims who are fighting for IS are wealthier and better educated than average. Similarly, a World Bank Study found in 2016, after reviewing 3,800 recruits of Islamic State, that:
"Poverty is not a driver of radicalization into violent extremism... Recruits to Islamic militant groups are likely to be well educated and relatively wealthy, with those aspiring to be suicide bombers among the best off."

Many of the 19 September 11th hijackers were well educated; some even studied at German universities. It is not social conditions that determine whether someone becomes a terrorist, but ideology. Thus suggested British Prime Minister David Cameron during a speech in Birmingham on July 20, 2015:
"When they say that these are wronged Muslims getting revenge on their Western wrongdoers, let's remind them: from Kosovo to Somalia, countries like Britain have stepped in to save Muslim people from massacres – it's groups like ISIL, al-Qaeda and Boko Haram that are the ones murdering Muslims.
Now others might say: it's because terrorists are driven to their actions by poverty. But that ignores the fact that many of these terrorists have had the full advantages of prosperous families or a Western university education.
Now let me be clear, I am not saying these issues aren't important. But let's not delude ourselves. We could deal with all these issues – and some people in our country and elsewhere would still be drawn to Islamist extremism.
No – we must be clear. The root cause of the threat we face is the extremist ideology itself."

The terrorists usually do not act out of desperation, but on the contrary out of hope. They act with the hope to kill as many Jews as possible, hoping thereby to be Islamic "martyr," hoping thereby to enter the Islamic paradise, hoping to be served by 72 virgins there and hoping to invite family members into paradise.

So when in 2016 a Palestinian terrorist killed a 13-year old Israeli girl asleep in her bedroom and was then killed by Israeli security forces, his mother said her son was "a hero" that had "made her proud":

"Praise be to Allah, Lord of the Worlds, he has joined the martyrs before him, and he is not better than them. Allah willing, all of them will follow this path, all the youth of Palestine. Allah be praised."

See also Tale: Motherly love.

If the terrorist survives the attack, there await high financial rewards from the Palestinian Authority.

However, it's different for female Palestinian terrorists. Their motives were investigated by Dr. Anat Berko, a psychologist at the International Institute for Counter-Terrorism, through interviews in Israeli jails. She blames a Muslim society with twisted and contradictory ideas about family, honor and religion.

Berko spoke with the terrorist Wafa al-Biss, who wanted to commit a suicide attack, but whose bomb-belt faulted. Her father had always beaten her, causing her health problems. From the perspective of her parents, Wafa was *"damaged material"*; she couldn't get a man because she was raped twice, first when she was eleven and then at age sixteen. Therefore her own parents actually encouraged her to become a "martyr." In this way, they would get rid of a financial burden – and their family honor would be restored.

This appears to be a typical example of female suicide bombers. Politics rarely plays a real role. Of course, the constant brainwashing to which Palestinian children are exposed from an early age makes empathy with the Jewish victims absent. But the real reason why women have the wish to die this way is almost always of a social nature, usually with a sexual background. The attack is a way to escape from a private hell. Not infrequently bombers were raped first and then blackmailed like this: *"When I talk about it, you will be already be dead socially. So you had better go straight to paradise."*

Phyllis Chesler, emeritus professor of psychology and women's studies, wrote a book about repressive sexuality in contemporary Islamic culture, which results in widespread sexual abuse of children – both girls and boys – and gives rise to paranoid, traumatized and revenge-seeking adults.

Another source of sexual frustration is the polygamy (men marrying more than one wife) in many Islamic countries. A study by sociologist Diego Gambetta from Oxford University found that all societies that recognize polygamy are more violent; when some men have more wives, other men can't get any, and that leads to violent behavior. This also applies to non-Muslim societies.

Suicide attacks however, according to Gambetta, are a typical consequence of Islam, because of the promise of 72 virgins in Islamic paradise.

Tale: Palestinian suicide bombers act out of despair.
Fact: They act out of hope for the Islamic paradise for themselves and their relatives.
Photo: Suicide vest with explosives.

122. Talmud

The Palestinian Tale: The Talmud is a hateful book against non-Jews.

This Tale is widely distributed, for example in the comments sections following Internet articles on Israel. This anti-Semitic accusation is indeed very old; it originated in the Middle Ages to motivate the persecution of Jews.

The "quotes" from the Talmud are often totally distorted, invented or taken out of context. If the quotations are not considered in their context and are interpreted without Jewish religious knowledge, it is impossible to assess what is really meant by them. Jewish law, as recorded in the 6,200 pages of the Talmud, gives non-Jews full respect as *"created in the image of God."*

This Tale is nevertheless widely spread, as is emphasized by the fact that Dutch journalist Theo van Gogh was killed by a knife to which was attached a letter; in it, van Gogh's Islamic murderer repeated exactly these accusations. The killer wrote it with references to the Talmud:

"What do you think of the fact that [Dutch politician] Van Aartsen supports an ideology in which non-Jews are depicted as non-humans? What do you think of the fact that the mayor at the helm in Amsterdam subscribes to an ideology where Jews may lie to non-Jews? What do you think of the fact that you are part of a government that supports the state with an ideology that advocates genocide?"

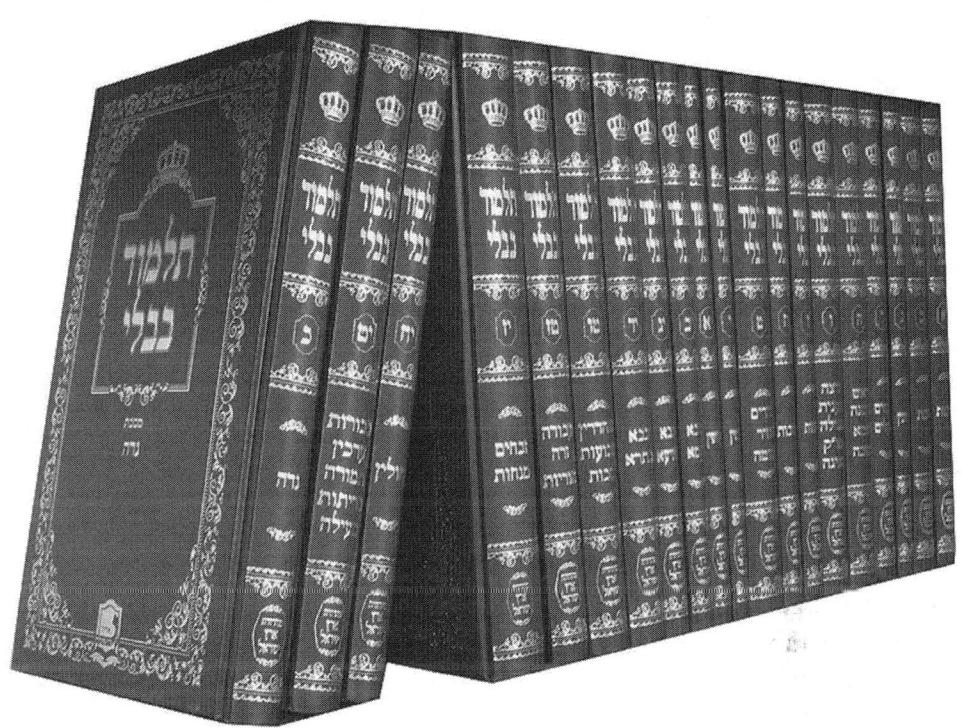

Tale: The Talmud is a hateful book against non-Jews.
Fact: The Talmud (photo) consists of 6,200 pages of discussions and therefore requires extensive knowledge of rabbinic legal texts to understand.

123. Temple Mount

The Palestinian Tale: The Jews want to destroy the mosque on the Temple Mount.

This Tale is very old and resurfaces often. The Grand Mufti (most senior Islamic cleric) of Jerusalem, Amin Al-Husseini, spread it way back in 1929, when it caused numerous pogroms against Jews throughout the British Mandate in which more than a hundred Jews were slaughtered (see Tale: Nazism). The Dutch-Canadian journalist Pierre van Paassen was in the country and wrote about the massacre in Hebron in 1929:

> *"Falsified photographs showing the Omar mosque of Jerusalem in ruins, with an inscription that the edifice had been bombed by the Zionists, were handed out to the Arabs of Hebron as they were leaving their place of worship on Friday evening, August the twenty-third. A Jew passing by on his way to the synagogue was stabbed to death. An hour later the synagogue was attacked by a mob, and the Jews at prayer were slaughtered."*

In 1996, Israel opened an ancient Jewish tunnel near the Western Wall to tourists. New evidence of historic Jewish presence, now visible to all, was again a sore spot for the Palestinians.

Palestinian leaders incited the public on the grounds that this tunnel would undermine the structure of the Al-Aqsa Mosque on the Temple Mount. Utter nonsense; the tunnel does not run under the mosque and had already been there for more than 2,000 years! But that did not stop the former Palestinian leader Yasser Arafat to describe the opening of the tunnel as *"a great crime against our religion and holy place."* During the subsequent riots more than a hundred people were killed.

In 1969 a mentally deranged Australian Christian set fire to the Al-Aqsa Mosque on the Temple Mount. There was limited damage; for example, a historic pulpit was burned. This fact is still used every year to keep the fire burning against the Jews. Thus reported the official Palestinian television on August 21, 2013:

> *"From investigations conducted by the Islamic Council it became clear that there was more than one perpetrator and that the fire was planned by senior Jews of high position."*

The accusation that the Jews plan to destroy the mosque is endlessly repeated. In an August 3, 2012, broadcast on official Palestinian television the presenter states:

> *"Experts on the Al-Aqsa Mosque and Jerusalem issued warnings that there are traces of chemicals under Al-Aqsa, which the occupation authorities are using in intensified excavations around the foundations of the Al-Aqsa Mosque in order to dissolve them.*
> *Israel's policies and schemes have never stopped and will never stop in Al-Aqsa's courtyards and surroundings in order to harm [the Mosque's] Arabness and holiness. What is new this time is the discovery of traces of dangerous chemicals in the Al-Aqsa foundations and other solvents used to cause the foundations to crumble and collapse in accordance with step-by-step plans."*

The Palestinian government is actively supporting this Tale. In a broadcast on official Palestinian television on February 25, 2014, the Palestinian minister of religious affairs, Mahmoud Al-Habbash, said of the Al-Aqsa Mosque on the Temple Mount:

> *"Israel is following a systematic, gradual plan supported by the Israeli government and protected by the Israeli army.*
> *Its goal is to remove the Al-Aqsa Mosque. As the final goal, they don't want to see the shining, golden, elegant Dome of the Rock."*

After this kind of constant brainwashing, it is not surprising that 86 percent of the Palestinians believe in this Tale (figure from a poll conducted by the Palestinian Center for Policy and Research in 2014).

It is a case of Arab projection, in which Israel is wrongly criticized of something that the Arabs do themselves. In reality, the Palestinians have wreaked enormous devastation on the Temple Mount, in order to erase the archaeological traces of the historical Jewish presence (see Tale: Archaeology).

Tale: Israel wants to destroy the mosque on the Temple Mount.
Fact: Israel has never done anything to damage the mosque.
Photo: The tunnel had already been there for more than 2,000 years.

124. Terror, cause

The Palestinian Tale: Terror against Israelis is the result of the Israeli occupation.

This is very obviously a Tale. The terror had started well before 1967, when the West Bank and Gaza were still under Arab control – occupied by Jordan and Egypt. Already then the terror was not directed against the Jordanian or Egyptian occupation, but against Israeli civilians in Israel. Thus in the 1950s – before the "occupation" – twice as many Israelis were killed by terrorists as in the 1980s – when there was "occupation."

The terror even started already in the 1920s, under the influence of a mixture of Islamic fundamentalism, Nazism and Arab nationalism (see Tale: Nazism).
That was almost 50 years before Israel got possession of the West Bank and the Gaza Strip – and 30 years before the State of Israel was founded.

So this proves that terrorism is not aimed against "occupation," but purely against the Jews (see Tale: Hamas). The PLO and Fatah were already formed before 1967 for that purpose, when there existed not one "settlement." And even after the Israeli withdrawal from Gaza, the terror from there continued and even intensified.

Incidentally, the Oslo peace accords have granted 98 percent of the Palestinians self-government. In return, the Palestinians pledged to renounce violence. Any act of violence is a Palestinian violation of the peace accords.

Muslim fanatics can always invent reasons explaining that Muslims are victims of some injustice and that is the reason that people of other faiths should be killed. In fact, the reason for their hatred is the mere existence of people with other faiths – including Shiites, Christians, Yazidis, and Jews – in the Middle East.

Tale: The terror is the result of the Israeli occupation.
Fact: Long before the "occupation" in 1967 there were already constant terrorist attacks.
Photo: An attack on an Israeli bus in 1954, which killed 11 of the 15 passengers.

125. Terror, right to

The Palestinian Tale: Palestinians are entitled to commit terror.

For this perceived right the Palestinians invoke UN Resolution 3236, which *"recognizes the right of the Palestinian people to regain its rights by all means."*

For example, a member of the Central Committee of Fatah, Abbas Zaki, said in a broadcast on January 1, 2013, on official Palestinian television, that this includes the right to armed struggle – Palestinian terminology for terror. Unfortunately, Abbas Zaki has only read half of the relevant sentence of Resolution 3236, for in the other half it says that these means have to be *"in accordance with the purposes and principles of the Charter of the United Nations."*

That UN charter prohibits deliberate attacks on civilians, even in war.
The Charter clearly states: *"All Members shall settle their international disputes by peaceful means."*

A terrorist fights without recognizable uniform, which is contrary to the laws of war. A terrorist targets civilians instead of soldiers, which is a war crime too. In this way, a terrorist is acting outside the law.

Palestinians who defend terror still like to call it the *"struggle against the occupation."* Small detail: the Palestinians are no longer occupied. A whopping 98 percent of Palestinians live in an autonomous region under self-rule. This autonomy is greater than the autonomy of, for instance, the Scots or the Catalans. And in exchange for autonomy, the Palestinians declared to renounce violence and are obliged to achieve a peaceful solution to the conflict, by negotiations for a final peace treaty.

That is precisely the problem that the international community – the Quartet: UN, EU, US and Russia – have with Hamas; that it does not honor that obligation. Therefore, this group of countries formulated three entirely reasonable conditions for Hamas to be acceptable to join negotiations: renouncing violence, recognizing Israel and honoring previously signed peace agreements. Thus, the major world players – the UN, the EU, the US and Russia – rebut this Palestinian Tale.

Tale: Palestinians have a right to commit terror.
Fact: Targeting of civilians is never allowed.
Photo: The remains of a disco at the seashore in Tel Aviv. It was blown up in 2001, and 21 people, mostly teenagers, were killed.

126. Terrorists

The Palestinian Tale: Terrorist violence is abhorred in Palestinian society.

Contrary to the Tale, approximately 80 percent of Palestinians support violence against civilians by Palestinian terrorists (see Tale: Violence). The glorification of terrorism and terrorists is central to Palestinian society. Assassins are the role models for Palestinian youth.

Imagine you decide to go shopping in the Palestinian city of Ramallah in the West Bank. When you have parked your car, you walk to the busy Abu Jihad Street, in the center of Ramallah, which is full of nice shops. That street is named after Abu Jihad, the mastermind behind many assaults on random Israeli civilians.

Or imagine you are a Palestinian boy of sixteen, living in Yaabad in the West Bank, and are a big fan of Real Madrid. Then as a student of the *Martyr Saddam Hussein school* you register, of course, for the football tournament in Tulkarem in memory of Abd Al-Basset, a terrorist who murdered 31 innocent civilians at a Passover Seder.

If you are a Palestinian boy who doesn't love football, you might take up fencing. Every year, the Palestinians in the West Bank organize the Abu Iyad fencing championship, named after the man who was in charge of the terrorist group that plotted the deadly attack on the Israeli Olympic team in Munich Olympics in 1972. Eleven Israeli Olympic athletes, coaches, and delegation members were killed as a result. Iyad's merit for sponsoring a fencing championship is apparently that under his leadership his group got Israel's Olympic fencing coach, Andre Spitzer, killed.

Terrorists that are convicted for murder in Israel receive a generous salary for the rest of their lives as a reward. The longer the sentence (the more Israelis killed) – the higher the reward. Mass murderers receive a salary equal to that of a Palestinian secretary of state or general. So, 6 percent of the Palestinian government budget is spent on these stipends – paid for with "development aid," mostly from Europe.

A statement by the official Palestinian news agency on December 27, 2012, confirmed that these salaries are paid as a reward: *"The government headed by Salam Fayyad considers the prisoners' cause as central, and has authorized regulations to support and protect them **out of esteem for their sacrifice and struggle**."*

The official Palestinian television shows programs that highlight imprisoned killers, to honor them. To name only one albeit horrible example, on January 19, 2012, there was a broadcast to honor of the murderers of the Israeli Fogel family. The father, mother and three of their young children were brutally killed with knives. The youngest member of this family, the three-month-old baby Hadas, had her throat slit with a knife. In the broadcast, the murderers were called "heroic" and "legendary."

There has been an uproar and motions in several countries to withhold the money that is funding Palestinian terrorists. In July 2016, Frank Lowenstein, the US special envoy for Israeli-Palestinian negotiations, told Bloomberg that the US has recently started withholding funding for this reason:

"We have robustly complied with legislation passed in 2014 that requires us to deduct from development assistance to the Palestinian Authority for Palestinian payments to individuals imprisoned for acts of terrorism."

The amount of development assistance that has been withheld is classified.

However, nothing has changed. On the contrary, at the early release of some Palestinian prisoners – as a goodwill gesture on Israel's part to relaunch peace negotiations in 2013 and 2014 – they were welcomed as heroes. With each release the Palestinian Authority celebrated, and Palestinian President Abbas went out to meet the prisoners personally and to kiss them. Every time, he called the killers "heroes."

What heroic feats had these freed terrorists performed? Well, for example, the stabbing of a 76-year-old Israeli man who was working in his garden. Or the throwing of a Molotov cocktail at an Israeli car, burning a mother and her son alive.

But according to the Palestinian government, murderers of Israelis cannot be regarded as murderers. Thus spoke the Palestinian minister of religious affairs Mahmoud Al-Habbash on official Palestinian television on March 28, 2014:

"All the Palestinian prisoners who protected [our] land, honor and homeland are prisoners of freedom; they are prisoners of war. They are not criminals, will never be and have never been.

Their hands committed no crime.
They were defending themselves. They are an inseparable part of this national Palestinian movement and one of its authentic elements."

This same minister said the exact opposite in English to Western journalists: *"We condemn the killing of any person. The principle of killing and violence is completely unacceptable."*

So this is an example of the double tongue of Palestinian leaders. In English they talk about peace, and in Arabic they encourage violence.

Terror is promoted; Tawfiq Tirawi, a member of Fatah's Central Committee, confirmed this goal in a speech broadcasted on official Palestinian television on December 19, 2013:

"I say, from a position of responsibility, that not a centimeter of Jerusalem will be liberated unless every grain of Palestinian soil is soaked in the blood of its brave people."

Tale: Terrorist violence is abhorred in Palestinian society.
Fact: Terrorists are revered as heroes.
Photo: Released terrorists are welcomed by Palestinian President Abbas.

127. Torah

The Palestinian Tale: The Torah (the Old Testament) orders Jews to commit violence and murder.

This Tale you hear even in Europe. For example, a Dutch journalist wrote in a national daily that *"radical orthodox parties would prefer to hunt Palestinians by to the sword, like in the Old Testament."*

In the Torah there is a lot of violence. But that does not mean that violent behavior is encouraged in Judaism. On the contrary, in the Torah it is written:
"When a foreigner resides among you in your land, do not mistreat him.
The foreigner residing among you must be treated as your native-born. Love them as yourself, for you were foreigners in Egypt."
– Vayikra / Leviticus 19:33-34

The Talmud tells that two thousand years ago someone asked the famous Rabbi Hillel to summarize the Torah as succinctly as possible. He replied: *"That what you do not want done to you, you should not do to your fellow."*
He added: *"That is the whole Torah; the rest is the commentary; go and learn."*

The Jews were the first people in the world to abolish the death penalty, already in the year 30, thus almost two thousand years ago. The most important Jewish religious scholar Maimonides wrote eight centuries ago that: *"It is better and more satisfactory to acquit a thousand guilty persons than to put a single innocent one to death."*

Compare that to the United States, where capital punishment is a legal penalty, currently used by 31 states and by the federal government.

This is a case of Arab projection, whereby something Israel is accused of misdeeds the Arabs are doing. For Arab countries often do have the death penalty, even for transgressions like adultery, sorcery or homosexuality. Muslim fundamentalist groups, such as Islamic State and Hamas, invoke their faith in order to kill. For example, in a sermon in the Gaza Strip which was broadcasted by the official Hamas television station on July 25, 2014:

"Our belief about fighting you [Jews] is that we will exterminate you, until the last one, and we will not leave of you even one.
For you are the usurpers of the land, foreigners, mercenaries of the present and of all times.
Look at history, brothers: Wherever there were Jews, they spread corruption: 'They spread corruption in the land, and Allah does not like corrupters [quote from Koran].'"

The Sanhedrin.

Tale: The Torah (the Old Testament) orders Jews to commit violence and murder.
Fact: The Sanhedrin (Jewish Supreme Court) abolished the death penalty 2,000 years ago.
Photo: The Sanhedrin according to an illustration from 1883.

128. Tourism

The Palestinian Tale: Israel is a country with a terrible atmosphere.

Israel is a hot spot for tourists because there is so much to enjoy in nature, culture, beaches, good food, religion and history.

Everyone is free to experience these in their own way. Tel Aviv was chosen in 2012 as the most LGBTQ-friendly city in the world. At that time, Tel Aviv surpassed Amsterdam – the city that previously held this title. In 2015, Israel ended in the seventh place in a global measurement of how well gay men feel they are treated in their home country. The United Kingdom was in 23rd place and the United States in 26th place (of the 30 worst countries, 27 were Muslim countries).

The atmosphere in Israel is very different from the false picture that emerges from the media. In 2014, British tourists who had visited Israel for the first time were surveyed. A mere 27 percent of tourists felt that their experience of Israel matched their expectations. A whopping two thirds (65 percent) assessed Israel to be more positive than they had expected before visiting. An even higher percentage (78 percent) said they wanted to visit Israel again, and 8 percent responded that they would recommend Israel to others as a vacation destination.

Tale: Israel is a country with a terrible atmosphere.
Fact: Tourists are surprised by how different Israel is in reality over its portrayal in the media.
Photo: Beach of Tel Aviv.

129. Two-state solution

The Palestinian Tale: Palestinians accept the two-state solution.

The idea of two separate states as a possible solution for the conflict is very old. In 1937, a British commission concluded – after ten years of Arab violence – that this was the only possible solution for the different wishes of Jews and Arabs. A proposal was made for a tiny Jewish state and an Arab state. The Jews agreed, but the Arabs rejected the proposal.

Arab leaders at the time said there was no such thing as Palestine, as it had never existed. What the British called Palestine, in their opinion, was southern Syria. The area should not become independent but should become a part of Syria.

In a statement, Palestinian leader Al-Husseini (see Tale: Nazism) stated that not an inch of "Islamic" country could ever be ceded, according to Islam. Also, there was no agreement that could be signed with the Jews, because:

> *"The Arabs have learned best how they really are, that is, as they [the Jews] are described in the Koran and in the sacred scriptures. The verses from the Koran and Hadith [Islamic tradition] prove to you that the Jews have been the bitterest enemies of Islam and continue to try to destroy it."*

Because of this, a Palestinian state was scuttled.

The idea was then picked up by the United Nations, in the Partition Plan of 1947 (see that Tale). This peace plan was also rejected by the Arabs, so again a Palestinian state did not come into existence. The Arabs then began a war to destroy the newly established Jewish State of Israel.

In that war, Jordan and Egypt conquered the West Bank and the Gaza Strip. The Jews who had lived there for 3,000 years were expelled. Egypt and Jordan had then, in 1948, the possibility to give these two areas to the Palestinian Arabs, as the United Nations had proposed in the Partition Plan. If that had happened, a Palestinian state would have been established in 1948. However, Jordan annexed the entire West Bank with all its Palestinian inhabitants and Egypt kept the Gaza Strip. The Palestinian Arabs thus got nothing, but became residents of these two Arab countries. In 1949, Israel asked, as part of the truce talks with the Arab countries, for self-determination for the Palestinian Arabs. The answer was: this is not open for discussion.

After the 1956 war Israel asked again for peace talks. It was rejected by the Arab countries.
In 1964 the PLO was founded with the goal to destroy Israel.

In 1967, Egypt, Jordan and Syria began another war against Israel. Israel won this war and captured the West Bank and the Gaza Strip, which for 19 years had been occupied by Jordan and Egypt. Israel wanted – in accordance with the binding Resolution 242 of the UN – to return these territories in exchange for peace with the Arab countries. That, however, was immediately rejected by the Arab countries with the three no's of their Khartoum conference: *"No peace with Israel, no recognition of Israel, no negotiations with it."*

Again a chance for a Palestinian state passed, and again this was caused by the Arabs themselves.

After the 1973 war, Israel again asked for peace talks. And, again, these were rejected by the Arab countries.

In 1979, after more than fifty years of violence, peace talks were held for the first time. However, these were only with Egypt. In exchange for peace, Israel returned the Sinai Desert, which had been conquered in 1967. The Israeli Likud Prime Minister Menachem Begin received the Nobel Peace Prize for this. The treaty also provided autonomy for the Palestinians. That, however, did not materialize, because Palestinians who wanted to implement these provisions faced death threats by the PLO of Yasser Arafat.

In 1993, the Oslo Accords were signed, again based on the principle of land for peace. This could be a prelude to a Palestinian State. These agreements stated that Israel would grant autonomy to areas with a predominantly Palestinian Arab population and that the Palestinians, once and for all, would renounce violence. So, the Palestinian leadership had to actively fight Palestinian terror and make clear to the Palestinian public that peaceful coexistence was now the goal. That did not happen (see Tales: Oslo Accords, Peace education and Rabin murder).

In 2000, US President Clinton tried again. He laid down a compromise proposal which was accepted by Prime Minister Barak of Israel. This proposed that the Palestinians would have a Palestinian state in Gaza and most of the West Bank, with East Jerusalem as a Palestinian capital. Arafat turned it down. Again, this resulted in no Palestinian state, and, again, it was the Arabs themselves who caused this. The same happened with a similar proposal in 2001. A Palestinian state was within close reach, but it was refused.

In 2003 the *Roadmap for Peace* was presented. Palestinian leaders signed it but immediately resolved not to carry out the first, most important step: ending terror and dismantling terrorist organizations. So nothing came of it. Incidentally, that "first step" was already a decade-long Palestinian obligation (under the Oslo Accords).

In 2005, Israel completely withdrew from the Gaza Strip. Again, this could have been a stepping stone towards the two-state solution. However, it was not long after Israel withdrew that the Palestinians began to bomb Israeli border towns with thousands of missiles.

In 2008, Israeli Prime Minister Olmert tried again with an even more comprehensive proposal than in 2000 and 2001: a Palestinian state in Gaza and the majority of the West Bank with East Jerusalem as its capital. As an extra, it offered a free passage between the West Bank and Gaza, via a newly planned road. This time, Palestinian President Abbas rejected it.

In 2009, Likud Prime Minister Netanyahu tried to move the Palestinians to a two-state solution.
He was the first Likud leader who suggested the two-state solution: two states for two peoples; Jewish and Palestinian:
> *"If we receive this guarantee regarding demilitarization and Israel's security needs, and if the Palestinians recognize Israel as the State of the Jewish people, then we will be ready in a future peace agreement to reach a solution where a demilitarized Palestinian state exists alongside the Jewish state."*

To stimulate negotiations, Israel announced in 2010 a building freeze for ten months in the "settlements." Nevertheless, the negotiations dragged on for years because President Abbas repeatedly put forward new requirements or blockades before even starting serious negotiations.

In 2013-2014 US President Obama tried. Israel released from prison "as a gesture of goodwill" as many as 76 Palestinian murderers. But the compromise proposed by the Obama administration was also rejected by Palestinian President Abbas.

Abbas rejected in 2014 both a full peace and the two-state solution, which are obviously the two most essential elements of the proposal. The two-state solution is based on the principle of two states, one for the Palestinians and one for the Jews. President Abbas has always refused to recognize a Jewish state: *"We do not accept a Jewish state; we will never accept a Jewish state."* (Official Palestinian TV, March 4, 2015).

He also refused to accept that after the Palestinians signed a peace treaty, the conflict must be regarded as terminated – Palestinians would have to desist from any further claims and of violence against Israel. This, of course, is the essence of any peace treaty!

So this was the sixteenth time that the Arabs rejected the two-state solution and / or peace!

> *"Palestinians never miss an opportunity to miss an opportunity."*
> – The then Israeli Foreign Minister Abba Eban after a Peace Conference in Geneva in 1973

Tale: The Arabs accept the two-state solution.
Fact: It was rejected each time it was offered, even the compromise proposed by President Clinton in 2000 and 2001.
Photo: Israeli Prime Minister Barak, US President Clinton and Palestinian President Yasser Arafat during those negotiations.

130. United Nations

The Palestinian Tale: Israel ignores all resolutions of the United Nations.

Whoever argues like this must first realize that many – often even the majority – of United Nations resolutions concern Israel. This is quite strange, taking into account all the horrible things happening in the world today. It is less strange, however, if we consider that no fewer than 57 Muslim countries have a seat in the UN and that they are all anti-Israel. Add to that the countries that are anti-West, what often means that they are anti-Israel too, for instance countries like Cuba and Zimbabwe. In this way, a majority of the 193 member countries is against Israel, so anti-Israel resolutions are easily approved. In the meantime beheadings continue in Saudi Arabia, China continues to torture Tibetans and Russia keeps prosecuting homosexuals.

Here are some examples of how this plays out at the UN.

The 2015 UN report on women's rights found only one country to be violating the rights of women: not the notoriously misogynistic Saudi Arabia, where women are even forbidden from driving, not Somalia, where 98 percent of women are genitally mutilated, and not Iran, where women who are victims of rape can be stoned. No, the only country mentioned was Israel.

The World Health Organization of the UN also condemned only one country explicitly, in its 2015 Annual Meeting, for its lack of appropriate health care. No, it was not Syria, Ukraine or Yemen, where the health status of the population by local emergency services has been described as "alarming," but it was Israel.

The 69th session of the United Nations General Assembly, which met in 2014, approved 25 resolutions condemning countries. Of these, 21 concerned Israel.

> *"If Algeria introduced a resolution declaring that the earth was flat and that Israel had flattened it, it would pass by a vote of 164 to 13 with 26 abstentions."*
> – The former Israeli Foreign Minister Abba Eban

There are other examples of the United Nations's lack of objectivity: Only in the case of Palestinians are the offspring of refugees also automatically considered refugees (see Tale: Refugee problem). Israel is the only UN member that is not allowed to preside over any UN Commission session. The Palestinians form the only group that has a "day of solidarity" at the United Nations – the millions of Syrian refugees of the Syrian civil war are not entitled to this privilege. The Palestinians are also the only ones to have their own agency, the UNRWA (see Tale: UN UNRWA).

By the way, the resolutions of the United Nations *General Assembly* have no legal value whatsoever. They are recommendations. They have no status in international law; no state can be "guilty" of violating such resolutions. These are political statements, dictated by any group of states that can muster a majority vote on a particular subject.

Given the fact that there are so many insanely anti-Israel resolutions adopted, it is not surprising that Israel does not feel obligated to fulfill these non-binding resolutions.

The resolutions of the United Nations *Security Council*, on the other hand, are often binding. They are more balanced and make demands of both sides of the conflict. Israel therefore expects the Arabs to meet their obligations as well.

This is where the real problem is, as is obvious when looking at the two most important resolutions in the Arab-Israeli conflict. Resolution 242 aimed to finally achieve peace after the Six Day War in 1967, on the basis of giving land in exchange for peace. It was the Arab countries that immediately pushed this resolution aside in rejection. This happened shortly after the passing of the resolution with the infamous "three no's" during a conference of the Arab League in Khartoum, causing peace talks to become impossible for decades. These three no's were: "no" to recognition of Israel, "no" to peace with Israel and "no" to peace negotiations with Israel.

This is evidently a case of Arab projection. Israel is accused of disregarding UN resolutions while the Arabs themselves refuse to carry out the binding and most important resolution regarding the Arab-Israeli conflict.

The same applies to the important (nonbinding) Resolution 181 in 1947, the Partition Plan, whereby the British would vacate their mandate and Palestine would be divided into an Arab and a Jewish state (see Tale: Partition Plan). The Jews accepted, and the Arabs reacted with maximal violence (see Tale: War of Independence in 1948).

"Supporters of Israel feel it is harshly judged, by standards that are not applied to its enemies – and too often this is true, particularly in some UN bodies. ...
Some may feel satisfaction at repeatedly passing General Assembly resolutions or holding conferences that condemn Israel's behavior. But one should also ask whether such steps bring any tangible relief or benefit to the Palestinians. There have been decades of resolutions. There has been a proliferation of special committees, sessions and Secretariat divisions and units.
Has any of this had an effect on Israel's policies, other than to strengthen the belief in Israel, and among many of its supporters, that this great organization is too one-sided to be allowed a significant role in the Middle East peace process?"
– Secretary-General of the UN Kofi Annan

The influence of the Arab / Muslim lobby in the United Nations is devastating for minority groups – not just for Jews. Some examples: the UN no longer condemns the death penalty for sexual orientation and Saudi Arabia, arguably the most misogynistic country in the world, is member of the UN Women Council.

"This is an unfortunate part of the UN institution. It's the theater of the absurd. It doesn't only cast Israel as the villain; it often casts real villains in leading roles: Gadhafi's Libya chaired the UN Commission on Human Rights; Saddam's Iraq headed the UN Committee on Disarmament."
– The Israel Prime Minister Benjamin Netanyahu in his speech at the UN, September 24, 2011

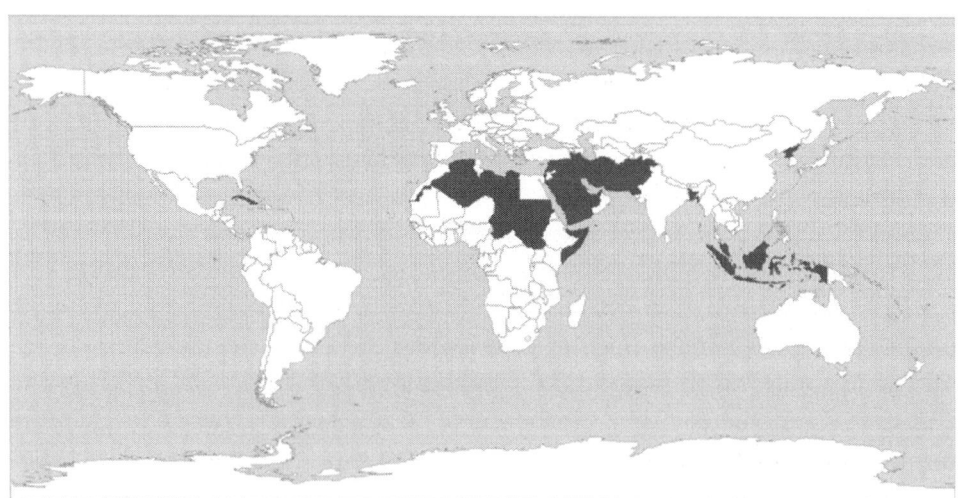

Tale: Israel does not take UN resolutions seriously.
Fact: Many member countries do not even acknowledge the existence of Israel (photo) and condemn it in advance.

131. UN Human Rights Council

The Palestinian Tale: Israel does not take the Human Rights Council seriously.

The one-sided anti-Israel attitude that applies to the United Nations General Assembly (see Tale: United Nations), applies even more so to the UN Human Rights Council. For example, Israel is the only country in the world that is standard on the agenda of each meeting to be discussed.
The Human Rights Council, due to the large number of Arab / Islamic countries that have a seat in it, is very much like an "Israel condemning machine." Over time, Human Rights Council has condemned Israel more often (61 times) than all other 193 states together! In fact, only ten other states were sentenced in the decade 2006-2015. Saudi Arabia, a country that discriminates against women, Christians and homosexuals by law, was not even amongst them. Perhaps, this is because Saudi Arabia is a member of the Human Rights Council itself.

The UN Human Rights Council has the ostensible task of promoting human rights, such as have been described in 1948 in the Universal Declaration of Human Rights. Islamic countries however, generally do not agree with all of these listed human rights, as they say some human rights are incompatible with Islamic values. Therefore, since 1990, Islamic countries have followed their own version of the human rights. For instance, freedom of expression is only valid if statements are in accordance with the *Sharia* (the Islamic law and code of conduct). Similarly, freedom of religion is not allowed. It is forbidden for a Muslim to withdraw from Islam or to convert to other religion. There is a fundamental inequality between men and women according to the *Sharia*. Therefore all kinds of rights and freedoms should be subordinated to the *Sharia,* according to this Islamic Declaration of Human Rights.

Given this, you may wonder why these countries still serve on the UN Human Rights Council. The answer is simple: because it is an excellent way to meddle in the affairs of Israel and the West. That is why a senior official of the Human Rights Council called the Netherlands racist because of its traditional celebration of Santa Claus.

It also explains why some hard to believe things happen at the UN Human Rights Council. Libya, when under the dictatorship of mass murderer Muammar Gaddafi, could become chairman of the UN Human Rights Council. The same Libya was praised by the UN agency for its excellent human rights situation. In 2014, there was a condemnation in which Syria was involved. But it was not, as you might think, regarding the 200,000 deaths and brutal attacks in during its civil war, but about the "human rights violations" by Israel on the Golan.

Many dictatorships have had or still hold seats in the UN Human Rights Council, such as Cuba and China. Saudi Arabia was elected chairman of the nomination committee for human rights experts in 2015 – in spite of their seemingly brazen denial of human rights to, say, homosexuals, among others. Even a Hamas leader was once invited as a guest speaker.

> *"As you all know, the UN Charter guarantees 'the equal rights of nations large and small,' and yet we have seen member states seek to use the UN Security Council, the General Assembly, and even the most arcane UN committees in ways that cross the line from legitimate criticisms of Israel's policies to attempts to delegitimize the state of Israel itself. The only country in the world with a standing agenda item at the Human Rights Council is not North Korea, a totalitarian state that is currently holding an estimated 100,000 people in gulags; not Syria, which has gassed its people – lots of them. It is Israel.*
>
> *Bias has extended well beyond Israel as a country, Israel as an idea – it even extends to Israeli organizations.*
>
> *Israel is just not treated like other countries. And so part of our posture in New York is dedicated to trying to ensure that the criticisms of Israel are about policies and not of the existence of the state itself, which is what it still feels as though a lot of that criticism is motivated by."*
>
>   – *U.S. Ambassador to the United Nations Samantha Power in 2016*

Tale: Israel is mistaken by not taking the UN Human Rights Council seriously.
Fact: The Council itself is not serious on human rights; they even praised the human rights situation in Libya under the rule of the dictator Gaddafi (photo).

132. UN peacekeepers

The Palestinian Tale: A UN peacekeeping force between the warring parties is the solution.

It sounds like a good idea, a peacekeeping force, but in the past it has been repeatedly shown that UN peacekeeping forces are not able to offer Israel protection from Arab aggression.
In 1967 the UN peacekeeping force left the Sinai Desert immediately after it was asked by Egypt to do so because Egypt wanted to attack Israel (see Tale: Six Day War). The UN peacekeeping force in southern Lebanon could not prevent the continuation of terrorist assaults on northern Israel. And the UN peacekeeping force on the Syrian Golan, when it was in 2014 attacked by Muslim fundamentalist groups, had to be rescued by the intervention of the Israeli army.

Foreigners are simply not willing to risk their lives to protect Israelis against enemy aggression.

Tale: A UN peacekeeping force between the warring parties is the solution.
Fact: That solution has repeatedly failed.

133. UN UNRWA

The Palestinian Tale: UNRWA promotes peace.

The UNRWA is a special agency of the United Nations for the Palestinians. UNRWA stands for United Nations Relief and Work Agency and was created for Palestinians refugees in 1948, making them the only group in the world for whom a separate organization of the United Nations has been created.
At its core, it is actually a welfare organization. Millions of Palestinians are dependent on the UNRWA for their income, education and medical care. Its annual budget is approximately one and a half billion dollars, paid mainly by Europe.

That money is then used to artificially label generations of people as "refugees" (see Tale: Refugees, numbers) and therefore keep them permanently locked up in camps – only because the Arab countries and even the Palestinian leadership want this to be the case.
A 2013 report from the UNRWA stated: *"1.9 million registered Palestinian refugees are living in the Palestinian state."*
How absurd to label people as refugees when they live in their own territory – often even in their hometowns – and under self-rule. However, such labeling enables them allowances and also provides UN staff with well-paid jobs. It is just as absurd that Europe and the US continue to pay the ever-rising bill for it.

The efforts of the UNRWA certainly do not contribute to peace. On the contrary, the UNRWA exists because of the Palestinians refugees and is therefore interested in keeping as many Palestinians dependent on the organization as possible. It is profitable for the organization and its employees because there is one staff member of the United Nations for every 165 Palestinian "refugees," resulting in approximately 40 times as many UN employees as for other, genuine refugees. About four times as much money is spent on a Palestinian "refugee" as on a real refugee.
The expenses per refugee could even be considerably greater, because the refugee numbers are inflated. The UNRWA reported in 2012 that 465,000 Palestinians in Lebanon would get support. But a well-researched study, made in 2010 for the same UNRWA, showed that in reality at most 280,000 Palestinians lived in Lebanon – so about half of the claimed number. The other approximately 200,000 Palestinians no longer exist as such; they have become Lebanese citizens or have left Lebanon, mainly to Europe.

The UNRWA identifies fully with the Palestinian cause. Of its 30,000 employees, 99 percent are Palestinian. This explains why Hamas missiles were stored in UNRWA schools in Gaza and that war tunnels were dug by Hamas under UNRWA clinics. These alarming facts were admitted by the UN itself in a research report in 2015.

Also, UNRWA schools falsify history. They teach that the Palestinians are descendants of the Canaanites (see Tale: Philistines), they promote anti-Semitism and deny Jewish history and Israel's right to exist. Thus, the UNRWA does not help in the resolution of the conflict but rather with the perpetuation and worsening of it. It is troublesome and alarming that the UNRWA has a significant financial interest in the conflict's continuation.

Tale: UNRWA promotes peace.
Fact: UNRWA was created to assist the Palestinian refugees from 1948 (photo). Seventy years later, their descendants are still detained in camps.

134. United States

The Palestinian Tale: Israel exists only thanks to the billions of aid money that the US provides.

In reality, the aid is not economic but military. It is important for the United States to have a strong military ally in the violent Middle East region. The reason is also not the Jewish lobby (see Tale: Jewish lobby).

The American support is about $3 billion a year. The entire amount must be spent on weapons and 100 percent of the money should be spent on the US arms industry. In this sense, Israel is supported with goods only; the money stays in the United States.

Other US allies have similar arrangements, like Egypt, which receives annual US support worth $1.5 billion.

And its cooperation with Israel in the development of weapons systems – particularly missile systems – benefits the US as well. It also profits from receiving access to information collected by Israeli intelligence and shared with other Western countries. This helps to prevent terrorist attacks in Europe and America. The need for this protecting this interest is unfortunately increasing.

In addition to the military support, Israel can rely on US loan guarantees. This means that Israel's loans are guaranteed by the United States and the lender runs less risk. But this will not cost the United States a penny (unless Israel goes bankrupt). The loan guarantees amount to $8 billion, but Israel has not made use of the guarantees since 2004 because of its strong domestic economy since. There remain only a $3.8 billion in loan guarantees, for loans from before 2004.

Would Israel not survive without those $3 billion of military aid, as the tale claims? Israel's economy – its GDP, gross domestic product – is about $300 billion. So the US support is only about 1 percent of Israel's economy. The Israelis themselves take care of the other 99 percent.

Tale: Israel exists only thanks to the billions in aid money that the US pumps in.
Fact: The armies of Egypt (photo) and Iraq, among others are also backed by billions of dollars.

135. Victim culture

The Palestinian Tale: The Palestinians are victims of Israel.

In the Arab world in general – and among Palestinians in particular – exists an enormous culture of victimhood. Anything that goes wrong is the fault of the Jews (see Tale: Arab anti-Semitism), the United States or Western colonialism. This culture paralyzes the taking of personal initiative to better one's own situation.

Regretfully, many leftist Westerners go along with this victim culture and the sometimes nonsensical statements that it propagates.

Few of the perceived misdeeds are true (see for example Tales: Economy, Palestinian and Suffering of the Palestinians). A number of reasons for the victim culture can be identified. The first one is that Arabs like to explain the success of the West and the Jews with conspiracy theories (see Tale: Conspiracy theories). This is caused by an essential difference in culture.

A blame culture prevails in the West, because of its Judeo-Christian foundation: It is important to recognize your mistakes. You may get penalized, but you can then be forgiven and carry on with your life.

The Middle East, on the other hand, has a shame culture. One is very aware of his place in the society or group and the dignity that goes with it. Damage to these factors leads to disgrace and should be avoided. Something which is seen as violation of that dignity, whether to the individual or to the community to which the person belongs, leads to aggression – as was seen in the riots following the Muhammad cartoons in Denmark and the attack on Charlie Hebdo.

It also means that mistakes and shame cannot be admitted. So we hear of petty criminals like pickpockets – and even of the worst Arab criminals and terrorists – from people who know them and judge them to be such good and kind persons.
A glaring example was the mother who, on June 6, 2013, lamented on Palestinian television the fate of her son, who was in prison for the brutal murder of an Israeli taxi driver. That mother said: *"By Allah, he is good, good. Ibrahim is honorable and a man. He's never harmed his Muslim brother, never harmed a neighbor, never harmed any person."*

Because of this victim culture the vast majority of the Arab world – and 68 percent of the Palestinians – does not believe that the attacks of September 11, 2001, were committed by Muslims. At the same time, a majority believes that these attacks were a just punishment for the United States because of *"their crimes against Muslims."* It is difficult to see how both can be true; this illogical position is only possible when you want to view Muslims as victims in both propositions.

Some Westerners go along with this wallowing in victimization. However, in this way they encourage it further. It ends up having completely negative ramifications, because this makes Arabs even less inclined to take responsibility for their own actions and future.

> *"There can be no greater mistake in assessing the current situation in the Middle East than to assume that the conflict continues because of a specific Arab grievance – the plight of the Arab refugees, the Israeli presence on the West Bank, the reunification of Jerusalem. The heart of the problem is what caused the Six-Day War.*
> *Simply put the root issue is the Arab attitude to Israel's very existence.*
> *They don't want us here. That's what it's about. It isn't true that they don't want us in Nablus or Jenin. They don't want us, period."*
>   – The then Israeli Prime Minister Golda Meir after the 1967 Six-Day War

Tale: The Palestinians are victims of Israel.
Fact: Arabs quickly see themselves as victims.
Photo: Demonstration in Sydney, Australia.

136. Violence

The Palestinian Tale: A majority of Palestinian citizens reject violence and desire peace.

An opinion poll amongst Palestinians in 2011 revealed that a whopping 73 percent agree with Article 7 of the Hamas Charter, which states that it is an Islamic duty to exterminate the Jews. A majority of Palestinians voted for Hamas in the 2006 elections.
According to another poll in spring 2014 (by Pew), 46 percent of Palestinians support suicide bombings – *"to defend Islam."*
The promotion of violence also appears in street scenes. When Israeli citizens are killed in Palestinian terror attacks, Palestinians take to the streets to distribute sweets and celebrate.

In November of 2014, there was a wave of Palestinian violence in Jerusalem. Four rabbis were killed with hatchets during their prayers, and Israeli citizens were deliberately run over at bus stops. Among the victims of these fatal attacks was a three-month-old baby. The Palestinian Center for Policy and Research (PCPSR) reported a month later that the Palestinians supported these murders. It showed that 80 percent approved of stabbings and car ramming attacks on Israeli civilians, including Israeli babies.

The Palestinian Authority encourages this (see Tale: Peace education).

> *"I am proud of him because everyone knows of Abdallah Barghouti and what he generously did for Palestine. I am proud of him, and I say: Praise Allah who gave me this hero, noble fighter for Palestine and its cause. I ask every Palestinian of noble soul to follow in the footsteps of Abdallah Barghouti for Palestine and Jerusalem."*
> – Interview on Palestinian television on June 22, 2015, with the father of Abdallah Barghouti, who prepared the bombs that killed 67 Israelis, including many children

Tale: Palestinians abhor violence.
Fact: The terrorists are widely worshiped.
Photo: Monument to terrorists of the extreme left-wing terrorist organization PFLP in Qalqiliya.

137. War crimes

The Palestinian Tale: Israel frequently commits war crimes.

The laws of war have two main criteria: distinction and proportionality.

The criterion of distinction means that the law of war distinguishes between civilian and military targets. Only the latter may be legally attacked.

Hamas puts warriors, munitions depots and rocket launchers among groups of civilians and public buildings, such as houses, schools, mosques and hospitals. These buildings are thus transformed into military targets. In complete violation of the law of war, Hamas combatants do not wear uniforms and thus cannot be distinguished from civilians.

Who determines whether a mark has turned into a military target? That decision is up to the military commander on the spot, on the basis of the best possible information available at the time. The Dutch military handbook says:
> *"Whether an object is a military target depends on the circumstances at that moment. This definition gives the necessary freedom to the discretion of the commander on the spot."*

So, the military commander determines the nature of each particular situation. Moreover, the designation of the attack as legal or illegal depends on the commander's intention. Rüdiger Wolfrum and Dieter Fleck write accordingly in *The Handbook of International Humanitarian Law* on the law of war:
> *"The prerequisite for a grave breach is intent; the attack must be intentionally directed at the civilian population or individual civilians."*

So long as the Israeli army does not attack civilians deliberately, and as long as the commander on the spot sees a military interest in each target based on the information available to him or her at the time, there is no question of a violation of the law of war.

Some who may still argue that on the surface some of Israel's military actions look like war crimes – solely on the basis of television pictures, for example – do not have the information to judge this accurately, according the laws of war. It is impossible for viewers to form an opinion about a commander's intention because they cannot know what information the commander possessed about the overall situation or the assessment of the likelihood of danger to the soldiers under his or her command.

The second decisive criterion in the laws of war is "proportionality." That criterion requires that the additional loss of life in the targeting of military objectives should not be disproportionate in relation to the anticipated military advantage.

The bar for proportionality is in actuality a lot higher than is often suggested. For example, consider the NATO bombing of Serbian radio and television studios on April 23, 1999. The station was, according to NATO, also used to communicate Serb military commands. Western journalists were warned to stay away on the day of the bombing, so it was assumed that the impending attack was also known to Serbs. In the bombing, 16 people were killed, all but one civilian, but the then British Prime Minister Tony Blair blamed the civilian deaths on the Serbs, since the broadcaster's employees were not evacuated. The military broadcasts were resumed within a day from another, undisclosed location. Yet the International Tribunal for Yugoslavia ruled that this studio had been a legitimate military target and that the number of civilian casualties was indeed high, but not excessive.

This example shows that when warnings are given to civilians to stay away from targets, it is considered sufficient care to minimize civilian casualties. Therefore, the NATO attack was not considered excessive.

We can note that on this basis of "proportionality" there can be no question of excess in the current practices of Israel. In the attacks on Gaza in 2014, for example, that was clearly the case, according to Dutch professor of international criminal law Gert-Jan Knoops:

> *"It was about the protection of thousands of lives that were the target of thousands of rocket attacks from Gaza. That seems a powerful military objective, which potentially subverts every argument on alleged disproportionality."*

Furthermore, Israel warns civilians away from military actions with several warnings and through various communication channels such as telephone, radio, email, SMS, pamphlets and warning shots. Israel's targets, such as command centers, tunnels and rocket launchers, also serve a clearer military purpose than disabling a broadcasting system for several hours, as happened in the case of Serbia.

The Israeli army takes the law of warfare very seriously. This is an important part of its military training. The higher an officer's military rank, the more extensive training they receive in the law of war. In addition, all divisions have legal experts that are consulted in operational decisions.

When it comes to air strikes, this policy is abundantly clear. Since these require an extensive preparation period, decision-making can be done very carefully. Therefore the Israeli armed forces follow a very rigorous and comprehensive protocol with standards that are more stringent than those required by the international law of war. Commanders have to adhere strictly to these rules, and they know that their process will be reviewed afterwards.

In reality, Hamas tries to influence these decisions by using civilians as human shields (see Tale: Civilian casualties). This is indeed a clear and very serious war crime – on Hamas's part (see Tale: War crimes, Hamas).

General Martin Dempsey, former chairman of the US Joint Chiefs of Staff, confirmed that Israel had done everything possible to avoid civilian casualties in the fighting in Gaza in 2014 (see Tale: Civilian casualties). For that reason an American team traveled to Israel to learn from the Israeli army how to minimize civilian casualties. In a television interview on November 6, 2014, the general said:
> *"I actually think that Israel went to extraordinary lengths to limit collateral damage and civilian casualties. The military did some extraordinary things to limit civilian casualties, including making it known that they were going to destroy a particular structure.*
> *The IDF is not interested in creating civilian casualties. They're interested in stopping the shooting of rockets and missiles out of the Gaza Strip and into Israel.*
> *It is an incredibly difficult environment. But I can say to you with confidence that they acted responsibly."*

Tale: Israel frequently commits war crimes.
Fact: This is not true according to the real experts, such as US General Dempsey (pictured).

138. War crimes, Hamas

The Palestinian Tale: Hamas does not commit any war crimes.

On the contrary, Hamas is clearly guilty of violating the two criteria for war crimes: distinction and proportionality (see Tale: War crimes).

Hamas fires missiles that make no distinction between civilian and military targets. The missiles are moreover deliberately fired at Israeli towns and cities – and on civil aviation airfields and a nuclear power plant. Hamas even boasts about it. Those missiles are specifically intended to kill as many civilians as possible. The missile attacks are therefore clearly disproportionate under international law of war.

During the fighting in 2014, Hamas committed in total 18 types of war crimes. The most important were: using its own civilians as human shields for combatants and rocket launchers, shooting deliberately at Israeli civilians, using medical facilities such as ambulances and hospitals for military functions, not providing shelter from hostilities for its own civilian population (Hamas had built tunnels, but these were only used by their combatants), not requiring combatants to wear uniforms to distinguish them from civilians, using child soldiers, and sheltering combatants, command posts, weapons, explosives and rocket launchers in civilian structures (such as houses, mosques and schools).

These Palestinian war crimes – and Israel's innocence – were even recognized by the Palestinian ambassador to the UN Human Rights Council, Ibrahim Khreisheh. He explained in a television interview on official Palestinian Authority television on July 9, 2014, why the Palestinian government could not seek Israel's conviction at the International Criminal Court:
> "The missiles that are now being launched against Israel – each and every missile constitutes a crime against humanity whether it hits or misses, because it is directed at civilian targets.
> Targeting civilians – be it one civilian or a thousand – is considered a crime against humanity.
> Please note that many of our people in Gaza appeared on TV and said that the Israeli army warned them to evacuate their homes before the bombardment. In such a case, if someone is killed, the law considers it a mistake rather than an intentional killing, because [the Israelis] followed the legal procedures.

As for the missiles launched from our side, we never warn anyone about where these missiles are about to fall, or about the operations we carry out."

Tale: Hamas does not commit any war crimes.
Fact: Missiles are intentionally fired by Hamas from densely populated areas (photo), which causes Palestinian casualties.

139. War of Independence in 1948

The Palestinian Tale: The Jews were guilty of instigating the War of Independence.

The war broke out because both the Arab countries and the leaders of the Palestinian Arabs rejected the Partition Plan proposed by the UN in November 1947. For years before that, Jewish leaders had constantly tried to reach a compromise. However, as an example, the secretary-general of the Arab League, Azzam Pasha said on September 16, 1947, to the Jewish leaders who wanted to avoid war:

"The Arab world is not in a compromising mood. It's likely that your plan is rational and logical, but the fate of nations is not decided by rational logic. Nations never concede; they fight. You won't get anything by peaceful means or compromise. You can, perhaps, get something, but only by force of arms."

After the plan met with approval by UN vote, the attacks on Jews by Arab armed gangs intensified. Just in the first month, 180 Jews were killed and many more wounded – both by Palestinians and by volunteers, mostly from Iraq and Syria. As before World War II, they were again under the command of the Nazi war criminal Al-Husseini (see Tale: Nazism), who gave the order: *"Kill the Jews to the last one."*

Even before the vote in the UN, Jamal Husseini, the representative of the Palestinian Arabs had promised that the Arabs would drench *"the soil of our beloved country with the last drop of our blood."*

Iraqi Prime Minister Nuri al-Said stated: *"We will smash the country with our guns and obliterate every place where the Jews seek shelter."*

The main Islamic university and religious center, Al-Azhar in Cairo, called for a holy war.

Al Husseini, the leader of the Palestinian Arabs, said in an interview in March 1948 that the Arabs were not going to stop only the partition, but *"would continue to fight until the Zionists were destroyed, so that the whole of Palestine would be a purely Arab state."*

The Palestinian spokesman Jamal Husseini spoke in the UN Security Council on April 16, 1948:

> *"The representative of the Jewish Agency told us yesterday that they were not the attackers, that the Arabs had begun the fighting.*
> **We did not deny this. We told the whole world that we were going to fight.**"

The Jews, on the contrary, in their Declaration of Independence of May 14, 1948, made an appeal to avoid war:

> *"We extend our hand to all neighboring states and their peoples in an offer of peace and good neighborliness, and appeal to them to establish bonds of cooperation and mutual help with the sovereign Jewish people settled in its own land. The State of Israel is prepared to do its share in a common effort for the advancement of the entire Middle East."*

However, the next day the armies of Egypt, Iraq, Jordan, Lebanon and Syria attacked, supported by units from Yemen, Morocco, Saudi Arabia and Sudan. That was already agreed upon in a meeting of the Arab League on April 20, 1948.

The result is known. Despite their overwhelming majority, the Arabs lost the war. However, the war killed 1 percent of the Jews living in Israel. The Arabs now call their loss the Nakba (the catastrophe). A curious term, for a disaster is something that happens to you. But this disaster was caused by them, so the word "failure" fits much better.

> *"We have always said that in our war with the Arabs we had a secret weapon – no alternative. The Egyptians could run to Egypt, the Syrians into Syria. The only place we could run was into the sea, and before we did that we might as well fight."*
> – Former Israeli Prime Minister Golda Meir

Tale: The Jews started the 1948 war.
Fact: Israel was attacked by nine Arab countries.
Photo: Shelling of Jerusalem by the Jordanian army.

140. Water shortage

The Palestinian Tale: Israel has a severe shortage of water.

> "Many Israelis feel that Israel cannot afford to completely withdraw from the occupied territories. Having the guarantee of sufficient fresh water will play an especially important role in the long term. Therefore Israel has also kept the Golan Heights occupied since the 1967 Six Day War."

This Tale can be found in many books including *World wise* (2012), a Dutch high school geography textbook. It shows yet again how many tales are spread about Israel, even in textbooks.

Fortunately the reality is quite different. Israel is a world champion in water conservation. Since 1948, agricultural production in Israel increased 16-fold and industrial production 50-fold. In this time period, water consumption actually fell by 10 percent.

Moreover, an increasing amount of desalination plants are being built in Israel. Through desalination, salty seawater is converted into fresh drinking water. Since the construction of its most recent factory in 2014, Israel has reached a production capacity of 600 million cubic meters of water per year. That's about 80 percent of Israel's total freshwater needs.

Add to this supply the fact that 70 percent of water in Israel is recycled – three times as much as in any other country in the world for that matter – and you will understand that Israel hardly depends on natural water anymore, by rainfall or rivers, and therefore doesn't need the water from the West Bank or the Golan.

On the contrary, Israel now has substantial surplus water. Israel is exporting more water than before. In the context of the peace agreements, Israel has been supplying water to the Palestinians and Jordan, and even provides much more than it is required to. If the need arises, these exports can be further increased.

Tale: Israel has a severe shortage of water.
Fact: Thanks to desalination plants, Israel has a surplus of water.
Photo: Nitzana water desalination plant in Israel.

141. Water theft

The Palestinian Tale: Israel steals water from the Palestinians.

This Tale shows that Palestinians blame even natural phenomena on Israel. It is true that rainwater flows from the high grounds of the West Bank to the lower-lying Israeli coast. But that has been the case for thousands of years!

So, on the contrary, Israel brings water to the Palestinians. To begin with, the water supply system in the autonomous Palestinian territories was almost entirely constructed by Israel after it took over the administration in 1967. Under Jordanian rule, the water supply was primitive and few houses were connected to running water.

While water consumption per capita among Israelis in 1967 was five times as much as among Palestinians, it is currently just about equal (150 and 140 cubic meters per year). In the West Bank, the price of water use is even lower for Palestinians than for Israelis.

Israel doesn't steal water from the Palestinians, but rather delivers water, under the peace agreements. Israel even provides approximately double the amount of what therein had been agreed.

It should be noted that Israel handles water sparingly by recycling as much as 70 percent of its own usage. The Palestinians barely recycle, and their poorly maintained facilities and pipelines leak a great amount of water. In the Gaza Strip about 40 percent of the amount of water carried through the pipes leaks into the ground.

The new main pipeline for the southern West Bank, which was built with foreign aid in December 2015, serves to prevent water wastage through leakages and illegal taps. Its necessity is instructive of the water wastage situation in the Palestinian Authority. The press release states:
> "Prior to USAID's intervention, residents of the region suffered chronic water shortages and supply interruptions due to water losses from the pipeline...
> The old Deir Sha'ar pipeline had a transmission capacity of 4.75 million cubic meters (MCM) per year, but nearly half was lost due to leaks...

The new pipeline is equipped with remote sensors that enable the Palestinian Water Authority and West Bank Water Department to detect any illegal taps or tampering, and to continuously monitor the system in real time for internal damages and leaks."

That's because the Palestinian authorities hardly invest in water collection, water reclamation and water treatment – despite the fact that the Palestinian Authority is so obligated under the peace agreements and that large sums of foreign aid money are available for this purpose.

So this is a case of Arab projection, in which Arabs blame Israel for something of which they themselves are guilty.
Furthermore, because the Palestinian Authority does not comply with the water provisions in the peace agreements, it affects both groundwater and surface water contamination. Ninety percent of Palestinian wastewater is not treated. Since the West Bank is situated on higher ground than the Israeli coastal plain, not only the Palestinian but also the Israeli population is very much affected.

For instance, Palestinian sewage is infected with polio. This disease has returned to Arab countries because the Nigerian Muslim fundamentalist Ibrahim Datti Ahmed says that the vaccination program against it is a Western conspiracy to make Muslim children infertile. So the disease has reappeared, and it has spread to all Islamic countries by Muslim pilgrimages to Mecca, and to Israel through wastewater. On this topic, however, you never hear protests, not from anyone.

Israel is therefore trying to catch the water at the border to purify it. It is apparently asking too much to expect from the Palestinian Authority to keep their autonomous region clean. Indeed, they obstruct Israel in this objective, as was demonstrated in 2013 when the Dutch company Haskoning was planning to build a water treatment plant near Jerusalem. Due to pressure from the Palestinian Authority and then – shockingly – the Dutch government, the company withdrew from the project.

The Palestinian authorities unfortunately have other priorities. For example, water and sewer pipes are used in the Gaza Strip to manufacture missiles. Because of that, drains regularly overflow. In 2007, five Palestinians, including two babies, were killed by flooding.

Moreover, everything is turned into politics. Plans by development aid organizations to build desalination plants in Gaza have been blocked for years because the Palestinian leadership did not want to allow Israeli companies to register, but the project was also met with much disapproval for other reasons. Dozens of Palestinian organizations have condemned the project and take action against it. Among them are many Palestinian "human rights organizations" and even the Council of Churches for the Middle East. Why are they opposed to providing good quality drinking water to the residents of Gaza? Because it *"helps the occupation"* and *"further isolates Gaza."*

That's right, these organizations want to maintain the dependent position to Israel at all costs, because Israel otherwise cannot be blamed for everything that goes wrong in Gaza.
That ordinary Palestinians must suffer because of these politics is deemed completely irrelevant.

Tale: The Palestinians have a shortage of drinking water.
Fact: The Palestinians have water parks.
Photo: The *Crazy Water Park* in Gaza, with many pools (however, this park was destroyed by masked men in 2010, just four months after its opening, most likely by Muslim fundamentalists because men and women were allowed to mingle).

142. West Bank claims

The Palestinian Tale: Only the Palestinians can rightfully claim the West Bank.

The West Bank was governed by Turkey from 1517 to 1917, as part of the Ottoman Empire. In 1917 it was conquered by Britain in World War I. In 1922, the League of Nations – the forerunner of the United Nations – assigned it to the Jewish people. All 51 member states of the League of Nations unanimously declared on July 24, 1922:

> *"Recognition has been given to the historical connection of the Jewish people with Palestine and to the grounds for reconstituting their national home in that country."*

Key in the Mandate is article 6, which states:

"The Administration of Palestine shall facilitate Jewish immigration and shall encourage close settlement by Jews on the land."

Jewish claims to the area are extremely strong. For more than 3,000 years, members of the Jewish people have lived there continuously. Such a long time is unique; no other people can make such a claim. The traces of historical Jewish inhabitation are everywhere and are much more widespread than that of Arab inhabitation. The recent development of the area is mainly due to Jewish immigration, as is clear from a comparison with the backward situation of Arabs in neighboring countries (see Tale: Land development).

The decision of the League of Nations in 1922 was the last binding decision on the area taken under international law. It is still valid, because the UN in Article 80 of its statute guaranteed the decisions of the League of Nations. The UN's later Partition Plan did not replace it, because it was only a recommendation – one that was, moreover, refused by the Arabs with much terror and war.

In 1948, Jordan conquered the West Bank and added the area to Jordan, a move that was recognized by virtually no country. During the Six Day War, Jordan invaded Israel from the West Bank – without provocation. In that war, Israel captured the West Bank.

The area thus was gained in a defensive war; according to international law, an aggressor can lose territory as a result of its aggression. By the way, Jordan later renounced its claim to the West Bank.

This book uses the term West Bank because Jordan called it that way after its occupation in 1948. It then signified the western bank of the Jordan River, while Jordan proper lay to the east. This name is well established because Arabs still refer to the area this way. However, for 3,000 years the correct geographical name of the area has been Judea and Samaria. The term Jew is derived from the area Judea, because it was a central area of the biblical Jewish state.

So, the legal status of the West Bank is disputed territory; two parties claim ownership.

In 1967, resolution 242 of the United Nations stated that Israel should (partially) withdraw from the territory that was conquered in 1967 in exchange for peace and secure borders. The latter means border corrections, because the armistice lines of 1949 have proven very unsafe for Israel (see Tale: Borders).

Israel agreed with partition in the Oslo Accords. In these treaties signed in the 1990s, the area of the West Bank is temporarily divided in advent of a future final treaty. Israel has withdrawn from the densely populated areas that were conquered in 1967. As a result, 96 percent of the Palestinians in the West Bank now live under Palestinian self-rule. In return, the Palestinian leadership promised peace. In reality, terror only increased.

In the Oslo Accords it is stipulated that a final, agreed-upon division of the area will be settled in a final, mutually agreed upon peace treaty. That has not yet happened because over the last two decades the Palestinian leaders have rejected all internationally proposed compromises and avoid negotiations – often for years (see Tale: Two-state solution). However, the Palestinian leadership is trying to unilaterally change the status of the West Bank through the UN. Thus they violate their obligations as defined by the Oslo Accords, which are guaranteed internationally, also by the UN!

However, in the negotiations that have taken place, a significant part of the final partition has already been agreed on. This emerged from leaked documents, called Palileaks.

Israel will hold a small percentage of the West Bank (in exchange for territory elsewhere). This involves areas settled almost exclusively by Jews – and in most cases, areas where Jews lived before 1948, before they were driven out by Arab armies. The best known examples are the Gush Etzion region south of Jerusalem and the centuries-old Jewish quarter next to the Wailing Wall in the Old City of Jerusalem.

The fact that there still is no final peace agreement has more to do with other issues, such as the Palestinian refusal to recognize the existence of Israel as a Jewish state (see Tale: Two-state solution).

The United States agreed with this territorial distribution in 2004, in return for the Israeli withdrawal from Gaza. This promise from then US president Bush received overwhelming support in the US Congress: in the Senate, the vote was 95 in favor, three opposed, and in the House of Representatives, 407 for and nine opposed. President Bush wrote a letter on April 14, 2004:

"The United States reiterates its steadfast commitment to Israel's security, including secure, defensible borders, and to preserve and strengthen Israel's capability to deter and defend itself, by itself, against any threat or possible combination of threats.
In light of new realities on the ground, including already existing major Israeli population centers, it is unrealistic to expect that the outcome of final status negotiations will be a full and complete return to the armistice lines of 1949."

Tale: Only the Palestinians can rightfully claim the West Bank.
Fact: Israel received the territory in a defensive war, after Jordan attacked it from there.
Photo: Jordanian artillery fire.

143. West Bank services

The Palestinian Tale: Israeli civil services in the West Bank violate international law.

Palestinian leaders argue that these services *"consolidate the occupation."* Therefore, even companies that would participate in it should be boycotted. The PLO – the Palestine Liberation Organization – of President Abbas started such a juridical procedure at the French Court of Versailles because several French companies were involved in the construction of a light-railway that was planned to run from western to eastern Jerusalem, to Arab and Jewish neighborhoods there.

In a crushing (for the Palestinians) verdict, the court ruled in March 2013 that Israel had acted correctly and responsibly within the applicable Hague Conventions of international law (specifically Article 43 of the 4th Convention The Hague, 1907):

> *"The authority of the legitimate power having in fact passed into the hands of the occupant, the latter shall take all measures in his power to restore, and ensure, as far as possible, public order and safety, while respecting, unless absolutely prevented, the laws in force in the country."*

It seems perfectly logical, this verdict that a state must provide good civil services for all citizens who are under its authority – regardless of creed or race. This includes ensuring that all citizens have access to good public transportation, anywhere. And that is not only justified but even obligated according to international law.

Moreover, the Court of Versailles went a step further by stating that the International Conventions of Geneva and of The Hague only apply to countries that are signatories, and that the PLO is neither. Therefore, all other accusations that were brought forward by the PLO held no legal status.

The Court of Versailles ruled that Israel acted entirely in accordance with the Geneva Conventions of 1949. The court therefore sentenced the PLO to pay compensation and legal fees for the accused companies.

The Palestinian Authority, since it was instituted 20 years ago, has done nothing to become independent from Israel in the field of public works, for example the supply of electricity or water – despite the fact that international aid funds are available for them. The Palestinian Authority even obstructs the progress of these services (see Tale: Water theft).

When Israel is accused of not providing equal access to public works for Arabs, it is projection; in reality Israel is often obstructed in providing these services. And in the typical mentality of those who always blame Israel: if Israel had done the opposite, and the Arab neighborhoods would not have been connected to the railway, then Israel would be undoubtedly also have been accused. But then it would have been of discrimination to Arabs, of withholding good public transportation from them.

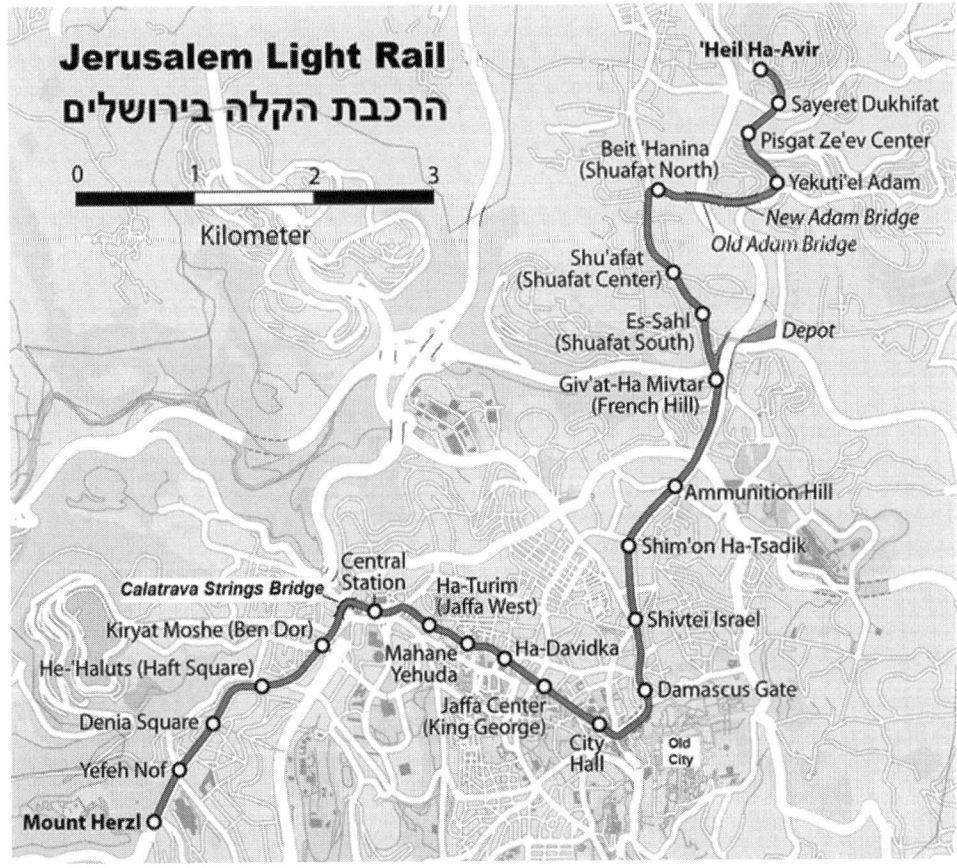

Tale: Israel grants the Arabs no access to public transportation.
Fact: The Jerusalem railway connects Arab and Jewish neighborhoods (photo).

144. West Bank withdrawal

The Palestinian Tale: Israel is in violation of international law because it has not yet withdrawn from the West Bank.

Regarding the West Bank withdrawal, Palestinians refer to Resolution 242 of the United Nations Security Council. However, the resolution, made in 1967, very explicitly states detailed conditions for potential Israeli withdrawal from disputed areas, namely:

> "The establishment of a just and lasting peace in the Middle East which should include the application of both the following principles: ... Termination of all claims or states of belligerency and respect for and acknowledgment of the sovereignty, territorial integrity and political independence of every State in the area and their right to live in peace within secure and recognized boundaries free from threats or acts of force."

These demands on the Arab countries to achieve peace with Israel were precisely the reason they rejected this resolution. They responded with three no's – adopted shortly thereafter at a conference in Khartoum: *"No peace with Israel, no recognition of Israel, no negotiations with it."*

And to this day Arab countries are still formally at war with Israel – only two have made peace – and most of them have no normal relations with Israel, execute Israelis and boycott Israeli products.

The resolution states that Israel is entitled to secure borders (in other words, borders more defensible than the pre-1967 ones; see Tale: Borders).

Claiming Israel has failed to comply with the resolution is another case of Arab projection. Israel has already withdrawn itself from 94 percent of the territory conquered in 1967, namely the Sinai, the Gaza Strip and the densely populated parts of the West Bank, while it has not gotten an end to violence in return.

> *"I cannot conceive of Israel withdrawing if Arab states do not recognize Israel within secure borders."*
> – Then president of South Africa Nelson Mandela

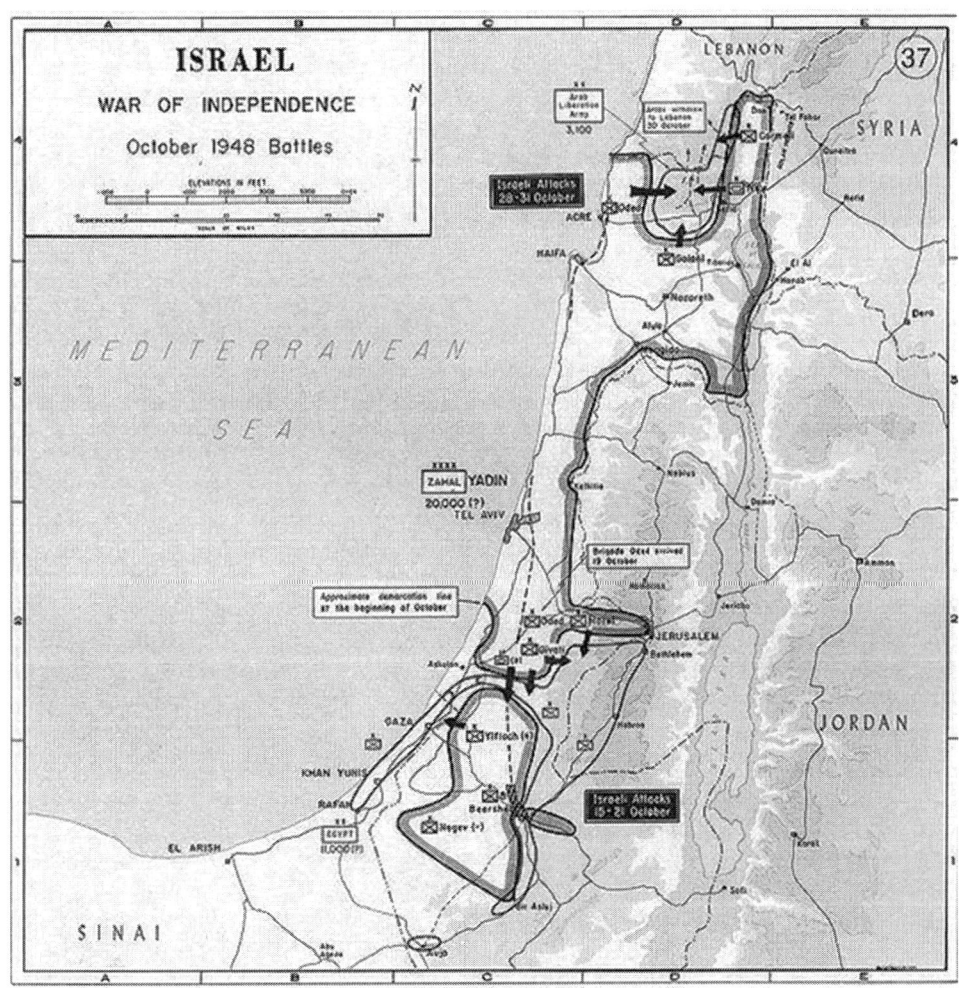

Tale: Israel is in violation of international law because it has not yet withdrawn from the West Bank.
Fact: Because the boundaries laid out for Israel in 1947 were very narrow, Israel could be intersected by hostile armies, as in fact happened in 1948 (photo). Therefore UN Resolution 242 has determined that Israel has a right to secure – thus, new – borders.

145. White phosphorus

The Palestinian Tale: Israel committed war crimes by the use of white phosphorus in Gaza.

White phosphorus is a chemical substance that can be used in chemical weapons because of its combustibility. However, it also gives off a thick white smoke; great for smokescreens. Of course, under international law of war, the use of white phosphorus as a chemical weapon is prohibited. However, it is permitted in grenades that create smokescreens.

During the Gaza war of 2008/2009 Israel used grenades with white phosphorus to generate smokescreens. However, it was nevertheless accused of also regularly deploying the substance as a chemical weapon against the people of Gaza. After investigation the accusation proved untrue, but, the Israeli army nevertheless switched to a different type of smoke grenade to prevent false accusations in the future.

Tale: Israel committed war crimes by the use of white phosphorus.
Fact: The use of white phosphorus for smokescreens (photo) is absolutely legal.

146. World domination

The Palestinian Tale: Jews manipulate the world and strive for world domination.

This Tale is very old. It was popular previously with the Nazis; Hitler said that Jews had to be destroyed because of their "conspiracies" (see Tale: Nazism).

The basis for this Tale is the book *The Protocols of the Elders of Zion*, which purports to reveal the Jewish quest for world domination. But the book is a fake, produced by the anti-Semitic secret service of the Russian tsars in the early 20th century. Due to the popularity of conspiracy theories in the Arab world (see Tale: Conspiracy theories), this book is nevertheless a continuing bestseller and is often referred to as "proof" by the Palestinians as well:

> *"[The historian and translator] Ajaj Nuwayhid worked on many books; perhaps the most outstanding is* The Protocols of the Elders of Zion, *a book that was widely distributed in the Arab world. He wrote [the translation] in the beginning of the 20th century, and attempted to trace the Zionist identity and its global and international scope.*
> *This man truly deserves our respect and appreciation."*
> – Ehab Bessais, Spokesman of the Palestinian Authority, on official Palestinian Authority television on July 7, 2013

This Tale is still very much alive today among Muslims. No less than 60 different editions of *Protocols* were available in Arab countries in 2002. Muslim world leaders spread this Tale, even in the conference of Islamic states.

The Hamas charter, deeply imbued with hatred of Jews, also tells this Tale:

> *"It [Zionism] does not hesitate to take any road, or to pursue all despicable and repulsive means to fulfill its desires.*
> *Zionism strives to demolish societies, to destroy values, to wreck responsibility, to disturb virtues and to wipe out Islam. It stands behind the diffusion of drugs and toxins of all kinds in order to facilitate its control and expansion.*
> *There was no war that broke out anywhere without their fingerprints on it."*

Thus the Palestinians are brainwashed:

> *"The Jews are behind each and every catastrophe on the face of the Earth. This is not open to debate. This is not a temporal thing, but goes back to days of yore. They*

concocted so many conspiracies and betrayed rulers and nations so many times that people harbor hatred towards them.
Throughout history – from Nebuchadnezzar until modern times – they slayed the prophets, and so on.
Any catastrophe on the face of this Earth – the Jews must be behind it."
– Hamas MP Marwan Abu Ras, a member of the International Union of Muslim Scholars, on Hamas television on September 12, 2012

This is an attitude that can be found across the Muslim world. The Iranians, too, believe this:

"It – the criminal, barbaric nature of Jewish power – has been there from the beginning, congenital from its birth.
Day by day, with the obvious meltdown of world order taking place and how much (most) of this is traceable directly to this one troublesome, meddlesome group of people and their control over the political, economic and military machinery of the West, the magic spell is wearing off and the deep sleep is coming to an end.
To invade, displace, mass murder, destroy, lie, show no mercy, destroy the culture, debase the economy and to reduce every land they 'possess' to utter ruination – the entire justification for which is that the Jewish God has demanded it."
– Article on the website of Iran's state news agency PressTV, published on December 11, 2013

It is of course total nonsense that just 15 million Jews worldwide – that also are much divided among themselves – would be able to control the world or would pursue that goal. Also, this is another case of Arab projection, where Jews are blamed for something that the Arabs are pursuing themselves:

"Tomorrow, our nation will sit on the throne of the world. This is not a figment of the imagination, but a fact. Tomorrow we will lead the world, Allah willing. Apologize today, before remorse will do you no good. Our nation is moving forwards, and it is in your interest to respect a victorious nation."
– Khaled Mashal, head of Hamas's political bureau, in 2006 in a Friday sermon at a Mosque in Damascus

"The Prophet Muhammad said that the Islamic caliphate would encompass the Earth.
The whole world will become subordinated to the Islamic caliphate one day.
I have said it before, and I say it again: Allah willing, Jerusalem will not be only the capital of the Palestinian state, but also the capital of the coming righteous Islamic caliphate."

– Islamic leader Sheikh Kamal Khatib on official Palestinian Authority TV on October 17, 2014

Tale: Jews strive for world domination.
Fact: In the Islamic world this idiotic conspiracy theory is believed eagerly.
Photo: *The Protocols of the Elders of Zion*, on sale at Kuala Lumpur International Airport in Malaysia.

147. Yom Kippur War

The Palestinian Tale: The Arab rejection of Israel does not result in an existential threat.

The best counter-evidence against this statement is the Yom Kippur War of 1973. Hundreds of thousands of soldiers from Egypt, Algeria, Bangladesh, Libya, Sudan, Egypt, Iraq, Saudi Arabia, Syria and even North Korea and Cuba attacked Israel by surprise; Israel at that time had a population of only 2.5 million people.

Only two of the 25 Arab countries recognize Israel nowadays. Products from Israel are boycotted and regularly calls are made to wipe Israel off the map. The majority of the Arab countries are apparently not yet ready for peace with Israel.

This is especially true for Islamic Iran, which has indicated many times its wish to destroy "the Zionist entity," which it equates with cancer.

Ayatollah Ali Khamenei, the supreme leader of Iran, declared on February 2, 2012: *"Iran will support any nation or group that attacks the cancerous tumor of Israel."*

Tale: Israel is not living under an existential military threat because of its rejection by the Arab world.
Fact: In the Yom Kippur War, Israel was attacked by 11 Arab countries.
Photo: Egyptian troops crossing the Suez Canal in the Yom Kippur War.

148. Zionism and anti-Semitism

The Palestinian Tale: There is a big difference between anti-Zionism and anti-Semitism.

Since at least 95 percent of Jews are Zionist – in favor of Jewish self-determination in the Jewish state, Israel – the distinction between anti-Zionism and anti-Semitism is very artificial.
For example, this racism shows from the fact that in Europe in the recent past, Jews that are recognizable as such are beaten up *"because Jews defend Israel."* But nobody beats up Moroccans because some of them defend IS.

The "anti-Zionists" even have little interest in the Palestinians themselves. They call for a boycott of Israel, though it will hit Palestinians harder than Israel (see Tale: Boycott). You also do not hear them speak out about issues such as discrimination against women, the lack of rights and the oppression of Palestinians in their autonomous Palestinian territory by Hamas and Fatah. They have not demonstrated over the 3,000 Palestinians (at least) who have been slaughtered in the current Syrian civil war.

> *"The hateful nature of anti-Zionism burns everything around it, and the Palestinians are its main victims.*
> *We therefore call for an awakening of conscience among the ranks of those who call themselves pro-Palestinian. If they truly are pro-Palestinian, and not simply anti-Israel, then we expect them to strongly condemn Hamas terrorism and Fatah corruption, which are the main causes of Palestinian suffering, rather than demonize Israel while ignoring the consequences of that demonization on the lives of real Palestinians."*
> – Bassam Eid, Palestinian human rights activist in 2015

German Prime Minister Angela Merkel has been clear about whether Zionism is legitimate:
> *"Anti-Zionism is not a legitimate position. For those who share my view that the Jews as a people have a right to self-determination, Zionism as a national movement of the Jewish people is the embodiment of this very right, which its opponents want to deny."*

The German court in February 2015 also ruled that the distinction is artificial: *"In the language of anti-Semitism, 'Zionist' is the code word for 'Jew.'"*

"How can someone say: 'I have nothing against the Italians, but I think that Italy should be destroyed'?"
– Morton Klein, president of the Zionist Organization of America

"When you see how the old anti-Semitism is growing again, linked to a new anti-Semitism, which hides behind anti-Zionism – but that is in fact exactly the same anti-Semitism – then I think we are facing a major challenge in European society."
– Commissioner of the European Union Frans Timmermans in the Dutch television program *Buitenhof*, March 15, 2015

"Anyone who does not recognize the Jewish people and the State of Israel – and their right to exist – is guilty of anti-Semitism."
– Pope Francis on May 28, 2015

"When people criticize Zionists, they mean Jews. You're talking anti-Semitism!"
– Dr. Martin Luther King in 1968

Tale: There is a big difference between anti-Zionism and anti-Semitism.
Fact: Egyptian propaganda showed how Nasser kicks a stereotypical Jew into the sea, with the help of soldiers from Lebanon, Syria and Iraq.

149. Zionism history

The Palestinian Tale: Zionism is a recent Jewish invention.

Zionism is centuries old. It is not a discovery from the colonial era as the Palestinians claim. Jews know that the longing for a state of their own in Israel is thousands of years old. It originated when most Jews were expelled from Israel by the Romans in the year 135. Since then, all Jews wish each other at the Jewish Passover Seder: *"Next year in Jerusalem."*

Non-Jews, including world leaders, have also long supported Zionism – the self-determination for Jews in their historic homeland. That was already the case long before the creation of modern Zionist movement (around 1890). The founder thereof, Theodor Herzl, already predicted in 1897, following the success of a Zionist conference organized by him:

"Were I to sum up the Basel Congress in a word – which I shall guard against pronouncing publicly – it would be this: At Basel I founded the Jewish State. If I said this out loud today l would be greeted by universal laughter. In five years perhaps, and certainly in 50 years, everyone will perceive it."

Herzl had it wrong by one year. In 1948 Israel was founded.

Napoleon Bonaparte said, at the time of his conquest of present-day Israel in 1799, that he wanted to establish a Jewish state:

"The almost 2,000-year-old ignominy put upon you; and, while time and circumstances would seem to be least favorable to a restatement of your claims or even to their expression, it offers to you at this very time, and contrary to all expectations, Israel's patrimony!"

US President John Adams in 1819 expressed the hope that the Jews would be restored *"to their national home in Palestine. This is a noble dream and one shared by many Americans."*

US President Abraham Lincoln said in 1863: *"The return of persecuted Jews to their national home in Palestine is a noble dream shared by many Americans."*

Winston Churchill said in 1921:

> *"It is manifestly right that the Jews, who are scattered all over the world, should have a national center and a National Home where some of them may be reunited. And where else could that be but in this land of Palestine, with which for more than 3,000 years they have been intimately and profoundly associated?"*

Even so, not everyone understood why the Jewish country should be established in Israel. As early as a hundred years ago, a British MP asked the future president of Israel, Chaim Weizmann, why it had to be there – was somewhere not also possible? Weizmann replied that he did not understand why the MP traveled a long way every weekend to visit his grandmother. Were there not enough old ladies living in his own street?

> *"O David, thou soughtest shelter*
> *From King Saul's tyranny.*
> *Even so I fled this welter*
> *And many a lord with me.*
> *But God the Lord did save me*
> *From exile and its hell.*
> *And, in His mercy, gave him*
> *A realm in Israel."*
> – The eighth verse of the Dutch national anthem Wilhelmus, 1572

Tale: Zionism is a recent Jewish invention.
Fact: For 2,000 years, Jews wish each other at the Jewish Passover fest: *"Next year in Jerusalem."*
Photo: Jewish Passover in Russia in the 19th century, by an unknown artist.

150. Zionism self-determination

The Palestinian Tale: Zionism is racist.

Zionism is the quest for self-determination of the Jewish people in the area where Jews form a majority. This is a widely accepted criterion for the self-determination of peoples, whether it's the French, Tibetans, Eritreans or Bosnians.

Zionist leaders have had always strived for peaceful coexistence as a basic principle. Already in 1919 Chaim Weizmann, leader of the Zionist movement, signed a peace agreement with Hashemite emir, Faisal ibn Hussein, then leader of the emerging pan-Arab movement. Because Britain failed to keep the associated promises (according to Hussein), the agreement was not implemented (see Tale: Colonialism).

From that time on, up to the proclamation of the State of Israel on May 14, 1948, Zionist spokesmen had hundreds of meetings with Arab leaders at all levels. All these talks were aimed at eliminating mistrust and preventing war. All Jewish leaders, from left to right, have always stressed the equal rights of non-Jews (see Tale: Jewish state creation).

So David Ben-Gurion, who would become Israel's first Prime Minister in 1948, stated in December 1947:
"In our state there will be non-Jews as well – and all of them will be equal citizens; equal in everything without any exception; that is: the state will be their state as well.
If the Arab citizen will feel at home in our state, and if his status will not be the least different from that of the Jew, and perhaps better than the status of the Arab in an Arab state, and if the state will help him in a truthful and dedicated way to reach the economic, social, and cultural level of the Jewish community, then Arab distrust will accordingly subside and a bridge to a Semitic, Jewish-Arab alliance, will be built."

Tale: Zionism is racist.
Fact: Jews demand self-determination in their historical homeland.
Photo: Jewish coin from Judea 2,000 years ago.

Bibliography

- Bard, Mitchell G. *The Arab lobby: The invisible alliance that undermines America's interests in the Middle East*. New York: HarperCollins, 2010.
- ---. *The complete idiot's guide to Middle East conflict*. New York: Alpha, 2008.
- Begin, Menachem: *The revolt: Story of the Irgun*. Jerusalem: Steimatzky, 1977.
- Boef, Johan. Ariel Sharon: Koning van Israël (Ariel Sharon: King of Israel). Soesterberg: Uitgeverij Aspekt, 2005.
- Danon, Danny. *The will to prevail*. New York: Palgrave Macmillan, 2012.
- Dershowitz, Alan. *The case for Israel*. Hoboken, NJ: John Wiley & Sons, 2003.
- ---. *The case for peace*. Hoboken, NJ: John Wiley & Sons, 2005.
- Fortuyn, Pim. 50 jaar Israël, hoe lang nog? (50 years Israel: How long will it last?) Amsterdam: A.W. Bruna Uitgevers, 1998.
- Gerstenfeld, Manfred. *Demonizing Israel and the Jews*. New York: RVP Press, 2013.
- Gilbert, Martin. *The Arab-Israeli conflict: Its history in maps*. Jerusalem: Steimatzky, 1991.
- Gilder, George. *The Israel test: Why the world's most besieged state is a beacon of freedom and hope for the world economy*. New York: Encounter Books, 2012.
- Haan, Jacob Israël de. Palestina. Kampen: Uitgeverij Kok, 1999. (First published 1925.)
- Herzl, Theodor. De Jodenstaat (The Jewish state). Translated by Sander Hendriks. Amsterdam: Mets & Schilt uitgevers, 2004. (First published 1896.)
- Hirschfeld, Hadassa. Kernpunten van het Israëlische-Palestijnse conflict (Key elements of the Israeli-Palestinian conflict). Soesterberg: Uitgeverij Aspekt, 2011.
- Hirsi Ali, Ayaan: Mijn vrijheid: de autobiografie (My freedom: The autobiography). Amsterdam: Uitgeverij Augustus, 2006.
- Jabotinsky, Ze'ev. *The political and social philosophy of Ze'ev Jabotinsky: Selected writings*. Edited by Mordechai Sarig. London: Vallentine Mitchell, 1999.
- Jansen, Hans. Islam voor varkens, apen, ezels en andere beesten (Islam for pigs, monkeys, donkeys and other beasts). Amsterdam: Uitgeverij van Praag, 2008.
- ---. Waarom mag Israël niet bestaan in het Midden-Oosten? (Why should Israel not exist in the Middle East?) Heerenveen: Royal Jongbloed, 2015.
- Karsh, Efraim. *Palestine betrayed*. London: Yale University Press, 2010.
- Kortenoeven, Wim R.F. Hamas: portret en achtergronden (Hamas: Its portrait and background). Soesterberg, Uitgeverij Aspekt, 2006.
- Kozodoy, Neil, Ed.: *The Mideast peace process: An autopsy*. New York: Encounter Books, 2006.
- Lewis, Bernard. *What went wrong? The clash between Islam and modernity in the Middle East*. New York: HarperCollins, 2003.

- Peeters, Frans. *Gezworen vrienden, het geheime bondgenootschap tussen Nederland en Israël* (Sworn friends: The secret alliance between the Netherlands and Israel). Amsterdam: Uitgeverij L.J. Veen, 1997.
- Peters, Joan. *From time immemorial: The origins of the Arab-Jewish conflict over Palestine*. Chicago: JKAP Publications, 1993.
- Praag, H.M. van. Joden-haat en Zion's-haat (Jew hatred and hatred of Zion). Soesterberg, Uitgeverij Aspekt, 2009.
- Rubin, Barry. *The Arab states and the Palestine conflict*. Syracuse, NY: Syracuse University Press, 1981.
- Senor, Dan and Saul Singer: *Start-up nation: The story of Israel's economic miracle*. New York: Twelve, 2011.
- Shimoni, Gideon. *The Zionist ideology*. Lebanon, NH: University of New England Press for Brandeis University, 1995.

Illustration Credits

The following individuals have given permission for the reuse of their work, but their views do not necessarily agree with the contents of this book. These individuals should be credited upon any further use of the material.

Front cover: Author's own photo.
1. Jonathan Nicholas
2. Wikimedia, Egyptian propaganda.
3. Wikimedia, English Foreign and Commonwealth Office.
4. Wikimedia, Radioman.
5. Wikimedia, MathKnight.
6. Wikimedia, zachi dvira.
7. Wikimedia, Hamed Saber.
8. Wikimedia, Ronen Marcus.
9. Wikimedia, Michel Wolgemut en Wilhelm Pleydenwurff.
10. Wikimedia, Israeli delegation.
11. Wikimedia, Neukoln.
12. Wikimedia, Débora Cabral.
13. Pixabay, ClkerFreeVectorImages.
14. Wikimedia, Maor X.
15. Wikimedia, Israel Defense Forces.
16. Wikimedia, Dough D.
17. Wikimedia, Arab League.
18. Wikimedia, author unknown.
19. Wikimedia, Robert.
20. Author's own photo
21. Wikimedia, Israel Defense Forces.
22. Wikimedia, Jonathan Klinger.
23. Wikimedia, 48Lugur.
24. Wikimedia, author unknown.
25. Wikimedia, Alt-x.
26. Wikimedia, Forum Kohelet.
27. Wikimedia, Ralf Lotys.
28. Wikimedia, Eic413.
29. Wikimedia, Jpatokal.
30. Wikimedia, author unknown.
31. Wikimedia, Roosewelt Pinheiro.
32. Wikimedia, Manar al Zraiy.
33. Wikimedia, Israel Defense Forces.
34. Wikimedia, Lencer.
35. YouTube, CulinaryTravellerAHM.
36. Wikimedia, Israel Defense Forces.
37. David Collier.
38. Wikimedia, Supreme Deliciousness.
39. Wikimedia, Hoheit.
40. Wikimedia, Ariel Palmon.
41. Wikimedia, American Colony (Jerusalem), Photo Dept.
42. Wikimedia, author unknown.
43. Wikimedia, Avraham Soskin.
44. Wikimedia, Kurt Alber.
45. Wikimedia, author unknown.
46. Wikimedia, Elmendorf, Dwight Lathrop.
47. Elder of Ziyon.
48. Wikimedia, Mielke.
49. Wikimedia, U.S. Army.
50. Wikimedia, James Emery.
51. Wikimedia, Chaim Molcho, Ezrat Niddachim Org.
52. Wikimedia, Beth Hashalom.
53. Wikimedia, Ariel Palmon.
54. Wikimedia, The Yorck Project.
55. Wikimedia, Israeli American Council.
56. Wikimedia, John Roy Carlson.
57. Wikimedia, CIA WFB.
58. Wikimedia, Briangotts.
59. Wikimedia, American Colony (Jerusalem), Photo Dept.
60. Wikimedia, author unknown.
61. Wikimedia, Humus sapiens.
62. Wikimedia, Adiral.
63. Wikimedia, Effib.
64. Wikimedia, author unknown.
65. Wikimedia, George Grantham Bain.

66. Wikimedia, author unknown.
67. Wikimedia, Jusmine.
68. YouTube, Memri.
69. Wikimedia, Marion S. Trikosko.
70. Wikimedia, Anon Moos.
71. Wikimedia, Gilgamesh.
72. Wikimedia, possibly Bernhardt Walter or Ernst Hofmann.
73. Wikimedia, Heinrich Hoffmann.
74. Wikimedia, Shuki.
75. Wikimedia, David Katz / The Israel Project.
76. Wikimedia, Doron.
77. Wikimedia, Torw.
78. Wikimedia, Stratforder.
79. Wikimedia, João Correia.
80. Wikimedia, Edi Israel.
81. Wikimedia, Kimberly Blaker.
82. Wikimedia, U.S. Embassy Tel Aviv.
83. Wikimedia, Moshe Pridan.
84. YouTube, Israel Defense Forces.
85. Wikimedia, Trango.
86. Wikimedia, Kaly99.
87. Wikimedia, Der Eberswalder.
88. Wikimedia, Avi Ohayon GPO.
89. Wikimedia, Alex D.
90. Wikimedia, User:Zero0000.
91. Wikimedia, Ynhockey.
92. Wikimedia, U.S. Central Intelligence Agency.
93. Wikimedia, Floris Van Cauwelaert.
94. Wikimedia, Israel Defense Forces.
95. Wikimedia, official portrait Israeli Government.
96. Wikimedia, US State Dept.
97. Wikimedia, webscribe.
98. Wikimedia, Michal Osmenda.
99. Youtube, AP Archive
100. Wikimedia, author unknown.
101. Wikimedia, Fargome D.
102. Wikimedia, Sridhar1000.
103. Wikimedia, author unknown.
104. Wikimedia, Rudi Weissenstein.
105. Wikimedia, author unknown.
106. Wikimedia, Khaldun Bshara.
107. Wikimedia, Yossi Zur.
108. Wikimedia, Jewish Agency for Israel.
109. Wikimedia, Borya.
110. Wikimedia, Bantosh.
111. Wikimedia, Georges Hayek.
112. Wikimedia, Ongayo.
113. Wikimedia, Eman.
114. Wikimedia, Hellochris.
115. Wikimedia, Maki1.
116. Wikimedia, AshSert.
117. Wikimedia, Her Majesty's Stationery Office.
118. Pixabay, Gazetasecret.
119. Wikimedia, author unknown.
120. Wikimedia, Israel Defense Forces.
121. Wikimedia, United States Army.
122. Wikimedia, Reuvenk.
123. Wikimedia, Yoav Dothan.
124. Wikimedia, Fritz Cohn.
125. Wikimedia, Avishai Teicher.
126. YouTube, euronews.
127. Wikimedia, author unknown.
128. Wikimedia, EdoM.
129. Wikimedia, US Government.
130. Wikimedia, Ravi84m.
131. Wikimedia, Jesse B. Awalt, U.S. Navy Photo.
132. Wikimedia, JoAnn S. Makinano.
133. Wikimedia, author unknown.
134. Wikimedia, Amr Farouq Mohammed.
135. Wikimedia, Greenatfifteen.
136. Wikimedia, Soman.
137. Wikimedia, Helene C. Stikkel.
138. Wikimedia, Paffairs San Francisco.
139. Wikimedia, Humus sapiens.
140. Wikimedia, Remi Jouan.
141. Wikimedia, Manar al Zraiy.
142. Wikimedia, Jordanian Military Photographer.
143. Wikimedia, Maximilian Dörrbecker.
144. Wikimedia, Department of History, U.S. Military Academy.
145. Wikimedia, Al Jazeera.
146. Wikimedia, Goldsztajn.
147. Wikimedia, author unknown.
148. Wikimedia, Egyptian propaganda.
149. Wikimedia, author unknown.
150. Wikimedia, CNG.

Back cover: Wikimedia, Godot13.

About the Editor

Tom S. van Bemmelen (1930) is a retired colonel in the Royal Dutch Navy, where he spent his career as an aviator in Dutch New Guinea, aboard the aircraft carrier HNLMS Karel Doorman and as commander of the naval base at The Hague. In his political career he was a legislator for the province of South Holland, a member of the Senate of the Netherlands, chairman of his party in The Hague and foreign secretary of the national board of the VVD Dutch liberal party. In the latter capacity he demonstrated his aversion to extremism of both the left and the right. For instance, he became known for being the first in Europe to work for the rejection of the Austrian right-wing Freedom Party by the Liberal International movement, a mission which he successfully accomplished. Tom van Bemmelen has been president of Likud Netherlands since 1998.